SOME KIND OF MIRROR

SOME KIND OF MIRROR

Creating Marilyn Monroe

A MANDA K ONKLE

RUTGERS UNIVERSITY PRESS

NEW BRUNSWICK, CAMDEN, AND NEWARK,

NEW JERSEY, AND LONDON

Library of Congress Cataloging-in-Publication Data

Names: Konkle, Amanda, 1982– author.
Title: Some kind of mirror : creating Marilyn Monroe / Amanda Konkle.
Description: New Brunswick : Rutgers University Press, 2018. | Includes
    bibliographical references and index. | Includes filmography.
Identifiers: LCCN 2018008405 | ISBN 9781978802629 (cloth : alk. paper) |
    ISBN 9781978802612 (pbk. : alk. paper)
Subjects: LCSH: Monroe, Marilyn, 1926–1962—Criticism and interpretation.
Classification: LCC PN2287.M69 K66 2018 | DDC 791.4302/8092—dc23
LC record available at https://lccn.loc.gov/2018008405

A British Cataloging-in-Publication record for this book is available from the
British Library.

www.rutgersuniversitypress.org

Manufactured in the United States of America

For Wes, Avalee, and my parents

"People had a habit of looking at me as if I were some kind of mirror instead of as a person. They didn't see me, they saw their own lewd thoughts."

—Marilyn Monroe, My Story

CONTENTS

SOME KIND OF MIRROR

CHAPTER 1

INTRODUCTION

PLAYING "MARILYN MONROE"

A story about Marilyn Monroe's 1954 performances for the troops in Korea concludes her autobiography, *My Story*.[1] Monroe, as the narrator, says the officer in charge of her Korean tour asked her to change the way she sang the George Gershwin song, "Do It Again," because her performance was "too suggestive." Although Monroe insists that she "hadn't sung the song with any suggestive meaning," she agrees to change "do it" to "kiss me," because she sees no point in arguing. She explains, "People had a habit of looking at me as if I were some kind of mirror instead of as a person. They didn't see me, they saw their own lewd thoughts" (183). With Monroe, this story suggests, sex appeal was wholly conspicuous, even if she intended her performance to be subdued or even classical. Eventually, when the individual formerly known as Norma Jeane Mortenson looked in the mirror, she would see not "herself," but Marilyn Monroe looking back at her. That she was "some kind of mirror" aptly describes Monroe's role in postwar culture, for, as I argue throughout this book, Monroe's star persona united many of the contradictory discourses of the postwar period. Her performances, onscreen and off, despite having been crafted to showcase her status as a sexpot, were more complex in that, at the same time as they acknowledged and resisted the conventions of the sexpot, they also mirrored, or reflected, the concerns and anxieties of many postwar Americans. Monroe played the sexpot role, but she also challenged that role with humor, sensitivity, and cultural relevance.

In fact, the sexpot role Monroe played—a performance of being consistently and conspicuously desirable and available—made Monroe's engagement with debates about postwar gender roles, female sexual desire, and the labor undertaken by actresses more palatable to audiences and critics—and thereby also obscured the range of cultural work undertaken by Monroe's star persona in the postwar period (as well as today). The very sexiness that is part of her persona has made it difficult for many writers to take her seriously as an actress, and yet, playing "Marilyn Monroe" meant not only being sexy, but also incorporating nuances of vulnerability *and* humor into her roles. Playing "Marilyn Monroe" meant not only being sexy, but also reflecting and advancing debates about women's roles in marriage and women's sexuality. Playing "Marilyn Monroe" meant not only being sexy, but also taking herself seriously as an actress, even when few others did. Playing "Marilyn Monroe" meant exposing and resisting many of the contradictions of the postwar era. How she did that is the subject of this book.

In spite of, or perhaps because of, Monroe's early, tragic, mysterious death, Monroe reflects what others want to see to this day; she figuratively, and sometimes literally, remains "some kind of mirror." For example, according to staff and guests at Hollywood's Roosevelt Hotel, where Monroe was photographed for her early modeling gigs, Monroe's reflection still occasionally appears in the full-length mirror that had once been in her hotel room. The hotel has since moved the mirror to the gift shop, where it can attract revenue. Monroe's films are still screened, both on television and in movie houses, and thus her screen image also persists.[2] Her offscreen image is nearly unavoidable: despite being dead, Monroe appeared in a Snickers Super Bowl ad (2016), a Coke campaign (2015), campaigns for Chanel No. 5 (1994, 2013) and J'Adore Dior (2011), campaigns for Levi's (1968, 1998), Gap (1993), and Max Factor cosmetics (1999, 2015), as well as campaigns for several automobiles, beers, and jewelry companies, among others (Gray).[3]

Monroe is useful to advertisers and exhibitors because she remains "some kind of mirror," reflecting viewers' desires and suggesting that our problems can be solved with easily attainable consumer goods. Monroe died while she was still young and beautiful, in the middle of production on *Something's Got to Give* (1962, dir. George Cukor), when she had not faced the dilemma of leaving Hollywood or acting only in "mature" roles. Indeed, Monroe never receded from the limelight in her lifetime, and her brief career and our memories of it, and her, have thereby escaped the vicissitudes of aging. She remains, to today's audiences, the same vibrant, fascinating woman she was when she died. (Aging might have been the necessary component for Monroe to escape the dumb blonde sexpot image to which she was bound. Ruth Barton argues that Hedy Lamarr "had to 'lose' her body" in death before her interest in invention could be reconciled with her star image [84].) Monroe has never "lost" her body, and while fans invested in her biography often remark on her intelligence, sensitivity, and curiosity, she remains a sex symbol.

But she also means much more to today's fans, hundreds of whom visit Monroe's grave every year,[4] and thousands of whom engage in lively conversation on fan social media pages, such as *Marilyn Remembered, Marilyn Monroe Forever in Our Hearts*, and *Immortal Marilyn*. Fans desire to honor the star, to save her from those who would exploit her image and story, and to bask in her beauty and glamour. But why should fans still have such strong feelings about a star who died over fifty-six years ago? S. Paige Baty argues that "rememberings of her end breathe life back into the dead star, casting her in roles and histories that relate her to the 'legitimate and illegitimate' bodies politic of the last several decades" (7). Baty focuses on Monroe as a figure that can cross "high" and "low" culture, and argues that her rich biography makes it possible for her to be used to continually refigure American identity (25–26; see also Ebert xvii–xviii).

Although many do engage in activities designed to remember Monroe's death, such as visiting her grave, many fans prefer to remember her work through discussing the merits of her films, sharing photos of her from throughout her career, and purchasing merchandise bearing her image in order to imagine her as one of their dear friends.[5]

Much has been written about Monroe's biography, and I do not intend to delve into who she "really" was or her complex personal life here (although it will, at times, be necessary to mention select details).[6] Instead, I focus on Monroe's career, which is unique in a number of ways that have nothing to do with her biography. For example, Monroe was obviously "built up" by her studio, Twentieth Century-Fox, to be a sexpot. That is, she conspicuously emphasized her sex appeal and sexual availability (including the "Mmmm Girl" campaign to promote *Love Happy* [dir. David Miller] in 1949, as well as such stunts as being photographed wearing a potato sack), was frequently cast in roles that were little more than decorative, and always played some version of the sexy blonde. And yet, she became a huge star, in a manner that differed from the blondes who copied her as well as from the few other sexpot actresses who had achieved similar stardom (e.g., Jean Harlow, whom I discuss later in the chapter). What's more, because Monroe's major film roles fell between 1949 and 1961, we can think of her career as a product of the 1950s, a decade in which many shifts in American cultural life took place, and in which, certainly, many changes in American women's lives occurred. It is perhaps counterintuitive that a sexpot should speak to American women's concerns, and yet, as subsequent chapters show, that is exactly what she did.

Playing "Marilyn Monroe" meant encompassing (at least) two meanings at once. The double entendres that filled reporting on her from the beginning of her career were so central to her persona that they became known as Monroeisms: for example, "In bed, she claims, she wears 'only Chanel No. 5,' and she avoids excessive sun bathing because 'I like to feel blonde all over'" ("Something" 88).[7] Monroe's double meaning was not limited to her offscreen publicity—her double entendres call attention to how she can say one thing while meaning another, and why should we think this differs in her film performances? And yet many writers, both then and now, doubt her acting skill. But encompassing at least two meanings at once, in a performance, has been praised, for example, in male Method actors, who have been described as delivering performances that, by expressing psychic conflict, "compet[e] with" the film as scripted (Wexman 174). Monroe has never been given the respect given to acclaimed Method actors, and yet, I argue that Monroe's performances always challenged the film as scripted, both resisting the sexpot role and referencing cultural debates about women's roles in marriage, sexuality, and acting.[8] Monroe was more than a sexpot—she was a star.

MONROE THE STAR

Monroe's performances simultaneously fulfill the expectations of a sexpot and a serious film star.[9] What do I mean by the designation "serious film star"? During the days of the studio system, all potential stars were given the studio buildup from the moment they stepped onto the lot, and even the studio wasn't sure which potentials would actually become favorites. More who were given the star buildup are forgotten than remembered, and so one aspect of being a star must be becoming well known enough to be remembered. In fact, predicting which "stars" were "Stars-of-Tomorrow" had been the subject of a *Motion Picture Herald* poll from the publication's beginnings in the 1930s. In 1952, the poll named Monroe the "Number One Star-of-Tomorrow" despite the fact that she had not yet had any major starring roles (Weaver 12). But, as Esther Sonnet points out, "the uncertainty and unpredictability of even Monroe's position at this point is historically confirmed by the lack of comparable historical impact of other Stars-of-Tomorrow actors that are named alongside her such as Danny Thomas, David Wayne, Marge and Gower Champion, and Forrest Tucker" (66). Studio publicity, then, succeeded in interesting audiences in Monroe, but her film performances had to complement that publicity to maintain audience interest and transform her into an enduring star.

Although there are many excellent articles that analyze specific films and Monroe's role in them, not enough emphasis has been given to the cumulative effect of her performances in shaping the interpretation of the films. The field of academic star studies boasts a number of useful approaches; P. David Marshall summarizes the ways film stars have been studied as, variously, "the economic heart of the culture industry," "a form of spectatorial pleasure and identification," and "a sociological phenomenon that exits the film roles and plays an active symbolic role in the lives of audiences" (12). Monroe has been examined, at least briefly, from all of these perspectives. I will incorporate what has been written about her films in later chapters, but an overview of the vast body of work on Monroe as a star is in order before proceeding.

Monroe often served as evidence of far-reaching patriarchy and Hollywood misogyny in the work of early feminist film scholars, and some of that persists even into the twenty-first century. Early feminist critics described Monroe as a product of "Mammary Madness" (Rosen 291), the "butt of all fantasies" (Rosen 287), or "breast fetishism combined with Lolita lechery" (Haskell 255). Molly Haskell admits that Monroe "was giving more to idiotic parts than they called for—more feeling, more warmth, more anguish; and, as a result, her films have a richer tone than they deserve" in that they "suggest the discrepancy between the woman (and young girl) and the sexpot, even as their directors (Wilder and Hawks) exploit the image, through exaggeration, more than they have to" (256). I agree with Haskell, but attend in more detail to Monroe's performances to demonstrate *how* she resisted the sexpot character. Haskell and Marjorie Rosen published their reflectionist studies of women in film in the 1970s, paving the way for further consideration of actresses, a task begun by psychoanalytic theorists of the late 1970s and early 1980s. Nevertheless, foundational feminist film scholar Laura Mulvey, in her early work, reads Monroe as a prime example of the passive female as "erotic object" in

Hollywood films ("Visual" 40).[10] Even into the twenty-first century, Jessica Hope Jordan, in her otherwise engaging study of the particularly feminine power of Hollywood "sex goddesses," isolates Monroe as the sole powerless Hollywood sex goddess, whose "true helplessness and desperation" disempower her (157). But Jordan does not acknowledge that while Monroe's film characters may have appeared helpless and desperate, they also challenged the expectations others had of the sexpot. When critics refuse to concede that Monroe was an empowered woman whom other women admired, they objectify her in just the manner of which they are critical. Directors did exploit Monroe as the sexpot, but we should not let that stop us from seeking signs of Monroe's resistance to that exploitation.

Complicating the insights of early feminist film scholars has provided later film scholars with tools to better understand Monroe's appeal as a star. By theorizing spectator desire and identification, psychoanalytic theory usefully illuminates the specific problems involved in discussing female stars. Mulvey's indispensable "Visual Pleasure and Narrative Cinema" posits that the camera and the other characters within the film have either a voyeuristic (watching the private without permission) or fetishistic (building up the beauty of the female star into a satisfying object to disavow castration anxiety) relationship to female stars. In either case, the filmic situation objectifies the woman ("Visual" 43).[11] Although Mulvey does not account for the pleasures of female stars for female viewers, nor for the camera's objectification of male stars, she has paved the way for subsequent theories regarding the kinds of pleasure viewers experience when watching Hollywood films, drawing at various points on notions of, as Gaylyn Studlar and Mary Ann Doane discuss, voyeurism, fetishism, masochism, and the masquerade.[12] Although such notions maintain rigid gender dichotomies, they nevertheless provide useful heuristics for considering the relationship between stars and viewers.

In contrast, by thinking of film as a fantasy structure housing a number of shifting identificatory positions, theorists such as Elizabeth Cowie and Judith Mayne propose that viewers respond to stars in ways that are not driven by gender binaries.[13] The work done toward disproving the hegemonic influence of the patriarchal gaze has resulted in a richer understanding of the ways female stars generate meaning for audiences. While female stars sometimes seem to embody the workings of patriarchy, at other times they demonstrate avenues of resistance to patriarchy, making these forms of resistance accessible to audience members. At still other times stars oscillate between being subjected to and resisting society's mores in a way that resembles the viewer's own experience of social existence. Thus, Lucie Arbuthnot and Gail Seneca use the principle of identification to argue that Jane Russell's and Monroe's performance of friendship in *Gentlemen Prefer Blondes* (1953, dir. Howard Hawks) encourages "the female viewer to join them, through identification, in valuing other women and ourselves" (113). Considering the sexpot's appeal to female audiences, then, challenges rigid understandings of viewer identification.

Studies of acting and performance also attend to the star's film work, but their focus is primarily on the language of performance, for example, determining whether a performance has been influenced more by the theories of Constantin Stanislavsky or Lee Strasberg. Although studies of film acting must attend to films as their key evidence, these studies rarely provide a comprehensive analysis of a star's significance, in terms of the star's agency, how the star's presence contributed to a film's meaning, or our understanding of the star's body of film work.[14] Because of the tendency to think of stars as popular with audiences, but relatively talentless as actors, many successful star performances have been interpreted as the outcome of directors' efforts. As Pamela Robertson Wojcik notes, attention to star performances is scant in star studies, which may "make some attempt at analyzing performance traits of individual stars; but rather than analyze individual performances in terms of acting style, these analyses tend to extract particular mannerisms or gestures that are repeated across a body of films as a feature of the star's persona" (7). Such a problem hampers Carl Rollyson's biography of Monroe as an actress. In this work, Rollyson emphasizes Monroe's acting instruction and its effects on her identity as an actress. When he addresses Monroe's creation of characters through gestures, he acknowledges the extent to which her film roles were her creations, but, because his project is primarily biographical, he thinks of these creations as mirrors of her psyche, rather than as crafted performances, and he therefore attends primarily to variations in those gestures across films rather than to each performance as a discrete entity.

Recent performance studies have added perspectives from which to consider the work of female stars. As Adrienne McLean notes regarding Rita Hayworth, "There are still many working in film studies who would hesitate to grant anything resembling subjectivity and agency to a female star image, much less a star so well known for her commodification, objectification, passivity, and one-dimensionality as a performer and as a pin-up" (*Being* 4). Nevertheless, in the last few years, critics have begun to analyze Monroe's performances. Matthew Solomon calls attention to Monroe's "metaperformances," in which "she often plays [performers, and therefore] two separate but not entirely distinct roles nested within one another" (108). In so doing, Solomon encourages us to read Monroe's performances as commentary on performing. Similarly, Kristen Pullen and Ana Salzberg have challenged us to see Monroe as a more complex figure. Pullen refers to Monroe as a "spectacular performer" whose physical appearance distracted audiences from the labor of acting (11). Salzberg documents Monroe's narcissistic female image, but also points out that such an image compels us to recognize the work that goes into making a star. In the context of these revised perspectives on Monroe's stardom, further examination of how her performances acknowledged and resisted the sexpot is in order.

Monroe exerted considerable control over the outcome of her performances, a little-known fact that encourages careful attention to her films. Although her star persona was largely "manufactured" through her new name, new look, and extensive acting and diction lessons, Ty Burr asserts that "she became big enough to understand that she was bigger than her studio, and that someone *that* big should be the author of her fame rather than its victim" (173). Once she acquired access to the movie-going audience, Monroe worked diligently to maintain their interest. As the author of her fame, Monroe first had control over personnel in 1954's *River of No Return* (dir. Otto Preminger): she demanded Jack Cole as choreographer (after working with him on *Gentlemen Prefer Blondes*) and chose Robert Mitchum as her leading man.[15] She also discussed script revisions with Preminger, thereby shaping her role (Leaming 90). More importantly, Monroe was an actress who dictated her own performances. She improvised scenes and created her character as she saw fit for the first time in 1956's *Bus Stop* (Leaming 213). Director Josh Logan confirms that he and screenwriter George Axelrod considered Monroe's "feeling about the whole story" when rewriting her scenes (qtd. in Rollyson 102). "Only very rarely have actors had the opportunity to influence a film so directly," insists Rollyson, "and Logan's supreme trust in Monroe, built on his belief that she was 'one of the great talents of all time,' has been occasionally matched by other directors but never surpassed" (102). Monroe continued to influence her roles not only in front of the camera, but also in the writing and editing stages. Billy Wilder and I.A.L. Diamond incorporated Monroe's suggestions into her entrance in *Some Like It Hot* (1959, dir. Billy Wilder) (Leaming 314). And although it was often necessary to shoot multiple takes of scenes involving Monroe, directors chose her successful takes over those of her costars because of her luminous screen presence (Banner 328).

This book's examination of how Monroe's performances acknowledged and resisted the sexpot persona complements the ideological understanding of Monroe that Richard Dyer established in his foundational works of star studies, *Stars* and *Heavenly Bodies*. Dyer begins his analysis of Monroe in *Stars* by suggesting her mannerisms reveal messages about sexuality and vulnerability, thereby pairing analysis of her performances with analysis of her ideological significance (158). Dyer notes that Monroe "seemed to 'be' the very tensions that ran through the ideological life of fifties America," underscoring how reading Monroe's films alongside popular cultural texts, such as *Playboy* magazine and Alfred Kinsey's reports on human sexuality, can help us understand how she engaged with American sexual ideology in a way that attracted and maintained audience interest (*Stars* 36). By establishing that films, as well as publicity materials and the stars themselves, are "texts" to be read, Dyer provides a framework for understanding stars within their cultural and historical contexts. These contexts are crucial for understanding what a star means to her audiences.

The few existing audience studies confirm that audiences connected to Monroe. Whereas psychoanalytic theory posits that the film's narrative positions the audience in fairly limited ways, scholars engaging in audience studies explore how actual audience members identify with film stars. Stars do not have a monolithic meaning, and different audiences identify with and react to stars in different ways. Jackie Stacey has found that Monroe represented for some British audiences the fantasy of a glamorous lifestyle (154), so they copied her fashion and hairstyles (192–193, 203).[16] Other British audience members identified with her "vulnerability and fear" (Stacey 162). Monroe's fans, then, understood her as more than a sexpot or a naive dumb blonde, in ways that I will address, drawing on fan letters, later in this chapter.

As a star with box office draw, Monroe was both a product of and participant in the Hollywood studio system. Influenced by Marxist principles, some star studies attend to the industrial conditions within which the star labored, shifting focus from the interpreting audience to the meaning-generating star and thereby acknowledging that stars have agency and are not objects or commodities. Danae Clark, in *Negotiating Hollywood*, argues that most star studies, influenced as they are by either apparatus theory or empirical audience studies, have privileged the subjectivity of the spectator over the subjectivity of the star, implying that the interpreting spectator creates all the film's meaning (10). Clark instead considers stars as active laborers within a network of industrial forces. She also considers the interaction between filmic and extrafilmic discourse, thereby calling attention to both the labor of the actor in creating the performance and the labor of the spectator in interpreting and receiving or resisting the film's message. Virginia Wright Wexman points out that female stars, while they are often "understood to play a subordinate and dependent role," are elevated to positions of power through the earnings they make by playing that role (133–134). The power stars have within the industry thereby underscores significant differences between themselves and their film characters.

Monroe was vital to the Hollywood industry of the 1950s. In recent books on stardom's role in branding film personalities, Paul McDonald analyzes the "symbolic commerce of stardom," or the extent to which the film industry is built upon selling star personalities (*Hollywood* 14). Monroe was a power player in this "symbolic commerce." Despite the low salary of her initial contracts, by as early as 1952, "it was estimated that Marilyn's name on a movie increased the gross by at least $500,000" (Zolotow 114), and by 1956, "every film that was made without Marilyn earned at least $1,000,000 less because her name was not on the marquee" (Zolotow 244).[17] Monroe's ability to generate revenue for the studio provided bargaining power when she walked out on her contract in April 1954, the same month she earned a top performer award from *Photoplay* magazine, the most popular fan magazine of the era. Monroe refused to work because the studio had failed to consult her on the script, a power that was not part of her contract. After holding out for over a year, Monroe garnered director, though not story, approval in a "new $400,000 contract for four pictures in seven years" that was, according to one industry veteran, "one of the greatest single triumphs ever won by an actress against a powerfully entrenched major studio" (qtd. in Manning 96). Later, Monroe was also paid $200,000 for two films she never made so she would not sue the studio (Leaming 327; Banner 322, 336). Finally, although Twentieth Century-Fox fired Monroe in 1961, some have recently suggested that she signed a new contract with the studio just before her death (D. Marshall 47).

Monroe exerted a degree of control over the Hollywood studio system, bargaining for the financial compensation she deserved as one of the decade's most popular stars. According to *Variety*'s annual grosses, Monroe rocketed from appearing in films grossing $3.5 million in 1952 to grossing $15 million in 1953, and in all other years in which she released films, she grossed at least $1.5 million (tallies by Higashi 18).[18] (Compare Doris Day's grosses in the same period, which peaked at $8.5 million in 1962, and Elizabeth Taylor's grosses of $12 million in 1956 and 1957.) Monroe was also vital to the publicity industry. For example, in 1953 she was the subject of five stories in *Photoplay*,[19] and appeared on the cover eight times; in 1954 these numbers were six and five, respectively. (Debbie Reynolds also appeared on eight covers in 1953, and Doris Day appeared on four covers [tallies by Higashi 22].) Not only did Monroe form her own production company and negotiate for a contract that gave her some official control over her film roles through director approval, but also many of her roles were created specifically for her, and when she failed to report to work, productions shut down. Monroe significantly contributed to the financial successes of both Hollywood and the publicity industry in the 1950s.[20]

Box office draw is certainly one important industrial marker of whether one can be labeled a star, and a star has box office power because an audience derives pleasure from seeing her on the screen, but a star also, as many critics have pointed out, has ideological significance that extends beyond her film roles. As Dyer argues, "Stars matter because they act out aspects of life that matter to us; and performers get to be stars when what they act out matters to enough people" (*Heavenly* 17).[21] This cultural role contributes to the star's dynamism over time. While the star's basic appearance and character types may remain roughly the same, a culture's concerns do not remain consistent over the course of a few years; consequently, the star's meaning is *not* stable and consistent over time—in fact, much of what interests us about stars has to do with their varying successes and failures. Through the star's offscreen and onscreen personae, audiences place them on the spectrum of acceptable behaviors and determine whether their behavior is to be emulated or criticized.[22] Monroe's merger of extremes—sexpot and star—required concerted crafting of her offscreen publicity, along with the support of a fan base that, from their experiences in the contradictory atmosphere of postwar America, understood that reconciling the extreme polarities established for women in that moment was remarkable, even admirable, and certainly star-worthy.

A number of writers have advanced the misinformed notion that women could not relate to Monroe, a notion that disregards evidence to the contrary found in letters from the 1950s and early 1960s. Haskell argues that "women couldn't identify with her and didn't support her" (254), and Dyer, while noting that "never" is too extreme, confirms, by casually asking a few women, that women wouldn't have been able to see her as resistant to the norms of 1950s sexuality (*Heavenly* 57).[23] I have no doubt that there are both women and men who didn't respond to Monroe, but evidence suggests that many women did in fact relate to her.[24] Female fans often responded not to Monroe's sexpot characteristics, but to the vulnerability and humor she brought to her roles. Gloria Steinem says she was "embarrass[ed]" by Monroe in *Gentlemen Prefer Blondes*, but why she was embarrassed indicates that she related to her performance: "How dare she be just as vulnerable and unconfident as I felt?" (12).[25] Women also saw Monroe as a fashionable woman to emulate. One of Stacey's respondents, Betty Cruse, remembers: "Monroe appealed to me deeply and desperately, little girl lost with the body of a desirable woman. She lit up the screen with her performances, the glamour, her movements were so exciting. Watching her made me feel she was in some way lonely and vulnerable, she was my cult figure, I felt like me, she was running away from herself" (162). Clearly, the fan response to Monroe is not as simple as it has been assumed to be.

In an era in which it was common for women's experiences to be silenced, cordoned off as "private" matters better left undiscussed, the star apparatus surrounding Marilyn Monroe exploited her private life to make women's matters heard.[26] Female fans responded to stories about Monroe's failure to have a baby, a frequent topic in fan magazines. A *Photoplay* article movingly imagined Monroe saying, "'Someday, when I grow up, I'm going to have a little girl of my own. And I'm never going to leave her, never. Never . . .'" (Dinter 93). This story inspired fans to reveal their own hardships under the guise of communicating with the heartbroken star. "I just read your article in *Photoplay* and it was the most heartwarming story I ever read that actually happened to a real person," wrote one fan. "I understand how much you want a baby. You see, my doctor told me chances were I wouldn't have one when I married, but the dear Lord was merciful. I did have a beautiful baby boy. . . . I want to say, Marilyn, please have patience" (Happy 10). A sexpot is not a figure we expect to warm a mother's heart, and yet this woman wished the supposed sexpot domestic happiness. Fans also responded to publicity analyses of Monroe's multiple identities. In response to a *Time* magazine report about Monroe's first suicide attempt, one woman wrote, "Turn in your couch, TIME, along with your amateur analyst's badge. That rundown of what makes Marilyn fun hit a new low in taste" (Pehowski 6), and another asked, "Is it really anybody's business (except Miss Monroe's) to be informed about her parentage?" (Citrin 4). The revealing story made these women feel protective, and they complained that it was unfair to expose Monroe's personal secrets of uncertain parentage and childhood abuses.[27] Women, it seems, identified with Monroe because, as a star, she spoke to women's concerns and seemed to need women's support; they saw not a sexpot, but a fragile companion—and audiences today also often see fragility in Monroe's performances.

After Monroe's death, her female fans expressed their various connections to her. Jennifer Frost reports that letters to Hedda Hopper after Monroe's suicide were primarily from men, "confirming scholarly conclusions that men, not women, constituted Monroe's fan base" (210). While Frost accurately captures the dominant scholarly interpretation of Monroe's fan base, archived letters indicate that many male and female fans felt an intimate connection with Monroe. Joan Tompkins, who met Monroe at a party, wrote to Hopper, "Monroe became admired by women too the world over" because of the details of her Cinderella narrative (4). Tompkins explains: "For they know of her hard life as a child and they too could see behind the façade of her acting life. She had suffered as many of them, two miscarriages and the same feelings of insecurity many have. . . . It would take a stone heart not to be touched by the story of her life. It was filled with more pathos, misery, drama than any story which she played in the movies" (4–5). Tompkins is certainly speaking from hindsight, noting how easily warning signs of Monroe's suicide could have been found if only fans had been sensitive and sympathetic enough, but she also points out what women felt they had in common with Monroe. Similarly, Mrs. Maurice Darone wrote that Monroe had many friends she never knew in "the every day, hard working, ordinary people who grew to love her, the little girl who never knew the love of parents and a happy home. I think that is why all hearts went out to her, everyone reaching out to help her, protect her" (4).[28] Because fans recognized more than the sexpot in Monroe's offscreen persona, they were likely primed to read more than the sexpot for which she was scripted into her film roles. And these fans' desire to protect Monroe from herself still resonates with audiences today, who look for signs of her life—and her death—in her screen performances.

Hollywood Sexpots

More than Monroe's fan base differentiates her from other Hollywood blondes designed to play the sexpot. Brief comparison of Monroe to a few Hollywood actresses of the 1930s and 1940s will illustrate her continuity with and difference from previous "eye candy" actresses. Hollywood has a long history of building up potential stars in sexpot roles. Jean Harlow, the "blonde bombshell" with whom Monroe is often compared, immediately comes to mind. Harlow's roles reflect pre-Code Hollywood's ability to present female sexuality openly and casually; her characters are tough rather than vulnerable, straightforward about their gold digging and often successful, but their toughness is also disarmed through "self-deprecating humor and habitual linking of sex and mirth" (Tremper 153).[29] Ann Sheridan, too, was most successful in "tangy" roles in the 1940s (*Screenland* 1940, qtd. in Schultz 164), roles she received after she won the rigged "Oomph Girl" campaign concocted in 1939 by Warner Bros. press agents Bob Taplinger and Daisy Parsons.[30] A year after Sheridan's "Oomph Girl" campaign, the small Hal Roach studio launched the "Ping Girl" campaign to promote Carole Landis, but then released her to Twentieth Century-Fox, where she often played second leads behind bigger stars like Betty Grable and Rita Hayworth (Gans 48, 66). While monikers such as "blonde bombshell," "Oomph Girl," and "Ping Girl" attracted plenty of attention, drawing attention to an actress's sex appeal was not all it took to make a star.

If that were the case, Monroe's imitators would have been stars of an equal caliber. There were plenty of them—March 1957's *Photoplay* cover touted "Blonde Explosions" Kim Novak, Jayne Mansfield, and Marilyn Monroe, and Mamie Van Doren is also part of this group.[31] Although the feature story inside asked, "Eeny, Meeny, Miny, Mo, Who Will Be the *First To Go?*," it also concluded, "We want all three of these young women here to stay" (Lane 38, 40).[32] Kim Novak is known as "the very last of the studio-created stars—an epithet she despised" (Brown 2), and as a somewhat respected actress for her performances in *Picnic* (1955, dir. Joshua Logan), *The Man with the Golden Arm* (1955, dir. Otto Preminger), and *Vertigo* (1958, dir. Alfred Hitchcock). Sumiko Higashi claims that Novak failed to achieve star status comparable to Monroe's because she did not "spark publicity and excite fans by marrying famous men" (98), and she did not have "a strong and distinctive personality" (99).[33] Monroe's distinctive off-screen persona may have attracted attention, but, as I will show, the way she both acknowledged and resisted the sexpot role also made her more than just another Hollywood blonde.

Other famous blondes of the period were known as Monroe knockoffs. Jayne Mansfield was a "road company Marilyn Monroe" (Saxton 121).[34] Her best role was a version of Monroe in *Will Success Spoil Rock Hunter?* (1957, dir. Frank Tashlin),[35] which film reviewers nevertheless called a "leadpipe travesty of Marilyn Monroe," commenting on how Monroe brought a lighter humor to her roles (qtd. in Farris 76, 68). Mamie Van Doren recognized herself as a Monroe knockoff, writing, "I became Universal's answer to Marilyn Monroe, though I (and they) had no idea what the real question was" (qtd. in Lowe 20), but, as Barry Lowe points out, she was the Monroe for the teen audience. Novak, Mansfield, and Van Doren were all built up as imitations of Monroe; Monroe's success was instrumental in creating the context for the limited stardom of her imitators.

Of course, there were other sexy stars during this period, though they weren't sexpots and stars in the same way that Monroe was. What makes Monroe unique among these actresses, such as Betty Grable, Lana Turner, Rita Hayworth, Lauren Bacall, or Jane Russell? Grable and Turner both contained an element of the "ordinary" within their images. Grable was famous for one pinup image, a wardrobe test that featured her smiling over her shoulder as her backside and legs dominated the foreground. Grable's pinup image, and subsequent stardom, "seemed to rest on a truly hyperbolic ordinariness," explains McLean, "marked as such on two levels: by a well-publicized absence of acting, singing, and dancing talent, and on an eroticism, if such it was, that was contained and made comforting by a domesticity and working life presented as being subsidiary to the needs of husband and children" ("Betty" 169). Turner, too, possessed what Dyer calls a "sexy-ordinary image" ("Four" 217), meaning an image that does not depend on the exotic for its appeal, although as her career progressed she became increasingly associated with an "attraction to bad" and was therefore pitiable ("Four" 226). Hayworth often played the femme fatale in a position similar to Turner's, but was both exotic and an extraordinarily talented dancer.[36] Bacall and Russell had stockier figures and played tougher women. Monroe's starring role with Russell in *Gentlemen Prefer Blondes* underscores how much sexier Monroe was than Russell, and literally makes Russell into a Monroe impersonator in the courtroom scene in which she pretends to be Lorelei.

Thinking of Monroe as just another sexy Hollywood blonde conceals her unique qualities as an actress and the skillful way in which her off-screen performance of "Marilyn Monroe" was crafted to inform her film roles and elevate her status as an actress. Monroe was never an "ordinary," girl-next-door type—her sex appeal was almost always exaggerated—and she brought humor and lightness to the majority of her roles. (Her non-comedic performances in *Don't Bother to Knock* [1952, dir. Roy Ward Baker] and *Niagara* [1953, dir. Henry Hathaway] are also quite good, but audiences wrote to the studio that they preferred her in comedy, shaping her subsequent roles.) Monroe's portrayal of the sexpot was not a parody (per Jayne Mansfield), nor was it an agonizing portrayal of the woman torn between desire for pleasure and desire for security (per Kim Novak). Neither was Monroe a sultry, femme fatale type like Lauren Bacall or Lana Turner—the punishment Monroe received for her sexuality in her films was being the butt of the joke, and her vulnerability, both onscreen and off, ensured that her sexuality wasn't only a joke.

What sets Monroe apart from these other actresses is that as Monroe transitioned into full-fledged film stardom, she didn't lose the sexpot qualities that established her career—she played "herself," or, more precisely, she played "Marilyn Monroe," both onscreen and off. I do not intend with this claim to undermine Monroe's acting talent. Rather, chapter 2 on her early performances and chapter 5 on the Method both argue that Monroe gave carefully constructed performances that challenged what was expected of a sexpot. These performances showcased her often imitated but really inimitable traits. One of those traits is her sense of comedic timing, which allowed her to defuse criticism with honest punchlines.

Another of those traits is her vulnerability, which allowed women to relate to her and men and women to seek to protect her, and which also lessened the sense that she was only sex and always available.

Monroe's films took advantage of both her comedic timing and her vulnerability, casting the sexpot in timely roles that engaged with concerns that were on the minds of many Americans. Monroe's roles engaged with the issues surrounding being a single woman in postwar culture. Because she was simultaneously a sexpot and a star, she subverted some of the repressive ideology around postwar gender roles, marriage, and female sexuality. Monroe held up a mirror that often reflected the way things were in postwar culture, but also often reflected the way things were becoming. And, although her desire to improve as an actress was often mocked, the Method films she made between 1956 and 1961 (*Bus Stop, The Prince and the Showgirl* [1957, dir. Laurence Olivier], *Let's Make Love* [1960, dir. George Cukor], and *The Misfits* [1961, dir. John Huston]) illuminate the process of confronting oneself as a joke, and in so doing acknowledge and contest the impulse to disregard Monroe as just a sexpot.

Monroe as Mirror

To better understand how Monroe combined the sexpot and star in the specific context of postwar America, I have examined a number of popular and archival sources. Fan magazines and mainstream media provide evidence of how Monroe's contemporaries were encouraged to think of her. Comparing Monroe's film roles and publicity to other cultural documents, such as marriage advice manuals, the Kinsey reports on human sexuality, and popular assessments of Method acting, illuminates how Monroe resonated with her culture. I have also examined reviews and contemporary criticism as well as film comment cards and letters to fan magazines and to studios in order to better understand how audiences responded to Monroe's films. Engaging with these various aspects of stardom simultaneously allows me to account for the multiple ways Monroe creates meaning onscreen and off, to determine how she served as "some kind of mirror" to postwar Americans.

Within the context of a few of the major cultural anxieties of the 1950s, I devote particular attention to Monroe as an actress and therefore to her film performances. Monroe said: "Rather than do so much talking I'd rather act. . . . To really say what's in my heart, I'd rather show than to say. Even though I want people to understand, I'd much rather they understand on the screen. If I don't do that, I'm on the wrong track or in the wrong profession" (qtd. in Goode 199). Her wish to be understood as an actress was not granted during her lifetime; critics were perhaps too blinded by Monroe the sexpot. Nevertheless, Monroe was popular with women as well as men, and it seems likely that this is because her performance of femininity—deployed in roles with ideological messages about marriage (chapter 3), female sexuality (chapter 4), and acting (chapter 5)— showed itself as a performance and thereby encouraged thinking of her as challenging both the sexpot stereotypes and the period's gender norms. Before she could engage in such ideological work, Monroe had to turn in performances that would move her beyond the simple sexpot for which she had been cast and turn her into a star. How she did so is the subject of chapter 2.

CHAPTER 2

BECOMING A STAR

THE PUBLICITY BUILDUP AND
EARLY PERFORMANCES

How did Marilyn Monroe make the transition from sexpot, eye candy, dirty joke to star? The conjunction of Monroe's offscreen publicity, which endeared her to audiences, and her film performances, mostly in minor roles from 1950 to 1952, effected that transition. Alan Lovell and Peter Krämer argue in their text on *Screen Acting* that star studies tend to focus on the star's ineffable charisma or on stars as texts to be read rather than on stars as actors (4). Elements inherent to the process of filmmaking encourage this; it has often been suggested that directors and editors cobble together stars' performances. Nevertheless, the stars speak the lines and produce the movements and expressions that create the characters they play. While it is not possible to wholly separate performance from other elements of film form, such as mise-en-scène, camerawork, and editing, examining Monroe's performances as performances will help us better understand her unique career and legacy.

Certainly, some attention has recently been paid to Monroe as a performer, but it remains worth considering how her performances, both onscreen and off, allowed her to create her own star quality.[1] Her early buildup situated her persona in competition with itself—the sexpot versus the shy and vulnerable childlike woman—and her early film performances, despite often revealing her lack of acting training, consistently brought more than over-the-top sexiness to the screen. The ease with which she performed her hurts, and the ease with which she alleviated tension with humor, allowed her to create a star quality that took her beyond the sexpot to the star.

OFFSCREEN PUBLICITY

Because stars are the sum of their offscreen publicity and their film roles, we must carefully examine the publicity that informs audiences' understandings of film performances. As a result of star "branding," Graham McCann explains, "the audience arrives to watch a well-known star, armed with certain preconceptions about the performer derived from knowledge of past appearances, generic conventions, advertising campaigns, and critical reviews" (25). During the classical Hollywood era, 1917–1960, studios "manufactured" their potential stars in order to increase the likelihood that they would in fact become stars and assume a prominent place in the collective imagination. Through makeovers and acting lessons, the studios both exercised a modicum of control over potential stars and gave the actors tools with which to challenge or exceed the roles as scripted through their performances.[2] These elements of star-making were relatively common knowledge: Fredda Dudley, for example, wrote a regular feature on "How a Star Is Born" in *Photoplay* in 1950 and 1951. Each article discussed how Hollywood newcomers were transformed into stars through acting lessons, makeovers, and conversation with other newly minted stars. Once a potential star participated in this training, the publicity agents went to work, telling the public about the newcomer's past and general outlook on life, and making sure people saw the newcomer in the right places with the right people.

Monroe received the standard studio buildup (after she signed her third contract, with Twentieth Century-Fox, having been dropped by both that studio and Columbia). In her case, this buildup was directed toward turning her into a sexpot—thus, during her first major publicity tour, she was dubbed the "Mmmm Girl" (Wilson 4), and in most photos of her during the late 1940s and early 1950s she wore a bathing suit. At the same time, however, elements of her persona challenged how the studio tried to exploit her. For example, she posed for cheesecake pictures, but the way she looked directly at the camera and smiled as she performed abdominal exercises or frolicked in the surf made her an active subject rather than a passive object. The Cinderella narrative the press agents developed for her stressed her working-class origins, but fans focused on how she was unloved, seeing her not as the tart from the wrong side of the tracks but as vulnerable and needy. These complex combinations allowed Monroe both to be a sexpot and to gain a prominent place in the public imagination as a star, first through her modeling work and then through her film performances.

Playing "Marilyn Monroe" in Still Photographs

Monroe's pre-stardom modeling work produced images of her that were soon nearly ubiquitous. These images, along with the most famous publicity stills from her film career, constituted a stable nodal point around which the instability of her identity, both onscreen and off, could coalesce without disintegrating. Carl Rollyson writes, "Marilyn Monroe's career is one of the finest examples of the way in which human identity in the twentieth century has been defined in terms of the replicated image" ("Replicated" 18). And yet, despite the stability they seem to offer, these images also invite viewers to seek more information about the star, to look for cracks in the apparently seamless identity. These images seem straightforward at first glance but become ambiguous upon closer examination, thereby allowing audience members with a number of interests to connect to the star through them. As McCann puts it, "The image thus displays the *absence of the absence*—what has gone seems to remain"—or what is really inaccessible, the star, seems accessible (77). Images of Monroe's body and face stabilized her star persona, thereby increasing her contemporaries' connection to her.

Because this chapter specifically focuses on the period in which Monroe transformed from sexpot to star, I'll discuss only the most famous publicity images from that period here (leaving aside, therefore, the [in]famous subway-grating shot from *The Seven Year Itch* [1955, dir. Billy Wilder]).[3] These include her early pinup and cheesecake photographs and her nude calendar photo, which was featured in *Life* in 1952. Even these images are not as simple as they might at first seem. While they all appear to contribute to the common understanding of Monroe as an emblem of 1950s "Lolita lechery," they do not lock Monroe into the role of sex object (Haskell 255). Each of these images of her body works simultaneously in two directions, at once suggesting a woman who has been objectified and a woman who controls her public image.

Monroe's pinup career began because of her wartime factory work, a fact that should make evident that her modeling work, and indeed her entire career, participated in the cultural struggle over changing gender roles. Monroe's pinup career began when she was painting fuselages for Radioplane during World War II; army air corps filmmakers and pinup photographer David Conover came to the plant to document women's support of the war effort. Conover photographed Monroe in a sweater in order to accentuate her figure, but at the same time as his photos emphasized her breasts, they also emphasized that she was a woman working to support the war effort, a Rosie the Riveter. After Conover "discovered" her, Monroe signed with Emmeline Snively at the Blue Book Modeling Agency; Snively thought she was "girl-next-doorish" (Guiles 91). Indeed, the public first saw Monroe on a *Family Circle* cover in April of 1946, wearing a pinafore and cuddling a lamb—certainly not a sexpot image.

Monroe's sexpot image derives from other modeling jobs in this period, when she posed for pinups for *Yank*, *Laff*, and *Stars and Stripes*. Pinups of the era are commonly thought of as passive objects, as Kathryn Benzel writes, "a spectacle for public consumption" (3)—think Bettie Page's bondage photos, for example, or even Betty Grable's derriere taking front and center as she smiles over her shoulder.[4] However, many of the earliest pinup images of Monroe stand out not because they document her exploitation, but because she seems to collaborate with the viewer.[5] She is often active, running on a beach or climbing a rock, looking directly at the viewer.[6] She may be scantily clad in these images, but that does not mean she is completely objectified. As Benzel explains, "Looking at photographs of Monroe, the viewer has the feeling that she will step out of her frame at any moment. In this illusion, the viewer is made to feel less a voyeur and more a participant because Monroe, her pose, her expression, her costume, all encourage interaction rather [than] anonymity on the part of the spectator" (3). Such a reversal empowers Monroe as the photograph's subject rather than its object.

Evidence confirms that these poses resulted from Monroe's skill as a model and control over her photographic image rather than from a photographer's direction. Monroe was well known for requiring approval of publicity photos, going so far as to destroy those she didn't like.[7] Photographer Richard Avedon explains, "She understood photography . . . and she also understood what makes a great photograph—not the technique, but the content. And she knew it was up to her to fill the page. She also knew that if she wasn't in the right mood, she couldn't give the right performance for the photograph" (qtd. in Hattersley 59). This indicates how her film performances draw on the skills she learned through her modeling work—she performed for both, and, therefore, could not produce the effect she wanted without the right conditions. Although she may have been difficult to work with, when the conditions were right, the results were worth the struggle.

Monroe maintained her agency despite the objectifying impulses of photography and film, even in her nude photos. In 1952, before Monroe had been featured in any starring roles, the public learned that she was the woman in the nude *Golden Dreams* photo taken in 1948 by Tom Kelley and printed as Miss February 1952 in "The Exclusive 'Hollywood' Calendar Line." To stop speculation in the entertainment columns about whether or not this nude was in fact Monroe, she admitted to posing for it in an interview with Aline Mosby of the United Press, whose article "Nude Calendar Beauty at Last Is Identified" appeared in the *Los Angeles Herald Examiner* on March 13, 1952. Mosby's article emphasized that poverty had led Monroe to pose, an excuse that *Life*'s article "Hollywood Topic A-Plus" repeated alongside a small color reproduction of the calendar image on April 7, 1952, with the caption, "Marilyn unclothed posed for calendar art when she was broke" ("Hollywood" 101). Monroe explained her nude poses in a way that made them acceptable to the general public. She told Hedda Hopper, "I was hungry and the fifty dollars I earned paid my board at the Studio Club. They had been carrying me along way past the time limit. I did nothing wrong and I am not ashamed to admit I posed for the pictures. Mr. Kelly [*sic*] took them and his wife was present" (qtd. in Hopper "Marilyn" 36, 85). Sheilah Graham stated that the studio urged Monroe to say nothing about the photo because "libel laws being what they are, they knew that, so long as Marilyn didn't admit she had posed for the photo, reporters would have thought twice before identifying her as the girl in the birthday suit. But—'I had to tell the truth,' says Marilyn, half closing her big, beautiful blue eyes. 'I just had to . . .'" ("Why" 97). Although the studio told her to deny the photo, she used this moment instead to begin shaping her resistance to those who considered her incapable of being anything more than a sexpot. Monroe took credit for the photos, refusing to allow them, and her detractors, to speak for her, making them instead just the result of a modeling job. Rather than a scandal, Monroe's nude photo was crucial in getting the public to like, even respect, the sexpot.[8]

The photo, in typical nude-spread fashion, exposes the entire length of Monroe's body. Richard Dyer criticizes the art photography tradition in which Kelley worked, noting that "the model is usually required to pose in willfully bizarre positions" in "this unpleasantly dehumanizing tradition of photography—and it was indeed a disreputable form, associated, quite correctly, with the dirty talk of men's locker rooms and toilets" (*Heavenly* 29). While Monroe's body is twisted into less than natural angles in Kelley's photos, they are not as unequivocally dehumanizing as Dyer suggests. In the two most famous photos from this shoot, "Golden Dreams" and "A New Wrinkle," she is looking at the viewer (albeit beneath lowered eyelids) and seems to push herself off of the canvas, suggesting that she knows she is being watched and that, far from passive, she is about to arise from this position.[9] Such activity, perhaps, made her more approachable. Richard Woodward writes that Monroe's nude photos "were not only the first photographs of a naked woman that many American males in the 1950s ever saw, they were almost certainly the first naked pictures of a celebrity" (23). Through her nude photos, Monroe represented a fantasy of access not only to a beautiful woman, but also to Hollywood glamour and success.

Given how well known images of Monroe's body are today, it is perhaps surprising to find that many images of just her face circulated in the 1950s. Fan magazines, as well as mainstream magazines such as *Life* and *Time*, frequently used a medium close-up on their covers; these images complemented Monroe's over-the-top sex appeal with approachability and vulnerability. Although even Monroe's, as *Time* describes them, "moist, half-closed eyes and moist, half-opened mouth" ("Something" 88) were associated with sex appeal, Monroe was not always photographed with this expression. A few of the poses suggest an effort at sexiness, but in many of her magazine covers (easily accessible through a Google image search), she is laughing, and several of them feature a benign smile. Emphasizing Monroe's cheerfulness over her sex appeal is an understandable approach to attracting a female readership for these magazines, but it also serves to depict Monroe as good-natured and fun-loving.

Still other images suggest a stillness, almost a "deer in the headlights" look—as if she has been photographed in the middle of a private thought (see, e.g., the October 1953 and June 1955 *Modern Screen* covers, accessible through the Media History Digital Library, www.mediahistoryproject.org /fanmagazines). According to British critic Gavin Lambert, "For all the wolf calls that she gets and deserves, there is something mournful about

Miss Monroe. She doesn't look happy. She lacks the pin-up's cheerful grin. She seems to have lost something, or to be waking up from a bad dream" (qtd. in Robinson 143). These images fix Monroe as enigmatic, a mystery about whom audience members can freely speculate. The close-up in a film, or the still image of a star's face that resembles a close-up, gives the audience a chance to purchase and possess intimacy with the star, to speculate about what inspired the look on her face.[10] The variety of poses Monroe deployed allowed her to present herself as something more than a sexpot. The distinction between who she appeared to be in posed images and glimpses of her pain in candid snapshots was at least partly responsible for Monroe's popularity: because it was clear that the images of her did not reveal all there was to know about her, either of her body or her inner life, audiences sought more information than the images themselves could convey. For this information, they turned to narratives circulated in the fan magazines and general press.

Playing "Marilyn Monroe" in Publicity Stories

How did the studio publicity help Monroe in the early days of her career, building her up from a sexpot to a star? Although they used many of the strategies familiar to the star buildup—a Cinderella narrative and exposing both private and public personalities, for example—these stories stuck in Monroe's case to make her an admirable sexpot. Monroe seemed to rise to stardom almost overnight, and, like many who suddenly achieve fame, she was a controversial figure. For instance, Roger Newland complained in *Silver Screen*: "Hillbillies who can't tell you who's president right now could probably recite the details of Marilyn's life." They could do so, Hedda Hopper pointed out, because stories about Monroe appeared in "the public press more often, with more pictures and more prose, than any other personality in the world" ("Marilyn" 36). Perhaps it is because she was in the right place at the right time, but there seems to be more to the public's love for Monroe—her vulnerable charm and humor made the sexpot relatable.

The studio press agents couldn't control aspects of Monroe's family, her love life, her body, or her psyche. These uncontrolled aspects generated ruptures in the controlled publicity story, and the public most likely attached to, identified with, and found sympathy for the star because her life wasn't perfect. As Hopper indicates, "A lot of the things that are being written about her, she says, are far from the truth" ("Marilyn" 36)—and this was the case whether Monroe contributed to the stories or not. Monroe shaped her publicity narratives through her answers to interview questions, which were frequently exaggerations of the truth or humorous aphorisms. She consciously used her story to elicit sympathy and become, as Richard Schickel characterizes the star-fan relationship, an "intimate stranger" with the audience.[11] Lauren Berlant writes that "intimacy . . . involves an aspiration for a narrative about something shared, a story about both oneself and others that will turn out in a particular way" (1).[12] Star publicity provides the foundation for a narrative that fans can share with the star. The star acquires more stardom if she has "a distinctive narrative, allowing [herself] to be subjected to constant scrutiny and a demand for perpetual performance, encompassing [her] private life and personality as well as [her] public roles" (van Krieken 10).[13] The Hollywood publicity machinery supplied this narrative, but Monroe chose some of its details, and fans responded by making Monroe one of their favorite stars.

From the beginning of her career, studio publicists drew on Monroe's difficult childhood to provide a story that, although extreme, made Monroe a relatable figure. Norma Jeane Mortenson, as Monroe was originally called, tried to please all of her foster parents (as many as a dozen), despite their contradictory demands—some, for example, forbade dancing while others encouraged her to develop her performing talents. None of them generous, they all burdened her with numerous chores, made her bathe in water that had already been used by the rest of the family, and, at the Los Angeles County Orphans Home, made her wash all the dishes for only five cents a month.[14] Such mistreatment carried over into Monroe's adult relationships; according to the press, she lacked female friends. Jim Henaghan wrote, "There is no star in Hollywood with less friends than Marilyn Monroe," because of Monroe's focus on improving herself, and because she has never been good at making friends with women (67).[15] Having few friends is a hazard of being a sexpot, but these stories presented Monroe as a lonely child seeking (and deserving) a companion.

These aspects of Monroe's story supported the studio's efforts to cast her as a deserving Cinderella. Like Cinderella, Monroe was an orphan who had been subjected to cruel treatment and manual labor, and, like Cinderella, Monroe was isolated from women whose camaraderie she desired. Writers drew on these similarities throughout Monroe's career. In an article that contributed to her iconography before she had any starring roles, Robert Cahn described Monroe as "a blonde apparition in a strapless black cocktail gown, a little breathless as if she were Cinderella just stepped from a pumpkin coach" (15). The Cinderella story was alluded to in subsequent stories. "Her background provided a story that was an all-time high in Cinderella yarns. The public was ready for Marilyn," noted William Bruce for *Movieland* (62). Both Twentieth Century-Fox's official biography of 1956 (Brand) and a 1959 news release from the Rogers, Cowan, and Jacobs press office invoked Cinderella in their descriptions of Monroe, conveying a message of hard-earned success.

At the same time as publicists drew on typical rags-to-riches stories, however, they also strove to prove that Monroe was not like other Hollywood sexpots. One of the first fan magazine profiles of Monroe, Cahn's "The 1951 Model Blonde" in *Collier's*, calls attention to her resemblance to "the standard Hollywood Blonde, traditionally equipped with automatic batting eyelashes, a vague smile that seems to include everybody, and a head filled with sawdust" (15). Nevertheless, Cahn insists that Monroe has "potential as a sensitive actress," that she brings an "indelible vitality" to the screen, and that one can occasionally read "several anguished chapters" of living and "the look of a lost child" in her face (50). Another early fan magazine profile of Monroe, 1951's "Pin Up #2," emphasizes her sexpot qualities—she sleeps in "neither nightgown nor pajamas"—but points out that she is neither a "loose" woman nor sleeping her way to the top; instead, "she snubs" the "Hollywood wolves" (23).

The *Life* magazine article discussing Monroe's nude photo in 1952 also points out that Monroe resembles Jean Harlow, but emphasizes her difference from her predecessor, insisting: "There is no hardness or tartness in Marilyn. She is relaxed, warm, apparently absorbed by whatever man she has her big blue eyes fixed on at any particular moment" (104). *Photoplay*'s 1952 article "Temptations of a Bachelor Girl" contradicts Monroe's sexpot image by insisting that her "work and other interests" keep her from becoming "promiscuous": she works from 6:00 A.M. to 7:00 P.M. and studies lines at home in the evenings (Monroe 44).[16] In another *Photoplay* article, Monroe pleads, "I Want Women to Like Me." Other early publicity neutralized her sex appeal by making it part of her screen persona rather than a trait possessed by the offscreen actress. Henaghan describes Monroe as a "lovable fake" "liv[ing] two distinct lives" at the studio and at home (67).[17] The onscreen Monroe, he suggests, might have been a sexpot, but the offscreen Monroe was lovable and differed from previous Hollywood blondes.

This publicity seems to have worked—many fans reached out to Monroe to form an intimate bond with her. "By 1954," Lois Banner states, Monroe "was receiving as many as twenty-thousand fan letters a week, setting a new record among film stars" (*MM* 113).[18] Fans found unexpected common ground between themselves and Monroe, the supposed sexpot. Although Monroe's early film roles cast her as a sexpot, Monroe continued the work of her early modeling and publicity in performing both the sexpot and the vulnerable comedienne, and this work made her a star.

EARLY FILM PERFORMANCES

Monroe could not have become a star worthy of such publicity coverage had she not attracted audience attention in her early film roles. Monroe's directors and many other members of the production crew certainly contributed to her film performances; shot angles and editing rhythms color our understanding of her characters and the films' overall impacts. Nevertheless, as Cynthia Baron and Sharon Marie Carnicke point out, actors create the gestures, facial expressions, postures, and vocal delivery that are captured by a director's camera and chosen in the editing room (1–2).[19] Although consistently cast as a sexpot, Monroe also consistently challenged expectations for the sexpot, complicating these roles sometimes with humor and sometimes with self-reflexive commentary on women's roles, both onscreen and off. Three such sexpot roles, *Love Happy* (1949, dir. David Miller), *The Asphalt Jungle* (1950, dir. John Huston), and *All about Eve* (1950, dir. Joseph Mankiewicz), brought Monroe into the limelight. In the interim, she appeared in a number of throwaway roles as a sexy secretary, although *Monkey Business* (1952, dir. Howard Hawks) stands out among other minor roles of the period for illustrating Monroe's ability to maintain the sexpot image for which she was cast while also complementing the performances of major stars Cary Grant and Ginger Rogers. *Clash by Night* (1952, dir. Fritz Lang) and *Don't Bother to Knock* (1952, dir. Roy Ward Baker) solidified Monroe's ability to turn in convincing, sensitive, and dynamic film performances, and paved the way for her breakout stardom in 1953.

At the time of Monroe's earliest film roles, she was known from her modeling. She failed to attract attention in bit parts in *Scudda Hoo! Scudda Hay!* (1948, dir. F. Hugh Herbert), *Ladies of the Chorus* (1948, dir. Phil Karlson), and *A Ticket to Tomahawk* (1950, dir. Richard Sale), but her thirty-second-long role in *Love Happy* with the Marx Brothers became a publicity goldmine. In this role, Monroe saunters into the office of detective Sam Grunion (Groucho Marx) as a criminal prepares to murder him. She knocks, opens the door, and pauses in the doorway as the shot lingers on her sultry beauty. Grunion had snuck out of the office after she walked in, but he can't resist her appeal. He runs back into the office and asks, "Is there anything I can do for you?," a question he recognizes as "a ridiculous statement." She presses herself against him, and, in a bedroom voice, explains that she needs his help because "some men are following me." With this line, she begins to saunter out, but smiles as she passes near the camera, suggesting her awareness of her sex appeal. In thirty seconds of screen time, Monroe established herself as a smiling sexpot, and the accompanying publicity tour dubbed her the "Mmmm Girl," but she was determined to become more than a sexpot. In her 1950 roles as a kept woman in *The Asphalt Jungle* and as a fledgling actress in *All about Eve*, Monroe captivates audiences with the characters she creates who, despite their apparent stupidity, and with humor and naivete, demonstrate an unswerving commitment to advancing their own interests.

The Asphalt Jungle

The story of Monroe's appearance in *The Asphalt Jungle* has become one of the contradictory legends of her stardom, with various versions of why director John Huston cast her in the role of Angela Phinlay, "niece" of the lawyer-turned-crime-boss "Uncle Lon" Emmerich (Louis Calhern)—whether to settle a gambling debt, or as a favor to Monroe's agent, Johnny Hyde. Nevertheless, the key element that appears in all versions of the story is that, because Angela was supposed to lie on a couch, but there was none in the audition room, Monroe read the part while lying on the floor. Whether this signals a dedication to her craft that is a rare find or a Method actress in the making is less important than recognizing that this role stands out because of Monroe's careful choices. As Angela, she was not content just to "be sexy"—she created a character and took command of the role to fully portray that character.

Critics have suggested that Monroe's portrayal of Angela is indeterminate and amorphous—she is "either an innocent waif floating through the filthy channel of the action or a canny, utilitarian grafter" (Pomerance 26)—but careful attention to her expressions in her first scene with Uncle Lon reveals the depth she gives to what has been scripted as a shallow character. When he tells her not to call him Uncle Lon, she pouts, "I thought you liked it," and he says, "Maybe I did; I don't anymore." Her reaction to this statement—which we see in a medium shot focused on her face—shows that she is playing more than just the dumb, sexy blonde. Her eyes roll downward in consternation, just for a brief second, as we see a woman registering a threat of having to soon fend for herself, without a male benefactor—a woman who, like the men in the film, is trying to negotiate the "asphalt jungle" Huston has created, in which crime is "endemic to all human behavior" (Munby 140) (Figure 2.1). She then returns to her "work," putting on a good front to make her benefactor happy as she tells him about the special food she has ordered him for breakfast (Figure 2.2). Her most "sexpot" maneuver here is to stretch her arms out, thrust her chest forward, and yawn, to indicate, within the confines of the Production Code, that she is luring Lon to bed.[20] And yet, when he repeats the line "some sweet kid" after she mentions the salt mackerel and again after she kisses him and heads to bed, we get the sense that Lon is aware of how she has shifted registers, from consternation to seductive manipulation, and that we, the audience, should be aware of Angela's maneuvers here as well.

Monroe also takes command of her role in her second appearance in the film. Lon encourages her to take a trip, and, with magazine spread of the beach she wants to visit in hand, Angela asks him to "imagine me on this beach here in my green bathing suit, yipe!" and lays her head in his lap. When the detective pounding on the door interrupts Angela's efforts, her face registers the anxiety that her trip might be in danger (she gave a statement to detectives the day before and therefore suspects they are pounding on her door now). When Detective Andrews (Don Haggerty) tries to get her statement, she initially acts tough, calling him a "big banana head," but when Andrews tells her Lon is a "dead duck," she switches to a seductive and sweet act, lowering her eyes and pouting her lips. As Angela crosses the room to approach Police Commissioner Hardy (John McIntire), the low-angle shot visually indicates her power to save or sacrifice Lon, but also underscores her confusion, as she tries to catch Lon's eye for a

Figure 2.1. Angela reacts to her benefactor's sudden disdain for being called "Uncle." Frame enlargement from *The Asphalt Jungle*.

Figure 2.2. The kept woman tries to remain kept. Frame enlargement from *The Asphalt Jungle*.

cue regarding what she should say. Again, when Hardy asks her if her previous statement was true, she looks to Lon for a cue, but his eyes remain fixed on the papers before him, and when she looks to him for a cue a third time, he tells her to "tell the truth." She looks downtrodden as she does so. Writer Budd Schulberg praised the direction, and, by extension, Monroe's performance, saying, "the thought-processes of the little kept blonde were for once accurate" (Meyers *John* 157). Many object to the naivete, or, from another perspective, callousness behind Angela's inquiry regarding whether her trip is still on as she grasps the hand of the man she has just implicated in a crime. But although Angela is self-centered, she expresses some sympathy for Lon, demonstrating the complexity of her character.

The role of Angela gave Monroe a small opportunity to demonstrate the emotional range she could bring to the sexpot. It is clear that the character has been written as a foolish woman of loose morals, but it should also be clear that Monroe played this role not as a "dumb blonde" or as a "vamp," but as a young woman just learning how to be "kept." As Carl Rollyson notes, "Angela had to be passive, seductive, innocent, solicitous, puzzled, vulgar, scared, angry, stupid, nearly hysterical, anguished, and calculating in just two brief scenes" (*Marilyn* 38). Far from being a throwaway sexpot role, Monroe's brief but complex performance in *The Asphalt Jungle* demonstrates how she could be both sexy and turn in a provocative, dynamic performance. Audiences responded to her sex appeal; the preview cards from the first screening praise the scene "with the babe in the old man's house" and scenes with the "hot blonde" ("First Report"). Louella Parsons warned Lana Turner to watch out for Monroe because she could play the sexpot and give a moving performance: "Marilyn has a scene in which she wears slacks and a shirt that demurely cover her from neck to wrist to toe—and not even in a shower bath have I seen a girl look so naked. What's more, in another scene where, under police duress, Mar [*sic*] has to 'sing' about her 'protector,' she's devastating" (123). Because her performance is subtle, rather than over the top, it set the stage for her to both remain a sexpot and ascend to stardom as something more than a parody of the sexy blonde.

All about Eve

All about Eve is crucial in continuing Monroe's work to move beyond the sexpot. In it, she is cast in a role that is meant to signify "window dressing," the kind of woman a man can wear on his arm, the way one might a Rolex, an accoutrement that draws attention to him, not her. But she steals the scenes she's in without deviating from her role or upstaging the principals. Monroe plays Miss Caswell, the arm candy of theater critic Addison DeWitt (George Sanders), who has brought her to superstar Broadway actress Margo Channing's (Bette Davis) party so that she might "do [her]self some good" and impress a director. Miss Caswell is the up-and-coming starlet, but one who is not in the same league as talented theater actresses—one, instead, whose sex appeal and (limited) abilities might better suit television.

Miss Caswell is there to be mocked as inferior to the other, serious actresses, but several moments in the film also laud a lower-maintenance brand of entertainment. Director Bill Simpson (Gary Merrill) (arguably the most likeable character in a cast of backstabbers and cutthroats) tells Eve (Anne Baxter): "You want to know what the theater is? A flea circus. Also opera, also rodeos, carnivals, ballets, Indian tribal dances, Punch and Judy, a one-man band—all theater. Wherever there's magic, and make-believe, and an audience—there's theater." Bill acknowledges actresses who provide a different kind of entertainment than the overblown theatrics of the stage actresses in *All about Eve*. Addison later tells Miss Caswell she might be better suited for television, but the film has already stated that middlebrow entertainment is still a version of theater.

Within this context, the performances Miss Caswell gives in the film become significant. Although we do not witness her theater audition, we see her holding her own among the fast-talking theater crowd at Margo's party. Despite her role as Addison's arm candy, in her scenes with Margo, the blocking sets her up to be at the center of most shots, and her light clothing and hair, as well as the height she has on Margo, draw our eyes to her. She is also a built-in audience for the bitter banter and doublespeak of the exchange between Margo, Addison, and Eve—as we can tell from her eyes (positioned in the center of the shot) moving back and forth, following the conversation, directing our vision. And yet she refuses to participate in the same doublespeak—instead, she plainly states how she met Addison—"in passing"—and that any woman has limited opportunity to "talk" when with Addison. When Addison directs her to speak with a producer, we see her begin her performance, throwing her shoulders back, smiling, and sashaying across and out of the shot. These factors encourage us to do more than notice Miss Caswell—they insist that we recognize the dynamics of her performance as she moves from honest conversation to obviously deploying her sex appeal.

Miss Caswell also gives a performance that attracts attention at the end of the party. As Addison waxes on about theater people as "a breed apart," Miss Caswell notices the sable coat Birdie (Thelma Ritter) holds and admits, "There's something a girl could make sacrifices for." She brings humor to these "maudlin and self-important" exchanges between the theater people. What's more, for all that has been written about how the framing situates Eve before an audience in Margo's dressing room, how the exchange on the stairs draws an audience to Miss Caswell is equally significant (Figure 2.3). As she explains that she "can't yell, 'Oh, Butler,'" because "maybe somebody's name is Butler," all eyes on the stairs are turned toward her. Yes, this is a stupid remark, but it's also comedic, and comes in the midst of Margo's overblown "salute" from "we who are about to die." This scene with Miss Caswell indicates another way to gain an audience, and, Addison, too, sees her "career rising in the east like the sun." Playing Miss Caswell was, in fact, central to Monroe's rising career, for in it she demonstrated her ability to steal scenes through her comedic timing despite being cast as a sexpot.

Figure 2.3. Miss Caswell's audience. Frame enlargement from *All about Eve*.

REMAINING THE SEXPOT

Between these breakout roles and the roles that transitioned her into star-ring material, Monroe played small parts as window dressing in a number of films. As the sexy Wac who moves into the apartment building run by her ex-army buddy Jim (William Lundigan) and his wife (June Haver) in *Love Nest* (1951, dir. Joseph Newman), her character lounges in a bikini and slowly undresses for a shower. She is clearly in the film to show how the sexpot causes difficulties for the happily married couple. In *Let's Make It Legal* (1951, dir. Richard Sale), a remarriage comedy, she plays Joyce, a beauty pageant winner and model "posing for cheesecake and trying to better her life," who becomes a tool for the jilted husband Hugh (Macdonald Carey) to use to come between his ex-wife Miriam (Claudette Colbert) and the rich bachelor Victor McFarland (Zachary Scott). When Joyce is no longer useful to the remarriage plot, she drops out of the film. In *As*

Young As You Feel (1951, dir. Harmon Jones), Monroe plays secretary Harriet, who mostly stands or sits in the background looking pretty, or calls attention to herself as vain and out of touch when she combs her hair while looking in the mirror just after she learns of a company takeover. Despite the acumen she demonstrated in *The Asphalt Jungle* and *All about Eve*, Monroe continued to be cast in roles that confined her to playing a shallow sexpot.

From this period, Monroe's small role in *O'Henry's Full House* (1952, dir. Henry Hathaway) does the most to complicate the sexpot. Monroe plays a Victorian prostitute whom an old beggar (Charles Laughton) talks to in an attempt to get arrested and spend the winter in jail. She demonstrates felicity at misleading the nearby police officer (David Wayne) by successfully pretending to be a lady. She is so successful, in fact, in alluding to a shared "cousin Fanny" that the old man cannot sacrifice her to the cop to satisfy his own scheme, and instead gives her his umbrella and continues on his way. Acknowledging that, despite the roles in which she had been cast, Monroe wanted respect, her punchline comes at the end of the scene, when the cop asks her to explain the situation, and she sniffs with pride, "He called me a lady." This small part does more than the other small parts of this period to challenge the stereotypes associated with the sexpot.

Nevertheless, in 1952, Monroe was cast in one of the shallowest dumb blonde roles as secretary Lois Laurel in *Monkey Business*. The counterpoint to the straitlaced and intelligent Dr. Barnaby Fulton (Cary Grant) and his wife Edwina (Ginger Rogers), she is the stupid sexpot whom the boss, Mr. Oxley (Charles Coburn), keeps around just for her sex appeal. For example, she explains why she's at the office early, stating, "Mr. Oxley's been complaining about my punctuations, so I'm careful to get here before 9." Throughout the film, she emphasizes her sex appeal in the double entendre for which Monroe was becoming famous. She places her leg on the sofa next to Fulton and lifts her skirt, asking, "Isn't it wonderful?" She is demonstrating the new "acetates" Fulton developed, but this project is never mentioned again, and seems to be a ruse to showcase her leg in this seductive position. After Fulton ingests a youth potion and begins to act foolish, she meets him at the car lot. In a series of double entendres, they discuss his new car. She begins, "It's a honey," and he replies, "It takes one to know one." When she asks, "Is your motor running?," he retorts, "Is yours?" She shows she can keep up by finishing the third double entendre. When he says, "It takes it a while to warm up," she replies, "It does me too." Nevertheless, she later ends up the butt of the joke when Edwina, under the influence of the youth potion, shoots rubber bands at her bottom, and she slaps both Oxley and Fulton, thinking they have pinched her. After much more hullabaloo, the film ends with Oxley, who has taken some of the potion, chasing Miss Laurel and squirting her backside with water. Monroe's comedic timing is apparent in this role, but she has little opportunity to challenge the stereotypes associated with the sexpot.

Clash by Night and Don't Bother to Knock

Monroe's two other roles of 1952, however, gave her a chance to enhance more complex characters with sex appeal. Rather than asking her to play a shallow sexpot, Clash by Night and Don't Bother to Knock ask Monroe to play women with strong opinions and complex psyches. Monroe received fourth billing in Clash by Night—Barbara Stanwyck was the star—and Don't Bother to Knock was the first film in which Monroe had the lead. Monroe is cast against type in these films: both of these roles make use of her sex appeal while not making that the sole focus of the character.

Clash by Night is the story of Mae Doyle (Stanwyck), a woman who returns to her hometown fishing village after ten years away and romantic disappointments. Torn between "protection" and passion, in the figures of the staid fisherman Jerry D'Amato (Paul Douglas) and the hard-drinking, rough-handling film projectionist Earl Pfeiffer (Robert Ryan), Mae marries Jerry but has an affair with Earl. When Jerry finds out about the affair, he threatens to keep the couple's child, and Mae eventually chooses the child and Jerry over Earl and passion. Peggy (Monroe) is a hot-tempered cannery worker engaged to Mae's brother, Joe (Keith Andes), who "push[es] her around," but, despite her flirtations with others, including Earl, she, too, chooses to marry in the end.

Peggy is a figure who focuses the film's pervasive anxiety about the working class, women, and marriage. Peggy is working-class, she challenges conventional gender roles, and she is both the object and agent of violence. The anxiety she provokes is signaled by her laughter, a key aspect of the sexpot persona that, the film insists, needs to be restrained. The beautiful women in the film routinely are threatened with violence, and Peggy has to choose between being a sexpot for one man or being a sexpot for all. In *Clash by Night*, she chooses the love of one man, thereby containing cultural anxieties about the figure of the sexpot and paving the way for Monroe herself to be both a sexpot for all and a star.

Monroe insisted her stardom was due to the "working people['s]" admiration of her (Miller *Timebends* 367), so it is fitting that this film, made on the cusp of Monroe's transition into stardom, should feature her as one of the working masses. We first meet Peggy waking up alone, but she does not roll around sensuously; instead, she climbs out of bed and sleepily puts on jeans. These first twelve seconds of her role give us no indication of the sexpot, and neither do later scenes. The second scene in which Peggy appears takes place in the cannery, and she does not stand out from the other women sorting through the fish—indeed, the women on the line are as anonymous as the fish. The only thing that draws our attention to her is that her skin and hair are a little lighter than those of the other women, and so the light reflects off of her more. Peggy emerges from the factory eating chocolate, and when Joe warns, "You'll spread," she retorts, "So spread" as she takes another bite. Peggy desires to escape from the small town, and she worries that she will still have to work in the cannery after she weds. Her statements draw attention to the "similarly hierarchical" position of "woman the worker and wife subordinate to man the employer and husband" (Pye 14). That is, although Mae and Peggy will choose marriage at the film's conclusion, it is clear throughout the film that marriage

is an additional job for women. Such an economy makes Peggy's independence and self-assuredness all the more engaging, because her independence suggests she resists becoming the subordinate of two economies.

The film's lyrical opening footage of violent ocean waves suggests the
overall theme of out-of-control passions being akin to the forces of nature.[21]
Clash by Night is replete with images of violence against women, which
arise when women don't do what is expected of them. Projectionist Earl,
discussing the female stars whom he projects daily, asks Jerry, "Don't you
ever want to cut up a beautiful dame?" (a comment that, as Julie Grossman has pointed out, "literalizes Laura Mulvey's concerns about film and
the male gaze" [60]). Jerry's Uncle Vince has "dirty pictures" of women in
his room, and proclaims, "I always said, women and horses, use the whip
on 'em." Of his wife, Earl says, "Someday I'm gonna stick her full of pins,
just to see if blood runs out." By contrast, Jerry is "nice" and "comforting" because, as Mae sees it, he's "a man who isn't mean and doesn't hate
women." The low expectations for the film's men effectively highlight the
complexity of the female characters.

Gossiping about the conditions of the other working women in the
community, Peggy tells Joe about women who fall asleep on the job and a
woman whose husband gave her a black eye. His responses demonstrate
his conventional attitude: "When a man pays you a day's wages, you owe
him a day's work"; and: "He's her husband." The first response in fact seems
to apply to both situations—a wife also owes a husband a day's work. Joe
is, as Douglas Pye argues, "aware . . . of potential threats to moral order
and harshly disapproves of the unconventional or deviant," both in his
woman and in his fellow workers (15). When Peggy challenges him, saying, "I s'pose you'd beat me up too, if I was your wife," he jokes, "Sure, on
the regular," but Peggy challenges "any man [to] try." Joe tries as a jest,
but the kicking and biting that Peggy returns to him indicate that she isn't
joking. A low-angle shot of Mae, who has been watching from the front
porch, interrupts this fight, but she nevertheless says Peggy "looks nice."
Mae condones Peggy's fighting spirit, seeing in her not a doormat or

Figure 2.4. Strangling the sexpot. Frame enlargement from *Clash by Night*.

sexpot, but an unconventional woman who stands up for herself and should therefore be respected.

The violence directed particularly at Peggy seems to be the result of the independence and self-assuredness that make her such a fascinating character. When she says, stroking the table with her finger, that Earl is "kind of exciting . . . and attractive," Joe strangles her until she says he's attractive. In fact, an image of Joe strangling Peggy featured in the publicity for the film (both the trailer and the poster; see Rollyson *Marilyn* and Figure 2.4), suggesting that publicity men thought the public would like to see Monroe strangled. What the publicity still does not show, however, is that as soon as Joe releases Peggy, she punches him across the jaw, demonstrating that she can give as good as she gets. Although Peggy is frequently the victim of violence, she also hands it out—just as often as Joe manhandles her, she kicks, bites, and punches him in return.

Peggy and Mae, as complex female characters who are attractive but assertive and independent, are the source of the male characters' anxiety. This anxiety becomes evident in the many scenes that feature Peggy's laughter on the soundtrack even when nothing funny is happening, and even when Peggy is not onscreen. For example, when a scene opens on a beachside diner, Peggy's laughter is crystal clear on the soundtrack although the image accompanying it is a long shot of Peggy in the surf, and the sound mix doesn't change with a closer shot. When Joe lifts her feet in the air to shake the water out of her ear, although she says, "You're hurting me," she keeps laughing, but her facial expressions, and the violent way he shakes her, suggest the laughter is a cover. Later in the same scene, her laughter dominates the soundtrack again, this time when she flirts with the misogynistic Earl—and her laughter continues on the soundtrack when the shot cuts to Jerry and Mae. Peggy's laughter is the laugh of the woman who resists convention, the laugh of a flirt, and it comes as easily with her lover, Joe, as it does with other men, including Earl.

Compounding the significance of Peggy's laughter is the role laughter plays in the Jerry/Mae/Earl story—the idea of laughter is, finally, what convinces Jerry to do something about the suspected affair. Jerry's Uncle Vince claims that everyone in town is "laughing" at him, so he snoops in his wife's things. In a confrontation over perfume and nightgowns Mae had hidden in her drawer, Earl begins laughing, and Jerry says, "What's so funny, Earl?"[22] After Jerry has kicked Mae out of the house, Vince encourages him to use violence against the couple, whom he claims have been "laughin' at ya, all the time laughin' at ya . . . yeah, laughin' . . . Shove the vinegar sponge in your mouth and laughin'. . . . Comin' in the house like a true friend, and laughin'." The tension escalates until Jerry begins chanting, "I can't stand it," and Vince repeats, "Batter his brains out, batter his brains out!" Jerry's violence is elicited by the idea of Mae as a sexpot who pretended not to be one.

A woman's laughter is tied to anxiety about the sexpot's presumed infidelity, which drives men to violence in this film. When Joe accuses Peggy of being like Mae, he warns, "The woman I marry, she don't take me on a wait and see basis. . . . If what you think is, 'Joe's alright until something better comes along,' honey, you better take another streetcar." The shot lingers on Peggy's face for three seconds as she contemplates, then the reverse-shot cuts to Joe pushing her for an answer, followed by a five-second shot of Peggy's face before she throws herself into Joe's arms sobbing. In the end, Peggy vows to be faithful to Joe, although, as Pye notes, "Her final capitulation in tears is eloquent of the potential cost at which she will marry" (15). More important than the personal cost to Peggy, however, is the potential social gain—in choosing to marry, she defuses the threat her independence had posed to postwar mores. Despite being a flirt and a sexpot, Peggy *chooses* monogamy—unlike Mae, who *settled for* monogamy. Peggy's competing needs—for independence and romantic partnership—in the end, are contained by marriage, but she has to be browbeaten into it. Such a resolution, however difficult it might be to believe, is in keeping with the star persona Monroe was developing, as a sexpot, but one who appealed to both men and women by complicating that sexpot persona in her roles.

This role, which already challenged the sexpot expectations associated with Monroe, proved she was ready for stardom. *Time* magazine reported that "neighborhood theaters now showing movies in which she plays supporting parts (e.g., 'Clash by Night') give Marilyn Monroe top-billing on the marquees over . . . well-established stars" ("Something" 88). *Variety* wrote, "Marilyn Monroe is reduced to what is tantamount to a bit role" ("Review: 'Clash'"). But note that she has been "reduced" to a bit role, a word choice suggesting that the writers saw Monroe as worthy of more. Soon after, she was given a chance to prove she was in her first starring role in *Don't Bother to Knock*.

Monroe's role as Nell in *Don't Bother to Knock* is a challenging one that significantly resists her sexpot buildup, for the role focuses on the character's complex emotional life rather than her beauty. Nell is a young woman whose lover Philip died while flying cargo across the Pacific following World War II. She was hospitalized for three years after Philip's death, and a close-up of thick scars on her wrists tells us why. Just released from the hospital, Nell begins her first job, babysitting at the hotel where her uncle Eddie (Elisha Cook Jr.) is the elevator man. After her charge, Bunny Jones (Donna Corcoran), goes to sleep, Nell puts on Mrs. Jones's (Lurene Tuttle) earrings, dress, and perfume and dances in front of open blinds, where Jed (Richard Widmark) can see her from across the courtyard. Having just split with his girlfriend, the hotel singer Lyn Lesley (Anne Bancroft), Jed calls Nell and invites himself over to take his mind off his heartache. When he arrives, Nell tries to maintain her ruse as a traveler and guest at the hotel, but when Jed mentions that he is a pilot, she slips into a delusion that he is her dead lover, only to be interrupted by the child, who fears they are stealing her mother's things. For the remainder of the film, Nell slips in and out of her delusion, at times admitting that it isn't real, and at other times violently reacting to anyone who interferes with her romance.

This film bears a complex suspense plot hinging on an actress who has to move through a range of emotional states, and even the film's director worried about casting the sexpot as a psychotic babysitter (see Mayer 24). Similarly, *Variety* twice commented on the disparity between the role and Monroe's buildup, saying, on July 11, 1952, "Miss Monroe scores nicely in a role demanding certain dramatic understanding, but change of pace isn't in line with her buildup as a glamour girl. She delivers solidly, however, and registers her star possibilities," and on July 16, 1952, "Her role seems an odd choice, however, since the studio has been giving her a big glamour buildup, and in this she's anything but glamorous, despite her donning a negligee" ("Don't"). Nell is, in many of her early scenes, an ordinary-looking girl. She first enters the film in a frumpy shirtwaist dress and beret—challenging audiences to find traces of the sexpot.[23] Her minimal makeup and the drab costuming keep us from seeing her as the kept woman or accessory she had

Figure 2.5. Playing the sexpot. Frame enlargement from *Don't Bother to Knock*.

played in *The Asphalt Jungle* or *All about Eve*. Now, we are asked to see her as a psychologically disturbed, overwhelmed, naive young woman. Although she is at times sexy, she is also manipulative, whimsical, violent, frightened, seductive, and suicidal. Monroe was challenged to sink or swim as the actress carrying the film's plot, and she swam.

Nell's early plain appearance gives her the opportunity to transform into the sexpot before the viewer's eyes. A bored Nell wistfully examines Mrs. Jones's things, then begins to put them on—and as she does so, we see the Marilyn Monroe of previous roles materialize. The medium shot places viewers in the position of the mirror Nell gazes into, so that, when she presses a sparkling earring into one ear, her eyes widening and her mouth opening slightly, the transformation into Monroe is apparent (Figure 2.5). But the sound of a plane flying overhead interrupts this process, and Nell gazes mournfully out the window. In a later scene, Jed glimpses

Nell across the courtyard, dancing before an open window, and he becomes the spectator within the scene, watching her as if she is on a screen. She murmurs, "Hello," but after he returns the hello, she closes the blinds. This resembles the twenty minutes of withholding Monroe's glamorous, sexy image from the audience—and shows that the sexpot is an image that the actress controls.

The film's narrative explains why Nell chose to transform into the sexpot. Eddie chastises her for putting on Mrs. Jones's things, and tells her she "could have stuff like this—kimonos, and rings, and toilet water with Italian names," but she insists that she can't, because "these people are married—that's what you have to be." Presumably, her desire to marry is her reason for flashing the blinds again after Eddie leaves. This time, she allows Jed to come over. Before he arrives, she sits at the vanity to apply lipstick, and we see the first of many mise-en-abyme mirror shots that will be used throughout Monroe's career. The camera tracks into a close-up on her hand mirror, drawing our attention to how much more glamorous she is becoming through accentuating her mouth, but then tilts down slightly to focus on the thick scars on her wrists, asking us to contemplate, perhaps, what the makeup hides, or the trauma that lingers behind her pretty face (Figure 2.6). Jed's knocking prompts her to stand up, place her leg on a stool, and rehook her garters, returning the focus to the sexpot image, but not until the film has established her loneliness and desire to marry as the reasons for her choice to use that image.

The film uses the sexpot performance self-consciously, so that it can explain its reasons and defuse any idea that it is manipulative, instead showing the sexpot to be a lonely and vulnerable woman's desperate maneuver for attention. Nell's sexpot performance, in her exchange with Jed, comes on too strong. He asks her how long she's staying in New York, and she invents an impending trip to South America, which he soon sees through. But when she sits on the bed and seductively says, "Maybe we'll go together, Billy" (using the name he had given her on the phone), he objects: "I ran outta girls like you when I was fourteen. And the name is

Figure 2.6. The sexpot and her scars. Frame enlargement from *Don't Bother to Knock*.

Jed, not Billy." And when he notices Mr. Jones's shoes under the bed, he says, "And what's his name? And where's my hat?" But she convinces him to stay, saying the shoes belong to her sister's husband, with whom she's traveling. Once he reveals that he's a pilot, she slips into the delusion that he is her dead lover—and creates him as such by narrating her lover's story into the full-length mirror, finally embracing him as her lover returned. Although Jed calls Nell "a gal with a lot of variations," she persuades him to stay by telling her story. "If you go, then none of it can be true," she pleads, and then, perched on an armchair, tells of poverty and abuse, and how her past led her to dress up in another's clothes, now in a subdued, sad way. The medium shots show none of the excessive moving mouth associated with Monroe; the actress instead uses a fluttering hand to indicate her anxiety. Several aspects of Monroe's own biography make their way into the film here. For example, similar to Monroe's foster parents,

Eddie "call[s] it a sin to be with a man—even to go to a picture show or a soda." Through calling on her past, this role reminds audiences that the sexpot is a likable, vulnerable figure, not a hardened vamp.

The film's trailer emphasizes Monroe's sexpot buildup, but the film's conclusion calls on the softer, more vulnerable aspects of her persona to make the sexpot endearing. Referring to Monroe as "America's *Most Exciting* Personality," "Every Inch a Woman . . . ," and "Every Inch an Actress!," the order of the trailer's text indicates a concerted effort to transform Monroe from just a "personality" into "an actress," using her sexpot qualities as the linchpin. The trailer promises that this film "rockets" "the most talked about actress of 1952 . . . to STARDOM!" The film's conclusion is designed to take this sexpot into stardom by eliciting sympathy when, because her chance at marriage is thwarted once again, she threatens to kill herself in the hotel lobby. As the camera tracks in on her, standing in the lobby with a razor blade between her fingers, her darting eyes and trembling hand convey a trapped creature. In the final moments, Jed makes Nell recognize that he is not her lover and sends her away with the police.

The film's final scene persuaded many that Monroe could be both a talented actress and a sexpot. Anne Bancroft, who played Jed's ex-girlfriend, responded to Monroe's acting: "I was just somebody in the lobby; and I was to walk over to her and react, that's all; and there was to be a close-up of her and a close-up of me—you know, to show my reaction. . . . There was just this scene of one woman seeing another woman who was helpless and in pain, and she *was* helpless and in pain. It was so real. I responded; I really reacted to her. She moved me so that tears came into my eyes. Believe me, such moments happened rarely, if ever again, in the early things I was doing out there" (qtd. in Tomlinson 29; Anne Bancroft interview with James Robert Haspiel for *Films in Review* in 1980). While some reviewers warned that "if [directors] also expect her to act, they're going to have to give her a lot of lessons under an able and patient coach" (Griffith, Richard), a review in the *Hollywood Reporter* asserted that "Monroe's sensitive, moving performance again stamps her as a very fine actress as well as a beautiful girl with a magnetic personality" ("Don't"), and an *LA Daily News* review insisted, "Marilyn Monroe fans may or may not be surprised, but in her latest picture . . . , she demonstrates she can act, also" (Bongard). These reviews emphasize both her beauty and her talent, paving the way for Monroe to act in starring roles, even if those roles also continued to draw on her sexpot persona.

Monroe, in photographs, publicity stories, and these early performances, converted herself into star material without abandoning the sexpot image for which she initially had been groomed. This transition occurred because Monroe repeatedly performed a range of emotions, resisting the stereotypes associated with the sexpot. A prototype for those that followed her, Monroe was never content to mean just one thing to her audiences. Monroe appealed to her contemporaries because her persona both maintained a few consistent characteristics throughout the years and changed with the mores of the day. As we will see, Monroe continued to be cast as a sexpot, but she also continued to resist that casting through performances that demonstrated she was more than a stereotype. Rather, she was "some kind of mirror," reflecting the concerns and desires of her contemporaries, both male and female. The remainder of this book is devoted to examining what Monroe the sexpot and star meant to postwar culture.

CHAPTER 3

MRS. AMERICA

MARILYN MONROE AND MARRIAGE ANXIETY

The sexpot could, of course, attract a man, but the sexpot does not readily suggest herself as marriage material. Nevertheless, in close succession, Monroe starred in four films specifically about marriage: December 1952's *We're Not Married!* (dir. Edmund Goulding), February 1953's *Niagara* (dir. Henry Hathaway), August 1953's *Gentlemen Prefer Blondes* (dir. Howard Hawks), and November 1953's *How to Marry a Millionaire* (dir. Jean Negulesco). The first two of these roles showcase the potential problems with marrying a sexpot, while the last two imply that, if the sexpot can be contained in marriage, her sex appeal provides a sound investment for a (not necessarily wealthy) mate. These films dramatize common marital problems at the same time as they draw on Monroe's offscreen identity; as Monroe was supposed to have said in a 1951 *Photoplay* article, "Let's be honest. A girl's Number One dream is to be ideally married" ("Make" 92). Monroe, as a single woman in Hollywood during a time in which most Americans were either married or seeking marriage, indexed the period's concerns about and attitudes toward marriage. Her film roles engaged with the advice of family life educators, a cultural context that the first section of this chapter discusses. At the same time as they participated in popular marriage discourse, these films also gave Monroe opportunities to continue to test the limits of the sexpot buildup the studio gave her.

FAMILY LIFE EDUCATORS

To better comprehend how audiences likely would have understood these marriage films, some attention to the postwar context is necessary. Monroe's roles in many of her early films as wife or eager bride functioned to index not just the marriage boom in the decade after the war but also the cultural anxiety surrounding unmarried individuals in the 1950s.[1] Typical of much commentary of the period, sociologists Judson and Mary Landis, in *Building a Successful Marriage* (1948), observe: "In our society marriage is not as inevitable for an individual as death, but it runs a close second" (36).[2] As Elaine Tyler May notes, "96.4 percent of the women and 94.1 percent of the men" who "came of age during and after World War II" would wed in their lifetime (23). This translates to a decline in the percentage of single adults over the decade from 23 percent in 1950 to 21 percent in 1960 (B. Harvey 69). Moreover, most Americans married young; the median marriage age in the 1950s "dropped from 24.3 to 22.6 for men, and from 21.5 to 20.4 for women" (B. Harvey 69). The younger marriage age often resulted in panic for unmarried women; according to a four-part series in *Ladies' Home Journal* in 1954 entitled "How to Be Marriageable," "By their 30th birthday 82 per cent of all American women are married. The woman of 30 who is unmarried has only about one chance in five of finding a mate. Fifty per cent of American women who marry are married by their 22nd birthday" ("How" 46). Single women, then, had a very brief window in which to become wives.

For couples in the postwar period, establishing a companionate relationship began to displace securing one's class status as the stated reason for marriage. Sociologists Paul Burgess and Ernest Wallin explain that the pre-World War II status concept of marriage, in which family members arranged many marriages and divorce was rare, "made mate selection relatively easy. Young people had only to marry within their social set, religion, and ethnic group to guarantee a satisfactory union" because marital satisfaction did not depend on the spouses' personal relationship (28). In contrast, sociologist Paul Landis describes "two family philosophies"—"the one rooted in the historic tradition which strongly emphasizes the *dutiful* or *institutional* aspects of family life; the other arises from contemporary individualism, which emphasizes the *romantic* and *companionship* aspects of marriage and family" (151, emphasis in original). Although gender roles under the companionate model were rigid, both parties expected "a reciprocal deep friendship" from their marriages (Burgess and Locke 319).[3]

Because the companionate ideal emphasized romantic love, it was believed to be partly responsible for the increasing divorce rate (around 25 percent) in the postwar period (up from around 20 percent in the 1930s and 1940s). Commentators feared that couples divorced when they felt any waning of romance.[4] When "the idea that love should be the central reason for marriage, and companionship its basic goal, was first raised," Stephanie Coontz explains, "observers of the day warned that the . . . very features that promised to make marriage such a unique and treasured personal relationship opened the way for it to become an optional and fragile one" (5). Even those who successfully found a spouse, then, had plenty to be anxious about.

These anxious Americans turned to a group of advisors who capitalized on fears of being "abnormal" or "failing" at marriage. Those who built a career from offering marital advice, including psychologists, sociologists, and marriage counselors (as well as university professors), offered a two-pronged approach to the difficulties spouses faced: carefully prepare future couples for marriage, but, if they are already married, offer extensive guidance on how to negotiate common marital problems. As sociologist E. E. LeMasters explains, "Parents, and young people themselves, have increasingly felt the need for outside help in thinking about courtship dilemmas and preparation for marriage. To provide this help, high school and college courses have been organized, and a new group of specialists, known as 'family life educators,' has emerged" (3).[5] According to sociologist Harold Christensen, whose manual was published in 1950 and reprinted in 1958, "Seven hundred colleges and thousands of high schools offe[r] special units and courses dealing with preparation for marriage" (4). Between 1945 and 1954, LeMasters tallies 1,031 research studies on marriage, courtship, and the family, the results of which had to be reported to the general public in a manner that would help them form their own successful marriages (13). Instructional marriage manuals for use in classrooms (with titles like *How to Prepare for Marriage, Marriage Analysis: Foundations for Successful Family Life, Modern Pattern for Marriage, Modern Courtship and Marriage, Your Marriage, Marriage for Moderns*, and *American Marriage: A Way of Life*) proliferated during this period.[6] Marriage advisors also often wrote regular columns and special features for national women's magazines.[7]

These commentators insisted that happy marriages required work. As marriage counselor and professor of family life education Oliver Butterfield succinctly puts it, "Nearly anyone can fall in love, but to stay in love with someone for all time demands more planning and intelligence than many people seem to possess" (3).[8] The "working at marriage formula," according to Kristin Celello, implies that "any married person who aspired to have a successful marriage could do so by trying hard enough" (8). Moreover, Celello explains, "Conceiving of marriage as work was a means of injecting realism into an institution that Americans increasingly looked to as a primary source of personal happiness. If experts could not altogether prevent Americans from romanticizing marriage, they could at least temper their enthusiasm with a more pragmatic approach to the marital relationship" (40). Advisors encouraged couples to determine compatibility prior to marriage (often using tests provided in their books) and, when married, to "work" to resolve problems related to careers, children, sex, money, in-laws, and religion.

Although marriage preparation courses addressed both men and women, the majority of advice outside of these courses targeted women, for whom, it was assumed, marriage would be a career.[9] Thus, women were expected to, as the advisors put it, "adjust" to the demands of both their husbands and marriage. "Adjustment," according to Judson Landis, "refer[s] to a working arrangement which exists in marriage. This arrangement could be one which is mutually satisfactory or one which is satisfactory to one spouse but unsatisfactory to the other. The term adjustment is used, then, to refer to the state of accommodation which is achieved in different areas where conflict may exist in marriage" (169). All experts advised adjustment; LeMasters's *Modern Courtship and Marriage*, for example, features these chapters: "Marital Adjustment," "Personality Factors in Marital Adjustment," "Family Background Factors and Marital Adjustment," and "Social Class and Occupational Factors in Marital Adjustment."[10] The burden of "accommodation" primarily fell upon wives, whose financial well-being depended on pleasing their husbands.

Just as commentators disagreed about the crucial aspects of a marital relationship—for example, finances, sex, in-laws, or careers—popular films emphasized varying difficulties associated with postwar marriages, a point Monroe's marriage films make evident. Monroe's films served, in a way, as family life educators—they focused on the woman's need to "adjust," to be, for example, an attractive sexpot before marriage but a demure housewife after, or to be a good catch for a millionaire by being sexy, but not a gold digger.

GOOD REASONS THAT *WE'RE NOT MARRIED!*

Monroe's first marriage film, the episodic *We're Not Married!*, dramatizes the fallout when five couples, all of whom think they have been married for thirty months, learn that the justice of the peace's authority to perform marriages was not in effect when he married them. The film peeks into each couple's married life and uncovers the problems that plague their marriages, then shows their responses to the news that they are not married.[11] One couple, the Melroses, split upon receiving the news that they are not married, making the much older "husband" (Louis Calhern) happy because it prevents the gold-digging Mrs. Melrose (Zsa Zsa Gabor) from getting a hefty divorce settlement. The other couples all remarry even though two of the four hardly seem happy. The Glad Gladwyns (Ginger Rogers and Fred Allen) are the hosts of the nation's most popular Mr. and Mrs. morning radio program, yet they have nothing to say to each other at home and argue at the office. While the two initially rejoice that they can escape their loveless marriage, their producer quickly informs them that without marriage, there's no show, so they decide to remarry. The Woodruffs, similarly, stay together, despite Mr. Woodruff's (Paul Douglas) sexually promiscuous past, which haunts his wife (Eve Arden) because it makes it impossible for him to remember what experiences he had with her. He therefore avoids reminiscing, rendering their home life silent. However, he burns the letter saying they aren't married, either because he doesn't want the substantial bar bills that accompany the playboy lifestyle or because he wants the thrill of knowing he's living with a woman to whom he isn't married. In contrast with these unhappy couples, the Fishers (Eddie Bracken and Mitzi Gaynor) find out, on the same day the husband deploys for military service, that they aren't legally married and that they are expecting, so they eagerly remarry despite a number of bureaucratic obstacles.

The vignettes contemplate the problems commonly associated with postwar marriages—gold digging, incompatibility, the sexual double standard that ensured men had more experience than their wives, children, military service. Monroe's ten-minute episode draws on her sexpot persona, casting her as a beauty pageant queen, and in so doing allegorizes both the dangers of marrying an ambitious woman and the dangers of marrying a sexpot. Annabel (Monroe) and Jeff Norris (David Wayne) happily remarry but must overcome a number of difficulties before they can do so. In confronting these difficulties, the film indexes debates about a woman's role in marriage. Annabel is competing for the pageant title of Mrs. America, which frequently takes her away from homemaking and caring for her infant. As Mrs. America, Annabel's sex appeal is conspicuous, but not threatening to her husband, who takes pride in seeing other men appreciate her beauty. We first see the couple when Annabel wins the Mrs. Mississippi contest. Jeff, holding the baby on his hip, grins from ear to ear as he applauds her victory. He also asks the man behind him, who is enthusiastically applauding Annabel, "Do you like her?" When Jeff boasts that the winner is his wife, the man "beg[s] [his] pardon," but Jeff encourages him to "keep looking." Although Annabel capitalizes on her hyperfeminine, highly sexualized appearance, her focus and determination, even if in the pursuit of a pageant title, suggest that Jeff is right to adopt the homemaker role as she strives for success outside of the home.

Annabel is an active and ambitious wife; this role capitalizes on Monroe's persona as an ambitious young star. Her ambition is evident in her queries about the disparity between the perks of being Miss America and the perks of being Mrs. America (Mrs. has to secure her own funding for pageant travel); in her plans to work the nightclub circuit in big cities, including Hollywood, after she wins the national title; and in the way her eyes widen with delight when she sees her pageant trophy. Although winning the Mrs. America[12] title is not a career path (such as a nurse, teacher, or administrative assistant) and will take Annabel away from the home for only a year, the film treats Annabel's pageant bid as though it were her job: to achieve success, she spends long hours making appearances and raising funds. But the episode is ambivalent about Annabel's ambition. After Annabel wins the Mrs. Mississippi semifinals, a newspaper headline reports that Jeff is "happy but glad it's all over," but the next scene illustrates, as he cooks dinner and feeds the baby while Annabel prepares for the national competition, that the pageant life that took her out of the home is far from over.

If Annabel ambitiously engages in work that takes her outside of the home, then Jeff has to be the homemaker. The episode doesn't indicate how the couple earns money, but Jeff is never depicted as the breadwinner; instead, he cooks, cleans, and feeds the baby. When Annabel comes home only to touch up her makeup before going out again, his complaint is typical of frustrated wives: "I cooked the supper already." The central joke of the Norrises' episode is that Jeff, whom the justice of the peace called a "jerk" because of his "foolish ideas about who was going to be boss in the house," is the boss of the house in terms of childcare, cooking, cleaning, and hanging diapers. Jeff wears an emasculating apron, and the mailman derides him: "Where's Mrs. Norris, at the office?" Even Jeff's attempts to end Annabel's pageant career by notifying the committee that she is ineligible for Mrs. Mississippi because she isn't married don't deter Annabel. Presumably, Annabel isn't fit for the role of Mrs. America anyway—Jeff is doing the job of Mrs. America. Not being married thus frees Annabel to pursue other goals. She squeals with delight at the prospect of entering the Miss Mississippi finals, which, as Jeff's fiancée, she wins. Jeff later happily bounces the child during the remarriage ceremony, demonstrating that he is ultimately willing to take on the unconventional role of caretaker in order to keep Annabel.

Although the men suggest that it isn't Jeff's place to care for his child, the film underscores his competence in doing so.[13] By making Jeff a competent and mostly willing caregiver, the episode challenges the popular advice that, instead of working outside the home, wives should focus on families. Although Evelyn Duvall and Reuben Hill admit that "women can work outside the home and carry on their functions as wives and mothers as well, with no serious damage to their husbands' happiness, their children's welfare, or their own adjustment," they nevertheless advise women to be aware of their responsibilities to their families and work outside the home only after the children are grown (415, 418).[14] Judson and Mary Landis, who studied college student dating, explain that marriage became more difficult in the postwar period because of women's new ambitions: "Wives who wholeheartedly accepted their role as passive and who entered marriage with no other expectation" were more suited to marriage than active, ambitious wives (284). The Norris family's episode in *We're Not Married!* indicates that marriage to an ambitious sexpot has its challenges, but it also underscores the pride the husband of the sexpot experiences.

While *We're Not Married!* indicates that wives, with the support of their husbands, could work outside the home, the film's production documents reveal how out of step with conventional advice this scenario was. On one of the first drafts of the continuity script, in the margins of the scene in which Annabel and her manager discuss fundraising, is handwritten: "The fact that this is MRS, it's always tougher being married" (25). While the note directly refers to Annabel's difficulty procuring funds to support her pageant bid, the phrase "it's always tougher being married" applies to the overall tone of the film. Although women, prior to marriage, might have been competent workers outside the home, as postwar wives they were expected to care for the house and children, which made it "tougher being married." It was also tougher for women to maintain and exploit their sex appeal while married, as few could expect a spouse as understanding as Jeff Norris. Nevertheless, in this film, what initially seems a pitfall of marrying a sexpot becomes a boon, for both members of the couple are pleased.

In the original story for the film, entitled "If I Could Re-Marry," writers Jay Dratler and Gina Kaus explain the transition from informal unions occasioned by hitting the bride with a club and dragging her to a cave, to formal, legal marriages. They refer to the marriage license as "a kind of Good Housekeeping seal of approval"—a trivial badge that transforms what would have been "a mere impromptu mating, without social sanction" into a socially approved relation, whether the two are suited to spend a life together or not (1–2). While the working title hopefully imagines "If I *Could* Re-Marry" (my emphasis), *We're Not Married!*, as evident in the title's exclamation point, cynically depicts the joy of discovering an easy out. Annabel is overjoyed when she learns she's not married, as being unmarried provides new opportunities for her, and to keep her, her husband has to accommodate her aspirations. By having the couples remarry, *We're Not Married!* reinforces the idea that marriage is the appropriate channel for adult relationships, but the Norrises in particular attest to the necessity for *both* spouses to adjust to changing gender roles. Monroe, in her first marriage film, thus contradicts the advice of most postwar commentators when the film imagines the possibility of being a sexpot, a wife, a mother, *and* a woman who works outside of the home.

We're Not Married! presented an upbeat perspective on what it would be like to marry a sexpot, but Monroe's next marriage film, *Niagara*, presented the sexpot as nothing but trouble and marriage as the postwar American nightmare.[15] Despite *Niagara's* dark outlook on marriage, *Good Housekeeping* recommended the film, presumably as an example of how not to behave for a successful marriage (Harbert 19). As it unites sex appeal with marriage, *Niagara* directs its "how-not-to" advice at women, who, as commentators warned, could make or break their marriages through their degree of interest in sex. By comparing characters on opposite ends of the sexual spectrum, *Niagara* illuminates the noirish cast of the period's marital discourse. This how-not-to advice can also be read as an allegory for Monroe's developing star persona, making *Niagara* a pivotal moment in the way her sexpot persona was used in films and publicity.

Niagara follows George (Joseph Cotten) and Rose Loomis (Monroe) on a second honeymoon, and Ray (Casey Adams) and Polly Cutler (Jean Peters) on a delayed first honeymoon. Both couples are staying at the Rainbow Cabins in Niagara Falls. The Cutlers, a seemingly happy if dopey couple, serve as a foil for the dysfunctional Loomises. Ray and Polly are initially happy to sightsee as a couple, but when Ray's boss, who is eager to welcome the winner of the company's best Shredded Wheat recipe contest, arranges for the Cutlers to join him and his wife on group excursions, it removes the romance from this honeymoon trip. Meanwhile, Rose arranges a rendezvous with her lover, during which they plot to throw George over the Falls, using his "battle fatigue" to make it look like suicide. When the police contact Rose to identify a body, she assumes George is dead and asks Polly and Ray to accompany her. When she sees that the body on the morgue table is not George but her lover, she faints and is hospitalized. No one knows if George is alive or still at the Falls, until he, seeking Rose, finds Polly in the cabin George and Rose had formerly shared. When George reveals that he killed Rose's lover, Polly tries to convince him to turn himself in. Instead, George stalks and eventually strangles Rose in the town's historic bell tower. In order to escape authorities, George steals a boat, unaware that Polly is on board. The boat runs out of gas and begins drifting toward the Falls. As the boat nears the edge, George pushes Polly to safety on a rock then careens to his death. The film concludes with Polly and Ray leaving the scene in each other's arms.

Heralded as an example of the noir style, *Niagara* features honeymoons rife with murder and intrigue, reflecting noir's preoccupation with the affiliation between sexual desire and violence. Drawing on many of the conventions associated with noir—chiaroscuro lighting, oppressive framing, the extreme high-angle long shot, voice-over narration, and unstable psyches—but featuring recurring images of yellow slickers and the waterfall's rainbow, *Niagara* is, in Jennifer Peterson's term, a Technicolor noir, perhaps an apt combination for a postwar film about postwar marriage.[16] Ideologically, noir represents, as Andrew Dickos states, "American culture at odds with its most optimistic illusions"—and marriage was certainly one of those illusions (xiv). Noir depicts America's dark underside, critics have suggested, because of anxieties engendered by World War II and its aftermath. Psychopathic men represent maladjusted returning veterans and a postwar masculinity crisis; femme fatales represent female resistance to domesticity.[17]

Niagara's dark representation of marriage is in keeping with noir's challenges to the norms of postwar American society; it is also in step with much postwar marital discourse.[18] Sociologist Henry Bowman, for example, echoed the fatalistic anxiety expressed in films noirs: "Any *type* [of marriage] can be made successful if the couple face and solve the special problems involved. This is not the same as saying that any marriage can be made successful. At times the *if* is practically insurmountable. There are individual marriages that are hopelessly doomed from the beginning" (171). Popular magazines reflected Bowman's attitude. In the year *Niagara* was released, Samuel Grafton, whose monthly column for *Good House-keeping* offered advice for "a Reasonably Happy Marriage," cautioned readers: "Almost any marriage is likely to run into its hour of terror" (March 1953, 44); "the American male has heard so much about woman's new freedom, her desire to express her individuality, etc., that he's a little scared of her" (April 1953, 46); and "about every marriage passes at least once through a kind of nightmare phase" (May 1953, 199).[19] February 1953's *Good Housekeeping* featured perhaps the most anxiety-ridden article of all, "How to Stay Married though Unhappy," by Reverend Fulton J. Sheen.[20] According to Sheen, even "when marriages sour and become either physical catastrophes or psychological nightmares; when the husband becomes unfaithful or the wife an alcoholic; when he becomes crude and cruel or she becomes nagging and jealous; when he stays out late or she becomes sloppy; when he becomes 'unbearable' or she becomes 'impossible,'" couples have no reason to divorce (59). As in most marital discourse of the period, divorce was not a realistic option because it would publicly indicate the couple's lack of dedication to American ideals. After all, "A man who marries a woman thinking he will divorce her when his mood changes," Sheen asserts, "is also capable of marrying her thinking that he might murder her" (116).[21] The noir undertones of popular marriage discourse are evident in Sheen's warning.

Niagara's honeymoon resort setting underscores the film's underlying message about sex's role in getting a marriage started well. As Karen Dubinsky notes, "Niagara Falls was where you went when you had your sexual 'papers,' a place that welcomed the only officially sanctioned form of sexual expression in Western culture—that which took place between two married heterosexuals" (13). But *Niagara* insists that simply having sexual papers is not enough to make a successful marriage. Rather, the film draws on anxieties about sexual adjustment that had been associated with the honeymoon for nearly a century. Since the Victorian honeymoon, according to Dubinsky, the "timid, fragile" woman has been contrasted with the virile and voracious husband (22). By the 1930s, this mind-set only slightly shifted to the "recalcitrant, terrified bride" and "blundering" groom (Dubinsky 160). Although Alfred Kinsey reported that about 50 percent of women and 90 percent of men in the late 1940s and early 1950s were sexually experienced before their wedding nights, experts nevertheless continued to give advice as though the participants were sexually innocent, and, as Dubinsky points out, to reinforce the notion that brides "possessed a vastly slower libido (desiring sex approximately half as often as men did, one said), were slower to climax, and more generally repressed than men" (218). In other words, popular commentators acted as if wives had no experience with or interest in sex.

The conventional understanding of the honeymoon as the first meeting of sexual opposites made Niagara Falls a terrifying, noirish setting even without the film's murder plot. In 1955, for example, psychiatrist Reginald Bennett characterized the honeymoon as an "ordeal," a "ghastly disappointment," and a "hopeless anxious fumbling effort." Imagining the combined effects of exhaustion, alcohol, and inexperience during the first sexual encounters of marriage, Bennett questioned whether marriages could survive the honeymoon, which was, after all, a relatively new institution and a sign of postwar prosperity ("Honeymooners"). That is, the way Americans reconceived marriage, as a companionate relationship that should be publicly displayed on the honeymoon, also constituted a threat to marriage.

Just as *Niagara*'s setting implies that the honeymoon can be terrifying, the femme fatale character, Rose Loomis, turns Monroe's good-natured sexpot sinister. The manipulative murderess Rose differs greatly from the primarily naive, good-natured roles that form the rest of Monroe's oeuvre. Nevertheless, this film most clearly inflected a debate that would persist throughout Monroe's life and career, a debate Jon Whitcomb named in a December 1960 story on Monroe entitled "The Sex Symbol versus the Good Wife." Was the sexpot always a threat, as suggested by films noirs?

Evidence suggests that Twentieth Century-Fox studio head Darryl F. Zanuck, infamous for his distaste for Monroe, saw the sexpot as a threat. Despite the public interest in her, he had been reluctant to sign Monroe and then to re-sign her a few years later because he thought of her as one in a long line of "casting couch" starlets. The way *Niagara*'s initial story treatment describes Rose is key to understanding how casting Monroe reflects Zanuck's distaste for her. The treatment describes Rose as "a handsome, sexy bitch in her late and desperate twenties. She is a woman who won't accept the hand life has dealt her" (Brackett, "Treatment"). Seeking an actress who fit this description, Zanuck landed on Monroe, who, as luck had it, was also less expensive than other actresses and had generated box office returns for her other films (Brackett, *Niagara*).[22] About his casting decision, Zanuck wrote, "For [George's] wife, Rose, I definitely want to use MM." He begrudgingly admitted, "Her performance in DON'T BOTHER TO KNOCK with Widmark brands her, curiously enough, as one of the best young dramatic actresses to have come up recently." He also expressed his personal opinion of her by concluding, "She is just ideal for the role of this slut" (Zanuck). Zanuck saw Monroe as suited to play a "slut" and "bitch," disregarding the sensitivity and comedic timing she had brought to her previous sexpot roles.

Niagara's poster alludes to the threatening female sexuality Zanuck associated with Monroe in the tagline, "Marilyn Monroe and *Niagara*: a raging torrent of emotion that even nature can't control!" By italicizing *Niagara*, the poster boasts that the film will illustrate the unbridled passion of Monroe's sexuality. That unbridled passion is directly aligned with the Falls themselves, which the poster depicts as streaming from Monroe's lounging body. For centuries, according to Dubinsky, travelers have described the Falls as "moan[ing]" while "the 'clinging curves' of water 'embrace' the islands, and water 'writhes,' 'gyrates,' and 'caresses the shore'" (43). With the image of the Falls streaming through Monroe's body, *Niagara*'s poster insinuates a sexual encounter with Monroe. At the same time, by combining the honeymoon resort setting and an image of aggressive female sexuality, the poster suggests that the film will address what many postwar commentators treated as a terrifying problem affecting postwar marriages: sexual incompatibility, particularly the unexpected problem of an experienced, libidinous wife.

Commentators underscored that sexual incompatibility was one of the most common problems leading to marital terror. Many of the most popular marital advice books had titles that emphasized sex's role in marital success, such as G. Lombard Kelly's *Sexual Feeling in Married Men and Women* and Hannah and Abraham Stone's *A Marriage Manual: A Practical Guidebook to Sex and Marriage.* In the foreword to Oliver Butterfield's 1953 book *Sexual Harmony in Marriage,* gynecologist Nadina Kavinoky writes: "The damage that can be done to individuals through an unsatisfactory sexual adjustment is recognized by physicians and psychiatrists; it is attested by the high divorce rate and the many lurid newspaper stories of marital strife and failure" (Butterfield ix–x).[23] Marital advice books frequently stressed that wives bore responsibility for most of the couple's sexual adjustment, but they gave these wives conflicting advice. If wives were sexually experienced and lustful, they would have to learn to control themselves; if they were disinterested in sex, as "normal" women were supposed to be, and found it difficult to achieve orgasm, they would have to work to keep their husbands satisfied and interested in the relationship.

Commentators encouraged couples to work through the wife's sexual restraint. Psychologist and marriage counselor Clifford Adams warns that "many married people, particularly wives, suffer from repression," and that "sexual maladjustment is still a problem for one-third of" well-educated married couples (52, 202). Male desire differs from female sexual desire, according to Henry Bowman, because sexual arousal "has been trained out of [females]. It has been so overlaid with inhibitions that it cannot find expression" (341).[24] The restraint encouraged before marriage could not persist into married life, Adams warns, because "when [orgasms are] absent or deficient, it" affects the couple's entire life, "show[ing] up first and most seriously in lack of agreement on showing affection. In descending order, other frequent disagreements relate to table manners, philosophy of life, conventionality, and matters of recreation" (203).[25] The wife's restraint, then, could ruin even the most mundane aspects of the couple's married life.

At the same time, however, women were advised not to express too much interest in sex. Those wives who had taken advantage of the period's shifting mores and engaged in premarital sex were in danger of placing too great a sexual burden on their husbands. Sexually experienced wives, according to gynecologist Lena Levine, "having been freed from taboos and superstitions about sex, desire intercourse more frequently, at times even more often than their husbands" (16). Bowman likewise warned: "It is true that some women do find physical satisfaction in their premarital sexual relations. Then their desire for repetition is aroused and there is created a problem of either promiscuity or control, which could have been avoided" (344).[26] Imagining the sexpot as a wife, then, means imagining her as a problem to be avoided.

From her first appearance on screen, *Niagara*'s Rose demonstrates the out-of-control female sexuality that commentators warned would plague wives who had had premarital sex. The scene opens on Rose smoking in bed. Her shoulders are bare, and, beneath the sheet, it is clear that her legs are spread, with one knee pointed toward the camera and one toward the ceiling. Her hand initially flutters beneath the sheet, and the next shot underscores her heavy breathing. Shadows from the blinds cross the entire shot. Rose's implicitly masturbatory behavior clearly threatens "healthy" marital sexuality.[27] Rose has what postwar marriage advisors called a "problem of . . . promiscuity" (Bowman 344). Later, George tells Polly, "She's a tramp. I'll tell you now so you don't have to ask." Polly looks at him disapprovingly when he says this, and when he complains about Rose's "dress cut down so low in front," according to George, that "you can see her kneecaps," Polly asks, "Why hide it?" But she also admits that she wouldn't wear a similar dress because she's "not the kneecap type." Rose, on the other hand, is open about her sexual desires. When George recognizes, immediately after she's gotten out of bed with him, that Rose is getting dressed to meet another man, he interrogates her, but she tells him she's meeting "just anybody handy, as long as he's a *man*." The couple's costuming makes their sexual incompatibility evident: Rose's blouse features a deep V-cut; George looks childlike in his two-piece pajamas.

In earlier versions of the script, Rose murders George for money; in the film, she acts only out of malice and a desire for sexual gratification. As Richard Sokolove points out in his analysis of the film for Zanuck, "All that Rose wants, apparently, is her physical freedom, not necessarily her *legal* freedom, which, incidentally, she could also get by divorce. And her physical freedom she could readily have simply by running out on Loomis" (8).[28] Merrill Schleier insists that throughout the film "Rose is . . . equated with trash," both in terms of being "lower class" and in the slovenliness indicated by the couple's messy cabin and the contents of her purse that spill behind her as she runs from George (34). Much of Rose's trashiness derives from her interest in sexual gratification above all else, and this interest disorders George's life by extension. George is thus unable to combat his battle fatigue and "get organized" not because of the ordeals of war, but because of the havoc the sexpot Rose brings to domestic life. She uses her sex appeal as a weapon, luring him into bed to throw him off the trail of her affairs.

In contrast, Polly, who is conservative and almost girlish, struggles to keep her husband interested in her sexually. We meet the Cutlers as they cross the border. When they announce to the Customs officer that they are on their honeymoon, Ray earnestly adds that he plans to "catch up on [his] reading." Polly, however, expresses her hope to rekindle their sexual relationship when she reminds Ray, "Delayed or not, we agreed to treat it like a regular one, didn't we?" Here, Polly coyly teases Ray, indicating that their honeymoon should not be accompanied by the typical anxieties about sexual initiation, saying, "Well, it should be better. I've got my union card now." The fact that Polly reminds Ray of the purpose of their trip suggests that she takes responsibility for correcting their sexual failures. As

Sokolove writes in his script analysis, Ray's "interest may have become cen-
tered more on his business than on Polly." Echoing marital advisors who
made women responsible for marital sexual adjustment, Sokolove explains
that "because she wants to correct it before it's too late, [Polly] has taken
the initiative in promoting this holiday, this 'delayed honeymoon.' After
all, they have been married for three years, and this development in their
relationship is quite possible, and highly probable" (64–65). Polly's girlish
ponytail and modest attire seem to explain Ray's disinterest—Polly is no
sexpot.

The contrast between Rose and Polly highlights the impossible situation many postwar wives found themselves in: wives should be sexy, but
"nice girls" are not interested in sex.[29] Ray frequently compares the bobby-
socked and ponytailed Polly to the scantily clad Rose. Ray stares at Rose
lustfully several times in the film's opening scenes, and when he watches
Rose walk away, he nudges Polly and says, "Hey . . . get out the firehose."
Noting Rose's low-cut dress, he asks Polly, "Why don't you ever get a dress
like that?" (to which she responds, "For a dress like that, you've gotta start
laying plans when you're about thirteen"). Later, when Polly sunbathes in
a modest bikini, Ray prods her to be sexier, begging her to "inhale" and
let him photograph a "profile," not of her face but of her bust. Although
Polly turns to her side, she does so begrudgingly and uncomfortably. But
before Ray can snap the photo, Rose's shadow falls over Polly. This moment
can be interpreted in two contradictory ways, both of which reflect advice
for postwar wives. Rose's shadow warns Polly that she fails to arouse Ray
(in the way that the sexpot Rose does), and the shadow also reminds Polly
that excessively sexual wives are dangerous. By interrupting Polly's posing, Rose, for better or worse, prevents Polly from being more overtly
sexual.

This message is reinforced later in the film, when, because the Cutlers
have moved into the Loomises' cabin, Polly naps in the same bed where
Rose had slept naked. But Rose reveled in the sunlight on her bare shoulders, whereas Polly closes the blinds and climbs into bed fully dressed

Figure 3.1. To Rose, the bed is a playground. Frame enlargement from *Niagara*.

(Figure 3.1). Although the shadow of the blinds falls over both women, Rose seems to embrace the shadows and shafts of light, while Polly seems disgusted by them; Polly's gestures seem as likely to ward off a lover as the sunlight (Figure 3.2). Beds are playgrounds for the sexpot but constitute a threat to the restrained wife. This threat materializes when George enters the dark, shadowy room, knife in hand, and approaches Polly. The fully clothed Polly, however, is no sexpot, and so George spares her, slipping out the back door while Polly screams.

George punishes Rose, on the other hand, for being a sexpot more than a wife. George strangles Rose in the bell tower at least partly because her out-of-control sexuality led her to plot murder. When the tower bells play "Kiss," which was to be the sign that Rose's lover had killed George, Rose recalls her scheming, and the song forces her to recognize that her "kiss," her sexuality, has turned George murderous. However, George must also

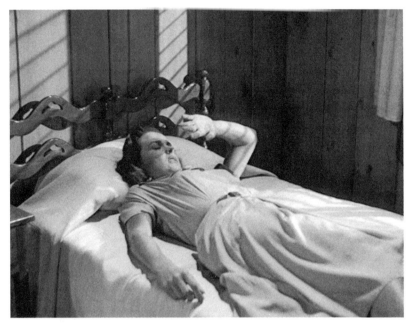

Figure 3.2. To Polly, the bed is dangerous. Frame enlargement from
Niagara.

contemplate his crimes, for when he descends he finds that he is locked in
the tower with Rose's corpse. When he finds Rose's lipstick on the stairs,
tears well in his eyes, suggesting that what angered him about Rose—the
way she accentuated her beauty and her sexuality—also drew him to her.
As George leans over Rose's lifeless body, he says, "I loved you Rose, you
know that." Attracted to the sexpot, even in love with her, George also feels
that the sexpot's appeal drove him to murder, for only with Rose dead can
he know who she is with and what she is doing.

   Rose ends up dead as a result of being an unfit wife—too aggressively
sexual, too manipulative—and serves as a warning to Polly.[30] George cau-
tions Polly not to emulate Rose's sexuality. When he tries to escape in a
stolen boat, he inadvertently takes Polly along. The boat runs out of gas
and, as the situation appears increasingly dire as the current draws the
boat toward the Falls, Polly unbuttons her skirt and throws it overboard,

ostensibly to swim to safety. Because Polly's undressing seems unmotivated, its importance is more figurative than literal. Figuratively, Polly is finally loosening up, removing her clothes around a man. George grabs her arm, warning, "You can't. You'll be torn to pieces." When George prevents Polly from undressing further, he indicates that if she succumbs to sexual passion, it will destroy her, just as it destroyed him and Rose. Thus, when Polly appears covered head to toe in a gray blanket in the film's final scene, her appearance confirms that she is no sexpot. Although Ray encourages Polly to be sexier, she is more in line with conventional wisdom, which encouraged wives to be willing sexual partners in private, but respectable and modest in public.

According to *Niagara*'s logic, the sexpot was a femme fatale and therefore had to be killed. Monroe's previous sexpot roles indicate, however, that she was better suited for the sexpot as a comedienne than for the sexpot as a femme fatale. In contrast with more compelling femme fatales, such as Cora (Lana Turner) in *The Postman Always Rings Twice* (1946, dir. Tay Garnett), whom feminist scholars assert are only "evil" from the male's perspective, Rose's strength and ambition are not apparent. "It is the leading female's commitment to fulfilling her own desires, whatever they may be (sexual, capitalist, maternal), at any cost," argues Julie Grossman, "that makes her the cynosure, the compelling point of interest for men and women. Film noir movies work to identify their tough women as victims whose strength, perverse by conventional standards, keeps them from submitting to the gendered social institutions that oppress them" (3).[31] Monroe's performance doesn't fit this mold—she doesn't seem particularly strong, the audience is not led to identify with her, and her motives are obtuse—only her excessive sexuality, which, in Monroe's star persona, had already been determined to be nonthreatening, makes her a femme fatale. Because Rose was a femme fatale with no real motive, the role isn't convincing, and Monroe's stint as the femme fatale type was abruptly ended. When George murders Rose, he also figuratively murders the dangerous, manipulative aspect of Monroe's sexpot persona.

Audiences voiced their concern that Monroe was not appropriate for representing the dark side of marriage or female sexuality. Many women worried that Monroe, who was already associated with sex, would, if she continued in these kinds of roles, make sex, including marital sex, "dirty," and the national press reported that Monroe's sex appeal was threatening her success. Women's clubs complained to the studio about her role in *Niagara*, and "movie-makers were worried about a United Press poll of editors which revealed that they are tiring of the sort of 'news' Marilyn and other starlets have been making lately. At week's end, the word was out to Hollywood's press agents: go easier on the sex angle" ("Go" 102).[32] Audience comment cards and letters to the studio also warned that Monroe was not suited to play the femme fatale. Reviewing the viewer comment cards, Zanuck wrote to Charles Brackett, the writer and producer, "You will note that the only bad ones are those that object to the sex values of MM. This of course we have to expect from a certain very minor percentage of an audience and particularly in a picture where she plays an unpleasant role" (Zanuck). One viewer insists that Monroe's performance as a femme fatale verged on making her a joke. The audiences at the three different showings of *Niagara* he attended weren't aroused by what he, as a chiropodist, identified as Monroe's "pathological," "abnormal" gait, but rather "they snickered—three times (and they don't know anything about gait!)" (Sauer). Audiences sent a clear message that Monroe's leading roles needed to capitalize on the persona she had been steadily developing playing secretaries and starlets—a nonthreatening sexpot persona.

The studio thereafter deliberately called attention to the shift in Monroe's persona. The headline accompanying the general publicity story (meant to be used in newspaper stories without revision) in the exhibitor's campaign book for Monroe's next film, *Gentlemen Prefer Blondes*, declares, "The Monroe Reforms, Changed Marilyn Promised in Film Bow." The article accompanying this headline explains: "The change in personality has been deliberate, the studio executives decreeing that her torrid sex appeal should be toned down and Marilyn herself deciding to be more dignified. However, as [director] Howard Hawks . . . says, 'nothing will change Marilyn's contours'" (15). The studio had tried to make Monroe a sexpot in the vein of her predecessors—hardened, tart—but the public saw her ushering in a new, comedic but dignified, sexpot.

IF *GENTLEMEN PREFER BLONDES*, BLONDES SHOULD LEARN *HOW TO MARRY A MILLIONAIRE*

At the same time as Monroe's sexpot image was toned down, it was also placed in marriage films that showed how the sexpot could speak to women's concerns. The sixth and seventh highest-grossing films of 1953, *Gentlemen Prefer Blondes* and *How to Marry a Millionaire*, solidified Monroe's stardom. Like *We're Not Married!* and *Niagara*, these films addressed postwar marriage, but they did so with a humor that defused their critiques of family life educators. What's more, the films achieved financial success despite the fact that, as Michael Abel reported to Zanuck regarding the story of *How to Marry a Millionaire*, the film was "not novel," but "basically similar to our current GENTLEMEN PREFER BLONDES" (1). Both films explore the woman's perspective on marriage. *Blondes* mocks the advice that compatibility is more important than financial security by advising women to use marriage to move up the social ladder and to embrace female friendship. *Millionaire* disregards any practical approach to marriage and, rather than advocate that women strive to "marry up," advises that they instead be content to marry men who aren't millionaires; in other words, to settle for horizontal rather than vertical movement (underscored by the film's CinemaScope format). Both films encourage women to make themselves into beautiful objects in order to attract and keep even middle-class husbands.

Blondes tells the story of "two little girls from Little Rock," Lorelei Lee (Monroe) and her friend Dorothy Shaw (Jane Russell); the former seeks financial security through marriage while the latter desires love.[33]

Dorothy accompanies Lorelei to Paris at the request of Lorelei's fiancé, Gus Esmond (Tommy Noonan), while he tries to convince his father (Taylor Holmes) that Lorelei is an acceptable spouse. But Dorothy is a distracted chaperone who falls for handsome detective Ernie Malone (Elliott Reid), whom the elder Esmond has hired to catch Lorelei in a scandal. Although Lorelei is technically faithful to Gus, Malone catches her in a compromising position with Piggy Beekman (Charles Coburn), from whom she procures a diamond tiara. Malone's report causes Gus to rescind his offer of marriage, leaving Lorelei and Dorothy in Paris without financial support. Although the two succeed as performers, they run into trouble when Piggy's wife takes legal action to reclaim her tiara, which Malone ultimately finds in Piggy's possession. After Lorelei is exonerated, she convinces the elder Esmond that she is not a "man-trap," but wisely is marrying for both money and love. The film concludes with a double wedding uniting Lorelei with Gus and Dorothy with Malone, but its final image is of the two women exchanging a knowing look, underscoring that, because they have joined forces as friends, they have achieved a fair exchange on the marriage market.

A sexpot seems an unlikely best friend for a woman, let alone a single, unmarried woman, and yet, Lorelei and Dorothy demonstrate genuine affection for one another. Both Monroe and Russell had sexpot personae, but while Monroe's was naive and vulnerable, Russell's was outspoken and assertive.[34] Nevertheless, the film aligns Lorelei, the seemingly stupid sexpot, with postwar family life educators: she considers it her "job" to teach Dorothy how to select a mate. One of the central jokes is that Lorelei insists that Dorothy, not she, is the stupid one. "Dorothy's not bad, honest. She's just dumb," she explains to Gus. She continues: "Always falling in love with some man just because he's good looking. I'm always telling her, it's just as easy to fall in love with a rich man as a poor man. She says yes, but, if they're tall, dark, and handsome, she never gets around to vital statistics until it's too late. That's why I'm her best friend, I guess. She really needs somebody like I to educate her."

In the context of contemporary warnings that top "husband-wife griev-
ances" included "w[ife]'s poor management of income" and "h[usband]'s
insufficient income" (Burgess and Wallin 586–587, 94), it makes sense that
Lorelei wants Dorothy to marry a wealthy man. "It's just as easy," Lorelei
advises, "to fall in love with a rich man as a poor man." Norman Himes
explains this paradox: "There is an old saying that a woman should not
marry a man for his money, but she should never let it stand in the way.
It is relatively easy for most of us to reject the idea of marrying for money,
but are our choices based on love, common experience, and similar back-
grounds any sounder?" (58).[35] In stating that marrying because of romantic
love is no wiser than marrying for money, Himes implies that it might in
fact be better to marry a rich man than a poor one, as such a move would
at least eliminate financial concerns. Because we tend to associate Lorelei
with Monroe's later film persona, which was certainly naive, if not, as
Sugar says in *Some Like It Hot* (1959, dir. Billy Wilder), "just dumb," it is
easy to overlook the extent to which the film actually confirms her assessment of herself as "smart" about marriage.

Another way Lorelei is smart about marriage is that she has partnered
with another woman to ensure her success. Rather than compete, the
women work together. The film makes this evident in the opening number, when the curtains open on Lorelei and Dorothy on stage, literally
working together. Harmonizing and dancing well together are staples of
musicals, but it is often a heterosexual couple (e.g., Fred Astaire and Ginger Rogers) that demonstrate their compatibility through their ability to
perform together. In *Gentlemen Prefer Blondes*, there are no male/female
duets—instead, Lorelei and Dorothy complement one another, demonstrating the benefits of having female friends.[36] Jack Cole's choreography
for "Two Little Girls from Little Rock" underscores how compatible the
women are: Lorelei's elbow fits perfectly into the curve of Dorothy's hip,
and Dorothy's outstretched arm perfectly curves into Lorelei's shoulder
and over her head (Figure 3.3). Their ability to work together also becomes
clear when they aren't singing—for example, when they join forces to

Figure 3.3. Perfect complements. Frame enlargement from *Gentlemen Prefer Blondes.*

retrieve a roll of film with incriminating images of Lorelei. The alternating shots show two girlfriends chatting on the phone, but they are in fact hatching a plot. Dorothy tells Lorelei to order dinner and drinks, saying, "If we can't empty his pockets between us, we're not worthy of the name Woman," and Lorelei replies, "I'll have everything ready." The women work so well together—Lorelei is, after all, accustomed to emptying a man's pockets—that they don't have to spell out the details of the plot.

But the women don't have to aim to exploit a man in order to work well together. The "When Love Goes Wrong" number is crucial in proving that Dorothy and Lorelei can provide for each other. The women spend all their money, then learn that Gus has cut off their credit, but they refuse Malone's aid, insisting that they can take care of themselves. A long shot shows the women considerately passing one cup of coffee back and forth across the table, demonstrating their genuine affection for each other. But as street

musicians join their song, the camera tracks in, and the two-shot demonstrates how, with only a knowing look and a subtle gesture toward the
musicians, the two women hatch a plot to get out of the café without pay-
ing. They increase the pace of their song, perform to the children who surround them, and eventually shimmy and dance in unison, despite that
they are spontaneously performing on the street, not on stage. The ease
with which they both sing and dance, as well as help each other out of
financial jams, suggests that a female friend is essential to a single woman.

Although Dorothy and Lorelei demonstrate their ability to support
themselves, the ultimate goal, for Lorelei at least, is a marriage that gives
her what she's worth—and Lorelei knows her value on the marriage market. Just after the head waiter collects $50 from Malone to be seated at
Lorelei's table, Lorelei comes to the head waiter to request that Mr. Spof-
ford be seated with her. When the head waiter says he can't do it, she persuades him by telling him about a time in Atlantic City when a head
waiter failed to grant her request. That head waiter had to give back all
the money he had collected because she "had all [her] meals in [her] room."
The shot lingers on the waiter's face as he begins to anxiously stutter and
swallow, and Lorelei gets what she wants. Lorelei's exchange with the head
waiter mirrors the more significant exchanges Lorelei hopes to make with
a rich man. Maureen Turim points out that the film's 1950s setting
"amplif[ies] the sexual play/exchange against a backdrop of the increasing reification of consumerist values" ("Gentlemen" 102). Within the film's
narrative, the women are "selling" themselves for love, but it's important
to note that they insist on getting their worth. And "'gold-digging,'" as
family life educator Christensen sees it, "is woman's way of 'working' a
man for all she can get" (248).[37] Lorelei knows that men are willing to pay
to simply be in her presence; why, then, shouldn't she expect a husband
who, as she tells Dorothy, "always does anything [she] ask[s]" and has "got
the money to do it with"?

Lorelei and Dorothy therefore seem to be objects of the gaze, but they
also, as many critics have noted, return that gaze and objectify men.[38] By

always chasing men, Dorothy seems to reverse gender roles.[39] When Dorothy freely pursues the disinterested Olympic team, she typifies behavior condemned by Robert Coughlan in *Life*'s 1956 special issue on women: "Spotily and sporadically, but increasingly, the sexes in this country are losing their identities. The emerging American woman tends to be assertive and exploitive. The emerging American man tends to be passive and irresponsible.... They are suffering from what the psychiatrists call sexual ambiguity" (109). On the other hand, though, the film suggests that, to get not only what they want, but also what they deserve, these women have to be "assertive and exploitive." When Lorelei looks at Piggy, she sees a diamond rather than a face, making him, as Ed Sikov notes, "even more of an object than she is" (79). Such a gender role reversal is much of the film's point—men want Lorelei for her looks, so why shouldn't she want them for their money? And, moreover, why shouldn't she encourage her friend to do the same?

The film's most memorable scene, the "Diamonds Are a Girl's Best Friend" number, visually underscores Lorelei's position as a woman navigating two conflicting camps of advice—one telling women to marry to secure their financial position, and the other warning women not to be gold diggers. The curtains open on a stage filled with sharply contrasted red, pink, and black décor; the color scheme makes the stage's close space both womb-like and sordid. Adolescent ballerinas wearing flowers in their hair and full skirts of pink tulle embody romanticism as they gracefully waltz with gray-haired gentlemen in tails. This first shot also indicates that romance is not the only perspective on love this number presents: women in black leather shorts, bikini tops, caps, and straps (costumes reminiscent of bondage wear) hang bound to the furniture, forming human candelabras beneath a human chandelier (Figure 3.4).[40] As Adrienne McLean has pointed out, choreographer Jack Cole's dances underscore "that women *and* men are prisoners of gender roles" ("Thousand" 141). The human furniture in this setting suggests that domestic life makes many wives extensions of their homes, fetish objects for the husbands who hold them in

Figure 3.4. A human chandelier. Frame enlargement from *Gentlemen Prefer Blondes.*

domestic bondage. But the costumes of the dancers in pink, who represent romance, also allude to bondage wear. In fact, the pink tops of the adolescent girls feature the same cross-chest banding as the costumes of the women who form the chandelier. This sadomasochistic attire visually suggests that it is just a small shift from being bound by romance to being dominated and objectified by a spouse. Because Lorelei wears the same pink as the dancers and sits at the base of one of the human candelabras, she is visually connected to both camps, indicating the common ground shared by the opposing ideologies of romance and exploitation.

Lorelei begins the number by rejecting men who offer red heart-shaped cutouts, repeatedly singing "no" while tapping each of them with her fan. This operatic trill (the only part of the famous song that is dubbed by Marni Nixon rather than sung by Monroe) and Lorelei's fan "referenc[e] eighteenth-century aristocratic women who used fans to flirt" (Banner

Marilyn 253). This reference to the subtle flirting of aristocratic women minimizes some of the crassness of Lorelei's refusal of "the heart." The sexpot can expect to receive offers of empty-handed romance. But just as she is often an accoutrement that improves or showcases a man's status, so should a man improve hers (if she is getting a fair exchange for her attractiveness). Because "a wife is usually accorded the social position of her husband," as Judson and Mary Landis explain, "marriage is a simple and effective way for her to achieve a desired social position" (44). If marriage is how women achieve status, Lorelei's pink dress underscores that she rejects romance because of her femininity—as a woman, she can't afford to be swayed by romance.

The lyrics seamlessly unite the advice of marriage educators with the consumerist impulses of the affluent era:[41] "A kiss may be grand, but it won't pay the rental on your humble flat. / Or help you at the automat. / Men grow cold as girls grow old, and we all lose our charms in the end. / But square-cut or pear-shaped, these rocks won't lose their shape. / Diamonds are a girl's best friend." Lorelei also educates the adolescent girls gathered around her: "There may come a time when a hard-boiled employer thinks you're awful nice. / But get that 'ice' or else no dice!" Lorelei exercises control over the adoring men by pulling on the diamond-studded straps they tantalizingly hold out to her. Because Lorelei accepts only this final offer of diamonds, this sequence suggests that women can make the most of their situations by insisting on the terms of their bondage in marriage. Lorelei's costume indicates her own diamond-studded bondage: she wears two diamond bracelets in the position of handcuffs and a diamond choker around her neck. She ends the number clinging to one of the human candelabras while a crowd of men wave diamond-studded straps in her face; this shot indicates that she will submit to a degree of "domestic bondage" for the right price.

When Lorelei insists she's in love with Gus, the film stops short of agreeing that women should marry for money. Although she admits to the elder Esmond that she wants to marry Gus "for your money," she convincingly articulates her reasons: "Don't you know that a man being rich is like a girl being pretty? You might not marry a girl just because she's pretty, but my goodness, doesn't it help? Would you want your daughter to marry a poor man? You'd want her to have the most wonderful things in the world. Why is it wrong for me to want those things?"

Esmond has to admit, "Say, they told me you were stupid. You don't sound stupid." In a line Monroe wrote herself, Lorelei responds: "I can be smart when it's important. But most men don't like it." To assume that the sexpot is stupid, or callous, is mistaken. Monroe's Lorelei is shrewd but warmhearted. She is only interested in getting what she deserves, and in an era in which women were encouraged to make marriage a career, it is wise to marry up, to ask for a return on the investment she has made in her sex appeal.

Blondes argues that women need to be gold diggers if they are to succeed in the postwar marriage economy. Although they submitted the lyrics to the Production Code Administration for approval, the filmmakers never recorded the following bridge for "Diamonds Are a Girl's Best Friend": "It's not compensation / It's self-preservation" ("Diamonds").[42] Nevertheless, these lyrics most clearly state that Lorelei's behavior is justified. The conflicting positions on money and marriage are "resolved" in the film's double wedding, when, as David and Christine Andrews explain: "The diamond that Lorelei has often equated with compensation for a short-term affair becomes the diamond in her wedding ring, the symbol of love *qua* long-term emotional commitment. Thus the closing sequence of the musical shifts the inflection of the phrase 'diamonds are a girl's best friend' by indicating that it holds true for committed marriages as well as for temporary flings" (65). Dorothy and Lorelei exchange knowing looks in the final shot, indicating that, while the film is ostensibly about marrying off two assertive, gold-digging women, it is really about female friendship.[43] Working toward a common goal, Lorelei and Dorothy have earned financial security by making their worth clear to the men who want them.

If *Gentlemen Prefer Blondes* exposes women's financial dependence in marriage, *How to Marry a Millionaire* works to make women happy to settle for middle-class lifestyles. Both in its narrative and in the effects of the CinemaScope format, *Millionaire* advises women to be content to move horizontally by marrying within their own social class, thereby stopping women from aspiring to "marry up." Although *Millionaire*, like *Blondes*, is structured around the conflict between marrying for love and marrying for money, the film depicts gold digging as untenable.[44] As Sokolove stated in his report to Zanuck about *Millionaire*, "The point, apparently, is that love, not money, brings happiness, but both are good to have" ("How" 1). Whereas *Blondes* illustrates how assertive women could be, *Millionaire* focuses on what Lisa Cohen has called 1950s "spectacles of domesticity"—both Hollywood visions of domestic life and domestic life as a spectacle enacted by private citizens (267). *Millionaire* makes the domestic spectacular, moreover, by showing off women's bodies. The film's CinemaScope format possesses an aspect ratio (2.25 to 1) that resembles a dollar bill; in this way, the film's form underscores its content by visually connecting women's financial security, however meager that may be, to their ability to make themselves husband-attracting spectacles. And yet, this film, like *Blondes*, underscores the friendships between women as they work to secure an acceptable exchange on the marriage market.

Millionaire begins with Mrs. Schatze Page (Lauren Bacall), a recent divorcée, renting an upscale Manhattan apartment and then inviting fellow model Pola Debevoise (Monroe) to room with her. Pola in turn invites another model, Loco Dempsey (Betty Grable), to join them in their plot to snag millionaire husbands. Initially, the women have a hard time attracting suitable candidates, but eventually, Loco meets J. D. Hanley (William Powell), a Texas oilman who, because of his attraction to Schatze, invites all three women to a meeting of the Oil Institute, where Pola and Loco meet unacceptable mates: swindler J. Stewart Merrill (Alex D'Arcy) and married, philandering millionaire Waldo Brewster (Fred Clark). In addition, each woman meets another man. Tom Brookman (Cameron

Mitchell), a young millionaire who dresses like a "gas pump jockey," woos Schatze, who resists his advances because she thinks he is poor. Loco falls for Eben (Rory Calhoun), a handsome forest ranger whom she mistakenly assumes owns all the trees in the forest. Pola becomes entangled with Freddie Denmark (David Wayne), the owner of the upscale apartment the women are renting, whose assets are tied up while he avoids the IRS. Loco and Pola do not marry millionaires, and Schatze eventually settles for Brookman, marrying him before she knows about his wealth. In the end, because each woman ends up married to her romantic match, the conclusion of *Millionaire*, according to *Time*'s review, proves that "filthy lucre loses out to nice, clean sex, and everybody goes to bed instead of to Bergdorf's" ("The New Pictures" 116). The review states that money is dirty and sex is clean, and Monroe in the role of sexpot has effected such a transition.

Like *Blondes*, *Millionaire* features a woman who wants to help other women secure acceptable spouses; in fact, she needs the help of these other women to make her plan work. Schatze has rented a swanky apartment as a kind of "bear trap," and she gathers her pupils on the terrace, creating a classroom space in which she can pace back and forth and check that they have comprehended her plan. When Schatze asks her gold-digging protégés, "If you had your choice of everybody in the world, which would you rather marry, a rich guy or a poor one?," she echoes Lorelei in the earlier film. But Schatze takes the marriage advice too far; her extreme rules for "intelligent consumer buying" establish criteria for shopping for a man: 1) "gentleman callers have got to wear a necktie," and 2) "a gentleman that you meet among the cold cuts is simply not as attractive as one that you meet, say, in the mink department at Bergdorf's." Schatze says this as she hands out sausages on buns and pours champagne, indicating, perhaps, how déclassé her proposition is.

After all, in the postwar period, people with relatively small incomes could, for the first time, project an image of wealth by purchasing a plethora of consumer goods. Status therefore hinged on making a spectacle of one's purchases. Postwar Americans had greater purchasing power than ever before: "Census figures show that between 1947 and 1959 median family incomes rose more than twice as fast as living costs—from $4,000 to $5,400, after taking inflation into account—and that by 1959 roughly 40 percent of the nation's families were in the $5,000 to $10,000 bracket" (Creadick 67). Although the median income in 1953 was $4,242, as *Fortune* magazine reported, 60 percent of the families who made between $4,000 and $7,000 a year were the families of "blue-collar workers" ("Rich Middle" 97). Therefore, while few women were married to millionaires, if they effectively performed the tasks of "household management, shopping efficiently, . . . and providing for the needs of an entire family on limited amounts of money," they could live a middle-class lifestyle with abundant material goods (S. Duvall 35).[45] Effective household management could even result in the appearance of being wealthier than middle-class. "Money must be translated into socially approved behavior and possessions," explains W. Lloyd Warner, "and they in turn must be translated into intimate participation with, acceptance by, members of a superior class" (21). Women didn't have to marry millionaires in the postwar period, because even working-class families were able to purchase abundant consumer goods, thereby giving the impression of wealth.

Millionaire's women teach each other how to be good consumers. While Schatze encourages the women to evaluate carefully the spectacle of wealth that potential mates project, her pupils are more interested in demonstrating how much they can acquire with just a little bit of money. Loco, is, as Pola points out, "awfully clever with a quarter" and can convert it into four sacks of cold cuts and champagne. Loco's industriousness, her ability to acquire practical items such as aspirin and shampoo caps from men she has just met, indicates her potential ability to run a home without a large income. Unlike Schatze, she has learned the lesson of "intelligent consumer buying" (S. Duvall 83) and can stretch a quarter to increase her purchasing power. Loco also knows how to make herself appear wealthy. When Pola wants Loco to participate in their millionaire-snagging endeavor, Schatze asks, "Is she class?" Pola responds, "Is she? Didn't I tell you she's been on the cover of *Harper's Bazaar* three times already?" Not only is she "class," but she's worn the clothes to prove it.[46]

The women are fashion models, and, as such, they also model for other women how to attract men. *Millionaire*'s fashion show scene (common to Hollywood films of the period[47]) depicts women as objects. The scene begins with a shot from over Brookman's shoulder, placing the audience in his position as he witnesses a private fashion show. The camera follows the women walking on a modified catwalk and posing for Brookman. As the camera tracks forward, Pola and Loco remove their outerwear, baring more skin. Pola and Loco cheerfully comply with their objectification. At the same time that this fashion show is directed at a man within the scene, it is also directed at both men and women in the film's audience. Audience members learn about the fashions, but they also see a "how-not-to" from Schatze, who glares at Brookman throughout the scene. When she tells her boss that Brookman is a swindler, the boss says he does not tell Schatze "how to put on a girdle," so she shouldn't tell him "how to run [his] business." This exchange indicates Schatze's place: her business is modeling the kind of clothing that will attract a husband, and, presumably, attracting a husband herself. Because Schatze refuses to make herself a complacent object, the scene ends with Brookman declaring, "I don't see anything I want"—he isn't ready to "invest" in Schatze as a wife. Although Brookman doesn't lose interest in Schatze, his parting shot suggests that Schatze has to learn to happily "dress the part" (of, perhaps, a wife with more money than she actually has)—as Pola and Loco do—before a marriage between them can work. As Figure 3.5 illustrates, *Millionaire*'s widescreen CinemaScope format[48] demonstrated that any woman, not just stars, could dress the part of the sexpot.

Any woman can dress the part of the sexpot with access to the right consumer goods. Just as the women in *Millionaire* demonstrate their status through their purchases, "Monroe," explains Laura Mulvey, "stood for a brand of classless glamour, available to anyone using American

Figure 3.5. A fashion show. Frame enlargement from *How to Marry a Millionaire.*

cosmetics, nylons and peroxide" ("*Gentlemen*" 216). Thus, both onscreen and off, Monroe suggested that women did not have to be married to millionaires to lead glamorous lives.[49] When the women convene in the powder room during their dinner dates, first Loco then Pola admires herself in a set of four mirrors (Figure 3.6). This scene displays the women from all angles. After the other women leave the powder room, Pola turns to the mirror in four different poses, observing her own profile, hips, behind, and bust while wearing her glasses. The glasses give her, as Cohen notes, "distance from (and therefore mastery) over her own image" (280). In this brief moment, Pola considers the way others see her and demonstrates that she is satisfied with the effect of her self-presentation. When Pola removes her glasses, however, she fumbles putting them in her clutch, allowing her to linger in front of the mirrors so that viewers can dwell on her body without the obstacle of her self-assessment. This scene raises Monroe "to the nth power," as the reviewer for *Newsweek* put it (qtd. in Buskin 155), and underscores how easily the star's glamorous image can be multiplied and copied. The mirrors capture multiple angles in order to better instruct female viewers in emulating Monroe's beauty.

The fashion show and the powder room scenes provide the film's real "how-to" instruction. As Ariel Rogers points out, "this massive and

Figure 3.6. Monroe "to the nth power." Frame enlargement from *How to Marry a Millionaire.*

repeated image can be read as a command to its female spectator, urging her to conform to this model of glamorous white femininity" (89).[50] Because the mirrors multiply this image, they call attention to how the widescreen format makes more of Monroe's body visible. "This on-screen manifestation of technology," Rogers notes, "emphasizes both the star's glamour and its means of construction, offering an enhanced view of Monroe's body while simultaneously identifying this possibility as a technological feat" (90). At the same time, the image underscores that the "technological feat" of Monroe's beauty was the collaboration of hairstylists, costume designers, and makeup artists.

If Monroe's beauty is partly the effect of cosmetics applied while standing before a mirror, then women in the audience could achieve the same effect with the right consumer goods. Publicity surrounding the film suggests as much. After praising the reaction Monroe drew from male audience members at the first CinemaScope demonstrations, *Photoplay* addresses its female readers: "What puts the M-M-M in Monroe? You can learn Marilyn's Beauty Secrets in the October *Photoplay*" (Johnson 83). Female fans appreciated the expansive spectacle of Monroe's body on the CinemaScope screen, which helped them access and emulate her beauty secrets. At the time of the film's release, Monroe and the other stars were also models for how to become wives: the young Bacall had charmed older tough-guy Humphrey Bogart into marriage. Grable, the most famous pinup of the wartime era, was married to musician Harry James, and Monroe, the nation's blossoming sex symbol, was dating Joe DiMaggio, whom she would wed in January 1954. Integrating the form and content of this how-to film by showing women how to look as attractive as its stars, CinemaScope also showed women how to snag husbands.

While this film offers much to female audiences, it also insists, through the CinemaScope widescreen, that men have no cause for anxiety: wives can learn to make do on a slimmer income, and sexpots make aesthetically pleasing wives. CinemaScope made it easy to display stars in horizontal poses that evoked Monroe's lounging nude figure in the by-then famous "Golden Dreams" photo. A *Life* magazine story about Cinema-Scope quoted Zanuck's awe at seeing Bacall "on a couch! . . . Her head was at one end of the screen and her feet were touching the other end! She filled the screen! *She was 64 feet long and in color!*" But the image accompanying this quote was of *Monroe's* body spread from one end of the screen to the other (Coughlan 81).[51] The caption reads, in part, "Miss Monroe, curves enhanced by curved screen, is 43 feet long" (Coughlan 83). *New York Times* film critic Bosley Crowther proclaimed: "The giant panel screen is without equal as a surface on which to display the casually recumbent figure of the temptatious Marilyn Monroe. Thirty-odd feet of the blond[e] charmer stretched out on a forty-foot chaise lounge . . . is an eye-filling sight which suits completely the modern-day taste for size, and, to that extent, anyhow, warrants this gigantic way of showing films" (X1).[52] Several shots enhance the sense of seeing the sexpot in a horizontal position on a horizontal screen—for example, she lounges on a chaise, and when she's on the phone, her legs stretch across the frame.[53]

The CinemaScope format thus makes getting married attractive in a larger-than-life way. When Denmark comes home to secure some documents and finds Pola stretched out on his chair, he does a double take, and his pause allows the audience to contemplate how attractive marriage could be—imagine Marilyn Monroe, your wife, relaxing on the sofa! Upon seeing him, Pola removes her glasses, exercising, as Cohen puts it, a choice "to go from seeing to being seen" (280). Becoming a spectacle in Denmark's home, Pola transitions from homebody to playmate. *Millionaire* thus anticipates the appeal of *Playboy* magazine, which emphasized, as Alan Nadel explains, "appreciating the seductive potential of women in even the most mundane settings" (131–132).[54] By extension, the film encourages viewers to appreciate the seductive potential of wives.

If the widescreen frame could project public sexuality, Pola's glasses frame a private spectacle. Later in the film, Pola accidentally boards the same plane as Denmark, which leads him to lecture her on the benefits of wearing glasses. Saying, "I've never seen anybody in my whole life that reminded me less of an old maid," Denmark convinces Pola to wear her glasses and, in doing so, he not only prevents her from becoming an old maid, but also confines her sexuality to a monogamous relationship. The shot/reverse-shot pattern reiterates Pola's status as marriage material: after she dons her glasses, shots feature the back of her head more often than her face or any of her other features, so that only her future spouse sees her. By encouraging her to wear her glasses, Denmark domesticates Pola, placing her sexuality within a frame that, theoretically, will provide boundaries for the sexpot and show other men that she has been contained. When she refuses to wear glasses, Pola can't see what she's getting into, but when she enters marriage with her eyes open (and glasses on), she can recognize a "compatible" mate (in the companionate sense), and her mate also benefits.[55] During a period when masculinity was in crisis, Monroe's film roles—as Lorelei, Pola, and later The Girl in *The Seven Year Itch* (1955, dir. Billy Wilder) and Sugar in *Some Like It Hot*—sent a reassuring message that she preferred feminized men, who, rather than paw at or manhandle her, would appreciate the sex appeal she brought to the relationship.

In order to make the shift from public sex image to private spectacle appealing to women, the CinemaScope format reiterates why women need men: to furnish a home and to satisfy them sexually. In a static shot, furniture disappears piece by piece from the apartment. Schatze admits that she has sold the furniture to pay the bills, and she bemoans her need for a man to support her, asking, "Where will we sit next week?" Instead of using CinemaScope's width to present expansive landscapes, *Millionaire* uses CinemaScope to show how empty homes are without men to furnish them.

The CinemaScope format also underscores how hungry the women are for sexual satisfaction. Recurring jokes about meat, in particular sausages, hint at the sexual desires the women have ignored in their pursuit of wealthy mates. The scene in which Schatze explains her plan begins with a close-up of a plate full of sausages long enough to fill the CinemaScope screen, which Schatze later distributes to her sex-starved friends. A later shot of the refrigerator reveals that their only food is hot dogs. Schatze and Pola have elaborate dreams of marrying men who bestow endless credit ("charge it," Schatze dreams of saying) and shower them with jewels; Loco dreams of a steaming pastrami sandwich. Catherine Johnson reads Loco's dream as "the truth of the matter: what these women really desire (or should desire) is physical pleasure, not cash" (69–70). The women of *How to Marry a Millionaire*, somewhat ironically given the film's title, learn that the wealth women acquire through marriage results from marrying for love. Neither Loco nor Pola marry wealthy men, but they're both "droolin'" with love; as a result of their romantic marriages, wealth is no longer necessary. While standing at the altar, Schatze also chooses a man whom she thinks "is nothing, a character straight from Characterville." Hanley tells Brookman not to "disillusion" Schatze by telling her about his fortune before the wedding: "She obviously likes gas pump jockeys better than millionaires."

The film's final scene emphasizes the middle-class lifestyles of the newly married couples as they sit at a diner reveling in their "dog-burgers." Schatze is married to a man who doesn't wear a necktie, Loco to an ordinary forest ranger, Pola to a shrimp in glasses with tax problems. While Eben estimates his worth at "about fourteen dollars," and Denmark can't "get his hands on" his wealth, Brookman lists all of his assets ("a little oil, some airline stock, a little steel, some cattle down in Texas, a couple of coal mines in Alabama, a bit of real estate here and there, some automobile stock, the Brookman Building, and Brookman, Pennsylvania"), then pulls out a thick wad of cash to leave a $1,000 bill to cover the $12.75 check.

As the camera zooms in on the $1,000 bill, a clatter echoes as the women faint and fall out of the frame. Because, as John Belton points out, CinemaScope bore "the shape of money," the $1,000 bill indicates Brookman's control not only over his wife's financial situation, but also over her status as a spectacle (223). The widescreen format, emphasizing width, rather than height, and horizontal movement rather than vertical, reiterates the film's plot. Indulging Schatze's efforts at control throughout the film, Brookman, at the conclusion, wrests control from her, making these marriages conform to the dominant postwar ideology. Brookman toasts, "Gentlemen, to our wives," and all three men stand, clink glasses, and look down at the floor with satisfaction, so that the final point of identification is the men, who have in the end outsmarted the women and been rewarded with sexpots falling at their feet. The film ends with a shot of the pleased men, their beers held high, laughing at their women, who have fallen out of the frame, presumably into domestic spaces they have earned for themselves by being pleasing spectacles.

From the Roles to the Persona

Although in both *Gentlemen Prefer Blondes* and *How to Marry a Millionaire* Monroe uses her attractiveness to secure wealthy mates, her ostensive stupidity—she isn't really capable of manipulating anyone—keeps her from being threatening. Both *Gentlemen Prefer Blondes* and *How to Marry a Millionaire* use "dumb blondes" to interrogate the relation between money and marriage, but do so in opposite ways that were equally popular with audiences. Lorelei shares some features with Rose—she uses her sex appeal to manipulate men, she puts her needs first—but she is a charmer rather than an aggressor. Pola is blind and passive. If, like Rose, Pola ends the film on her back, she is not being punished for her aggressive libido but being rewarded for being a pleasing spectacle. When Pola falls out of the frame in *Millionaire*, she becomes, as Lorelei had in *Blondes*, the partner of a man who owns spectacles, one of which, it seems, is her.

The first two films discussed in this chapter suggest the dangers of marrying a sexpot; the last two suggest the pleasures. Monroe's marriage films confirm her assertions in early publicity that, despite career success, like all women, she was preparing for marriage, and "a girl . . . never knows when or where she may meet the right man" (Monroe "Make" 92). Monroe's own marriages suggested the first two films better indexed reality—her husbands complained about her desire for a career, saying it prevented her from being a "good" wife. The remainder of Monroe's career would confront marriage's demands on postwar women. Shortly after *Niagara* was released in February 1953, James Dougherty, Monroe's husband from 1942 to 1946, published "Marilyn Monroe Was My Wife" in *Photoplay*. Dougherty said he was glad he never became "Mr. Monroe" (47).[56] "To Marilyn, [modeling and movies] seemed a better security than marriage," he complained (83). Criticizing Monroe's obdurate aspirations, Dougherty laments, "I think she'd give up anything for stardom—she already has" (85). Dougherty surmised that the marriage failed because of Monroe's career, and that the fame associated with her career was sure to disrupt traditional gender roles to the extent that it would make marriage difficult. Monroe was never able to sustain a long-lasting marriage—she divorced Joe DiMaggio the same year they wed and her marriage to Arthur Miller ended in 1961, after five years. Reporting on Monroe's divorce from DiMaggio, the press recognized "the conflict in their two careers seemed inevitable" ("Last" 53). Miller, too, understood why Monroe prioritized her career over her marriage to him: "Her stardom was her triumph. How would I feel if the condition of my marriage was tractability, the surrendering of my art?" (*Timebends* 483). Monroe's ex-husbands recognized that she prioritized her career over her marriages, but they did not unanimously fault her for that.

Perhaps this is why Monroe was cast as a single woman with little interest in marriage in several subsequent films (*The Seven Year Itch, The Prince and the Showgirl* [1957, dir. Laurence Olivier], *Some Like It Hot, Let's Make Love* [1960, dir. George Cukor], *The Misfits* [1961, dir. John Huston).[57] While her early marriage films called attention to a goal she presumably had in common with a majority of postwar women—to attract a husband and establish a new phase of life as a homemaker—her offscreen life in many respects contradicted the goals of these characters. Nevertheless, the marriage films began to express how the sexpot could appeal to women. The films Monroe made after this paved the way for more explicit representations of the sexuality of unmarried women, and thus, as chapter 4 shows, solidified the sexpot's appeal to postwar women.

CHAPTER 4

"IT'S KINDA PERSONAL AND EMBARRASSING, TOO"

MONROE, THE KINSEY REPORTS, AND THE DOUBLE STANDARD

Nudity bookended Marilyn Monroe's career, demonstrating that, even after she achieved stardom, she remained a sexpot. Monroe's first nudity scandal broke in 1952, before her highly successful starring roles, when the public learned that a nude calendar featured her image. The image associated with that scandal moved out of the realm of garage calendars when it was printed as a small inset in *Life* in 1952; in 1953, it helped establish *Playboy* magazine's prestige.[1] Rather than outrage the public, the stories accompanying the nude image made them sympathize with the sexpot (see chapter 2). Nudity also played a prominent role in the final months of Monroe's life. September 1962's issue of *Photoplay*, dated after but clearly printed before Monroe's August 5th death, features an article entitled "Marilyn Poses Nude—Again!," which asks, "Is publicity—bold and blatant publicity—all that's left of Marilyn's career?" (Rowland 46). Sadly, this article's title could also apply to reports of her death, which reiterated that Monroe's lifeless body was found in the nude.[2] Salacious publicity—in keeping with Monroe's sexpot image—suffuses, but does not define, her career. In many instances, such publicity made both male and female audiences sympathize with, rather than chastise, the sexpot. Monroe's stardom ascended alongside changing attitudes about female sexuality in the wake of Alfred Kinsey's reports on human sexuality. Monroe represents the 1950s female's engagement with her own sexuality, and three of her film roles (*The Seven Year Itch* [1955, dir. Billy Wilder], *Bus Stop* [1956, dir. Josh Logan], and *Some Like It Hot* [1959, dir. Billy Wilder]) evidence how, from her mid- to late career, she spoke to a female audience through her expression of sexuality. In these films, she is in fact not sexually available—instead, her characters engage in brinkmanship and insist on their own sexual pleasure. Monroe's films participated in a broader cultural project of advancing a single sexual standard. In keeping with the 1958 article "Ten Indiscreet Proposals," which warned "Don't be a sexual fascist!" by "believ[ing] the double standard of morality is legitimate" (Ellis 10), the transgressions associated with Monroe's career ushered in a new era of sexual mores beyond sexual fascism.

As previous chapters of this book show, Monroe's sexpot status, rather than limit her star potential, provided the conditions for its existence. After several events of 1953 and 1954, Monroe as sexpot could fully index the growing national interest in how sexual mores and sexual behaviors differed. At the same time as the nation reacted to Kinsey's findings on American sexual practices, several events in Monroe's personal life, events that contributed to her persona, coalesced in a way that made it acceptable for her to play women who weren't eager to wed. Early in 1954, she married Joe DiMaggio, but by the time *The Seven Year Itch* was released in 1955, Monroe had experienced a very public divorce. The press implied, in fact, that the film's famous scene of Monroe's skirt blowing above her knees contributed to that divorce. Whether she was married or not, Monroe's sex life, or fantasies about it, drove much of the reporting on her by the mid-1950s.[3] Her films during this period—*The Seven Year Itch*, *Bus Stop*, and *Some Like It Hot*—draw on Monroe's persona to interrogate Kinsey's findings by representing the women who, as Kinsey said, were sexual though unmarried.

THE PUBLIC'S AMBIVALENT ATTITUDE TOWARD KINSEY'S REPORT

Although a number of previous studies of female sexual behavior had produced findings similar to Kinsey's, his report generated a unique furor.[4] Kinsey's 1948 report on male sexual behavior, controversial for its findings on the incidence of male homosexuality, paved the way for public interest in what he might reveal about women's sex lives.[5] Kinsey ensured, through a publicity coup that shrouded his report in secrecy (he made reporters attend weeklong retreats to read advance copy and receive story approval from his team), that the second report would generate interest and become a bestseller.[6] Even before its publication, the press extensively covered Kinsey's *Sexual Behavior in the Human Female* (1953), and, after its release, journalists compared its impact to that of the H-bomb ("Bombs" 57). Hundreds of stories debated the merits and dangers of the report, such that a Harvard sociologist, among others, called society itself "sex-crazy" ("Sex" 14).[7] Kinsey's book reached number three on the *New York Times* Best Seller list just after it was released in September 1953 and stayed on the list until December, selling over 250,000 copies (C. Lewis 31). Kinsey appeared on the covers of *Time, Life, Newsweek, Collier's,* and *Woman's Home Companion,* and he developed a public presence afforded few zoologists despite the fact that, as the magazines joked, the report was a "least-read bestseller" ("Behavior" 79).

What most Americans knew about the report they derived from the hundreds of popular magazine and newspaper stories summarizing its findings. Kinsey's findings, particularly the incidence of premarital sex (about 50 percent of women) and extramarital sex (about 26 percent), were shocking because they revealed that the behaviors of the study's subjects— who were primarily white, middle-class women—did not correspond to professed moral standards. The reports in the popular press underscore Kinsey's insistence that, contrary to the beliefs of many psychiatrists and laymen, women were rarely "frigid." Rather than confirm that frigidity was common, the reports reiterate Kinsey's finding that women's sex lives "often become more satisfactory with age" ("5,940" 51–52). The press also underscores Kinsey's finding that "both men and women experience the same pleasure in the sex relation" (Bergquist 23).[8] Kinsey insisted that women were interested in sex, and many postwar Americans acted as if this surprised them.

The reportage painted a picture of sisters, wives, and mothers interested not only in sex, but also in pleasure. Some of the reportage praised Kinsey for proving women's interest in sexual pleasure; other reports condemned him for blaspheming American women. A number of writers praised the report for opening dialogue about sex. Gallup public opinion polls regarding both reports found that people approved of having information about sexual behavior publicly available at the ratio of 5 to 1 for the male report and 3 to 1 for the female report (379, 381).[9] Many writers even laud Kinsey for publicly exposing hypocrisy.[10] Bruce Bliven, writing for the *New Republic*, explains: "We still pay lip service to a Puritan idea of monogamy and chastity that probably never existed except in a highly neurotic minority and certainly does not exist today. This dichotomy between what most Americans do and what they say appears in many forms" (18). Bliven finds Kinsey's reports reassuring: "For those whose Puritan load of guilt is extra heavy, Kinsey's two books taken together offer a sort of ready-made self-psychoanalysis: your wickedness is not unique as you thought but has been shared by 71 percent of the sample" (18). That is, many commentators pointed out to readers that they would likely find common ground with Kinsey's subjects.

At the same time, several prominent psychologists and sociologists criticized both Kinsey's methods and his subjects, whom they discredited as "neurotic" liars (Bergler and Kroger 7). As Miriam Reumann explains, critics heralded the male study as evidence of "Kinsey's interviewing skills and scientific acumen," but the female study generated public criticism of Kinsey's scientific methods (99). Dr. Karl Menninger, cofounder of the Menninger Clinic, for example, wryly claimed that Kinsey's book "should have been labeled 'What 5,000 or 6,000 rather talkative ladies told me about sexual behavior of women in the U.S. under certain conditions,'" insisting, "I don't much care what they said because I don't believe them" ("Can" 75). Menninger, like many social scientists, faulted Kinsey for disregarding love and other psychological motives behind sexual behavior.[11] More extreme critics accused Kinsey of undermining the nation's morality and exposing America to Communist infiltration.[12] Nevertheless, Kinsey had located subjects who engaged in the sexual behaviors in which American women presumably did not engage, including premarital sex and adultery. Thus, Kinsey's findings clearly demonstrated that mores needed to catch up with behavior.

Despite public criticism of Kinsey's findings, several women's magazines advised their readers to compare themselves to Kinsey's subjects, thereby suggesting that Kinsey's findings might alleviate the guilt of women who assumed that their behavior was "worse" than that of their peers. In *Pageant*, Laura Bergquist asks readers, "Can you find some helpful clues about *you*? Can you learn what's a 'normal' sex life for a woman your age? Whether your sexual experience differs from that of other women? Can the report shed light on problems you don't discuss even with close friends?" (16–17).[13] Bergquist's questions underscore the role Kinsey's findings played in shaping the beliefs of American women. Those who praised Kinsey even associated his work with the feminist movement. According to Bergquist, Kinsey exposed "that a single standard is evolving, and that the sexual freedom once extended only to men—traditionally less controllable in their sex activity—is being extended to women" (20). Marriage counselor Bill Davidson, writing for *Collier's*, notes, "If years had names, 1953 might be called The Year of the Second Emancipation of Women. There have been books to prove the equality of women, books proclaiming the superiority of women [Ashley Montagu's *The Natural Superiority of Women*] and books assailing the brutality of men for preventing women from becoming equal or superior [Simone de Beauvoir's *The Second Sex*]" (19).[14] Davidson counted Kinsey's book as one of a handful arguing for gender and sexual equality.

Sexual Behavior in the Human Female led Americans to contemplate the sexual double standard, a pivotal accomplishment. While "objections to a double standard have usually implied that the male should accept the same restraints which our culture has been imposing upon the female," Kinsey's team found that in reality "the double standard is being resolved by the development of a single standard in which pre-marital coital activities have become extended among females to levels which are more nearly comparable to those in the male" (324). *Newsweek* reported that this shift stemmed "from freer consideration of sex matters in our times; the 'emancipation' of the female, increased knowledge of contraception, anonymity of persons living in urban areas, control of venereal infection, draft armies which allow American men and women to observe foreign cultures, and drives against organized prostitution" ("All" 70). Even Margaret Banning, who was confident that Kinsey's subjects were "neurotic," warned that the report "is almost certain to break down belief in virginity, or belief in a woman's desire for virginity" (110).[15] Kinsey reported that such a shift had already occurred.

Kinsey's reports shaped the 1950s, and, although the double standard was not eliminated, the culture's attitude toward female sexuality shifted. Sociologist Ira Reiss described the 1950s attitude as a "transitional double standard," in which "exceptions are made, and the woman who engages in premarital coitus because she is in love or engaged is not condemned. This is still the double standard, for men are allowed to engage in coitus for any reason—women only if in love or engaged" (97). Reiss predicted a shift to a moral standard under which affection would be the sole criterion determining whether sexual relations were morally acceptable (236). The "conflicts and confusions" E. E. LeMasters attributed to slowly shifting mores occurred because, while sexual behaviors had changed, *the code has not been changed*—it just is not observed very much any more" (185).[16] Monroe's sexpot persona demonstrates the tension between mores and behavior: she both publicly challenged mores and was beloved.

MONROE EMBODIES KINSEY'S FINDINGS

Monroe, as the period's preeminent sexpot, exposed sexual hypocrisy and promoted a single standard through her films. Several commentators, discussing Monroe in the context of Kinsey's findings, insisted that she only represented a prurient fantasy. For example, film critic Hollis Alpert argues that women in the movies, including Monroe, represent an unrealistic "Hollywood Siren—the woman who simply by existing, or at most sprawling on a rug or sauntering up a street—is supposed to imply all the vigorous, kaleidoscopic possibilities of human sexuality, past and present" (38). Aligning such sirens with "caricatures out of some evil little boy's imagination," Alpert explains that "not Hollywood alone, but the entire press of the country has made Marilyn Monroe into an animated pin-up, to be looked at, perhaps laughed at, and certainly whistled at" (38). Similarly, in a 1953 analysis of Kinsey's second report, Ernest Havemann writes, "In movies the standard close-up shows the heroine with eyes closed, breathing hard, as she melts into the arms of the hero; Marilyn Monroe is the most publicized movie star of all because she can convey this impression of total passionate surrender even while walking rapidly away" (48, 53).[17] Monroe's characters at times seemed available, that is, but Havemann's comment also insists that they often walked away from the men who pursued them. Although these writers insist that "real" women did not behave like Monroe's screen characters, it is important to note how Monroe represented both the male fantasy of female sexuality and the sexual women Kinsey studied.

Monroe's sexpot persona generated its share of criticism, but, for every critic, there seemed to be two more who insisted she should not be criticized. For example, columnist Sheilah Graham insisted that Monroe had single-handedly shifted Hollywood's emphasis to sex appeal. She describes the "Monroe Doctrine" thus: "Open your mouth, remove the underwear, pose in the nude, show your legs, show your bosom, split your skirts. V to the waistline, front as well as back, and never mention anything quietly domestic" ("Is" 37). Graham's disapproval reflected the opinion of many,[18] but, at the same time, many were also saying Monroe was just what Hollywood needed. Hildegard Johnson summarizes these contradictory positions: "For years, Hollywood has been awaiting a Marilyn Monroe: the essence of sex, a personality so exciting that column after column of free publicity, photo after photo would be devoted to recording her latest sayings and doings." Instead, "all the town's heavy artillery was hauled out to assail her with a walloping barrage of criticism" (42). William Bruce, writing for *Movieland*, insists that "Marilyn had that unique quality in her make-up that prevented anything she did from becoming sordid" (62). Monroe's public affairs late in her career with Yves Montand and Frank Sinatra seem to evidence this: they elicited more sympathy for her broken heart than censure.[19] For example, in a story on Monroe's relationship with Sinatra, Jack Tracy points out, "To Marilyn Monroe, sex and love are as far apart as the Poles. To Marilyn Monroe *love* can exist without *sex*. And if this is so, does it follow that she also believes *sex* can exist without *love*?" (43). Although Tracy recognizes this perspective as "unusual," he nevertheless publicly acknowledges that for Monroe, sex without love might be possible, without criticizing her for it. By the early 1960s, fan magazine writers demonstrated that Monroe helped usher in a new era of sexual standards for women.

Monroe's great box-office appeal provides additional evidence that her sexpot attracted audiences. "Vulgar?" Graham asks. "Of course. But everyone flocks to her films. So . . ." ("Is" 84). Twentieth Century-Fox publicity attributes Monroe's nearly universal appeal to her combination of sexiness and comedy: "Career-wise, the Blowtorch Blonde's torrid sex appeal has been toned down with comedy in the conviction that women will more readily expose their boy friends to her charms via the screen if the girls can giggle while the guys sigh" (Johnson Publicity 1).[20] This strategy must have been successful: Monroe was voted one of *Photoplay*'s ten most popular performers in 1954. Monroe's appeal persisted to the end of her career. A 1961 *Photoplay* article reiterated Monroe's charm for both male and female fans: "Ninety-nine percent of the men in this world find her desirable as a woman. They go to see her on the screen. So do most women—they're seething with curiosity. That is Marilyn's chief worth" (Rowland 86). But Rowland misses another possible appeal Monroe had for women—she was a likeable sexpot who showed them how to advocate for their own desires and their own sexual pleasure.

While official publicity insisted that Monroe was concerned only with pleasing men and asked nothing in return, comments she made on her thirtieth birthday suggest that she advocated for female sexual pleasure: "Kinsey says a woman doesn't get started until she's thirty. That's good news—and it's factual too" ("Marilyn at 30"). Monroe's films drew on this aspect of her persona to index the concerns of the larger culture; each of the film characters discussed in this chapter represents a different controversy raised by the Kinsey report (*The Seven Year Itch* alludes to Kinsey; the others reference the debates his reports engendered). Although each of these characters is a sexually experienced woman, the profit-motivated studio system and the Production Code kept the films from fully depicting sexually active, unmarried women. However, as the decade progressed, the Production Code's power diminished, such that Monroe's characters increasingly reflected Kinsey's findings that over half of American women engaged in premarital sex and, implicitly, his call for a single standard governing sexual behavior. Thus, in *The Seven Year Itch*, The (nameless) Girl makes no demands for her own pleasure, but also doesn't succumb to the man's pressures. In *Bus Stop*, however, Cherie acknowledges her sexual experience and expresses her demands for reciprocal pleasure before she agrees to marriage, and in *Some Like It Hot*, Sugar admits to her past affairs, seduces a man, and defies moral conventions. Each of these films increasingly supported Kinsey's claims that (even unmarried) women desired, and achieved, sexual pleasure.

The Seven Year Itch

Best known today for the image of Monroe's skirt blowing above her knees, *The Seven Year Itch* revived Monroe's career after she left Hollywood to negotiate a better contract and study at the Actors Studio. While Monroe, known only as The Girl, was featured heavily in the film's publicity, the central character in the film is Richard Sherman (Tom Ewell, reprising his role from George Axelrod's 1952–1955 Broadway play of the same name). After sending his wife, Helen (Evelyn Keyes), and child (Butch Bernard) to Maine for the summer, Richard struggles with his sexual fantasies, seemingly brought to life when The Girl, who has moved upstairs for the summer, rings his buzzer to get into the building. Shortly thereafter, she knocks a potted tomato plant from her balcony, an event that spurs Richard to not only fantasize about making love to The Girl, but also to engage in fumbling attempts to seduce her, attempts she resists while maintaining a casual friendship so she can take advantage of Richard's air conditioning. Although Richard and The Girl share two kisses, their relationship never advances (a point where the film deviates from the play), perhaps because he fears his wife may be having an affair with Tom MacKenzie (Sonny Tufts) and therefore demands a leave from his job to join his family in Maine, leaving The Girl behind with his air conditioning.

This plot outline reveals none of the subtleties that make *The Seven Year Itch* a commentary on the sexual mores of the postwar period. The film opens on a scene of "Manhattan Indians" who, staying behind while their wives vacation for the summer, follow an attractive young woman (Dorothy Ford) like a pack of dogs. This scene is immediately echoed in the train station (Dorothy Ford again playing the attractive young woman), where the film compares the behavior of the natives to that of the more "civilized" modern man. "In all that time," the film's narrator states, "nothing has changed." This scene, unrelated to the rest of the narrative, refutes the sentiment reflected by physicians Edmund Bergler and William Kroger: "*What Kinsey never takes into consideration is that jungle-sex and cultured sex are two different entities"* (52). The film, on the other hand, reflects Kinsey's findings when it insists that "cultured sex" has much in common with "jungle-sex."

The film also uses a fictional psychoanalyst, Dr. Brubaker, to allude to Kinsey. Richard is publishing a pocket edition of Brubaker's *Of Man and the Unconscious*, a highly technical book that, like Kinsey's, was an unusual choice for popular reading material. In Axelrod's play, the jacket of Brubaker's book boasts that it is "hotter than the Kinsey report" (71). Although the film does not directly refer to Kinsey, Richard diagnoses himself with the "seven-year itch" in the same way readers compared themselves to Kinsey's subjects. Richard reads that Brubaker claims the seven-year itch "strikes 84.6 per cent of the married male population, [and] rises to an alarming 91.8 during the summer months." As he notes this statistic, Richard compulsively scratches himself.[21] But although Richard has the itch, unlike Brubaker's subjects (as well as Richard's boss [Donald MacBride] and handyman Kruhulik [Robert Strauss]), Richard resists the urge to scratch.

Richard is about to turn thirty-nine; his wife is thirty-one, and yet he does not acknowledge Kinsey's key finding regarding the difference between male and female sexuality: that men's sex drive peaks around the age of sixteen and then steadily declines, while women's sex drive slowly ascends to its peak in their late twenties and early thirties but remains consistent into their fifties and sixties (Kinsey et al. 714–715). Perhaps most damaging to the postwar male ego, already made fragile by white-collar work and the togetherness model that insisted husbands help with childcare and domestic labor, Kinsey writes that "the steady decline in the incidences and frequencies of marital coitus, from the younger to the older age groups, must be the product of aging processes in the male" (353). Richard soliloquizes, "Helen is worried. I just know she is. . . . She probably figures she isn't as young as she used to be. She's thirty-one years old. One of these days she's going to wake up and find her looks are gone— then where will she be? Well, no wonder she's worried. Especially since

I don't look a bit different than I did when I was twenty-eight. It's not my fault that I don't. It's just a simple, biological fact: women age quicker than men." This speech disavows another simple, biological fact. Although he may look young, his sex drive is declining when Helen's is ascending, and therefore the seven-year itch may be hers.[22]

Even Richard's fantasies make it overwhelmingly apparent that his age impacts his potency. When the fantasies begin, a pan opens up some eye-room, upon which the first moments of the fantasies are superimposed. These dual images allow viewers to see the sagging cheeks of the fantasizer at the same time as we see his fantasy about women throwing themselves at him. After he rebuffs each woman, however, utter exhaustion sweeps over his face, and, in the fantasy that draws on the famous beach scene in *From Here to Eternity* (1953, dir. Fred Zinnemann), he limps into the tide, unexplainably dragging his right leg behind him (Figure 4.1). The "extraordinary" "animal" magnetism Richard thinks he possesses stems from his psyche, not his body; his wife, even in *his* fantasies, only bemusedly remarks, "The only extraordinary thing about you is your imagination."[23] His body betrays him in reality, too. When he first meets The Girl, his neck audibly cracks as he gazes up at her ascending the stairs and again when he looks up at her on the balcony, highlighting an age difference similar to that between Richard and his wife (Tom Ewell was forty-six when he was playing Richard and Monroe was twenty-nine when playing The Girl). These cues make it apparent that the sexual appetites of young women threaten Richard's aging body.[24]

If Richard is the prototypical aging male, The Girl is the prototypical sexpot—that is, she is Marilyn Monroe. The Girl's sparsely drawn character capitalizes on Monroe's persona in a number of ways. She seems to embody sexual availability, a character trait that is attributed to her by drawing upon Monroe's previous sexy roles and the publicity stunt for the film that allowed the average New Yorker to see a movie star's undergarments. The Girl's work as a model draws directly on Monroe's biography: The Girl's "artistic" photo appears in *U.S. Camera*, a magazine that featured

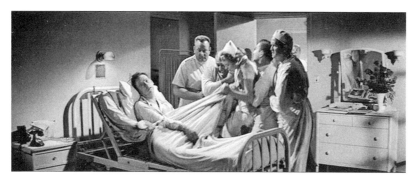

Figure 4.1. Exhausted, aging Richard. Frame enlargement from *The Seven Year Itch*.

Monroe on its cover in 1946. Moreover, explaining the "blonde in the kitchen" to MacKenzie, who has stopped by to retrieve Ricky's paddle, Richard remarks, "Maybe it's Marilyn Monroe." The joke lies in the improbability of the situation in which Richard finds himself—the ultimate sexpot is in this bumbling man's kitchen preparing breakfast.

The Girl as sexpot clearly derives more from Richard's fantasies than from any of her own behaviors.[25] In fact, the fantasy scenes, when contrasted with Richard's actual interactions with The Girl, demonstrate that Monroe had to give two very different performances within this film. In Richard's fantasies, The Girl is a cold, sultry vamp (Figure 4.2). But when The Girl actually joins him for a drink, she wears not the tiger print gown he had imagined, but pink matador pants and a pink linen shirt. Rather than speak in the deep tones of the vamp, her voice is light and airy, and she sits casually on the sofa arm, making eye contact with Richard. In contrast with his fantasy, she has little interest in seducing him. Although The Girl later goes upstairs to change into a thin-strapped white dress (because "it just isn't right to drink champagne in matador pants") and then joins Richard at the piano, her expressions, rather than oozing the sex appeal of the vamp of Richard's fantasies, suggest how intent she is on having fun (Figure 4.3). She is more of a casual sexpot, one who arouses Richard by mundane behaviors, like lifting her blouse before the

Figure 4.2. The Girl of Richard's fantasies. Frame enlargement from *The Seven Year Itch*.

Figure 4.3. The Girl just wants to have fun. Frame enlargement from *The Seven Year Itch*.

air conditioner, or asking him to hook the straps of her dress. The Girl "who ultimately joins him," according to Sabrina Barton, "fails to follow his script" and throw herself at him (130). This puts The Girl beyond his control, just like his wife in Maine. Because Richard cannot abandon his seduction script, he doesn't recognize that The Girl is spending time in his apartment for air conditioning, not sex.

While The Girl is more than a product of Richard's imagination, Monroe's presence in the film as an unnamed character underscores the predicament of the movie star as a fantasy figure for the masses—and of the sexpot as a performance, not a reality. "She's an angel," James Harvey writes, "and that full-hearted speech she makes to the beady-eyed Tom Ewell about his desirability ('If I were your wife, I'd be very jealous of you') makes her mission on earth clear. She has come to us . . . not only to turn us on but to shore us up, provoking our lusts, but then redeeming them by her innocence" (66). But Harvey might be speaking from his own fantasies, for the film makes clear that her sex appeal is not inherent, but is rather a performance. To demonstrate her television commercial work to Richard, she says, "I kinda sit there like this . . ." as she lifts her chin and turns her body so that her chest is in profile. She hoods her eyes and rounds her mouth as she speaks her advertising lines, but abruptly resumes her casual posture and wide-eyed, subtle smile when speaking to him after her performance. When Richard asks, as The Girl stands over the subway grating, using the commercial's words, if her breath really is "kissing sweet" and steals a kiss from her, he reveals he has fallen for her performance. Neither of them can, as Richard Armstrong puts it, avoid "the throwaway culture in which all America is immersed" (74). The sexpot seems to be another aspect of America's "throwaway culture" in that she is just a fleeting act. Monroe's performance within the film, and her performance within the performance, underscore the extent to which the screen sexpot "Marilyn Monroe" is a construct.

Several images in the film hint that the sexpot of male fantasy (in contrast to what Monroe actually brings to the film) is in fact more a nightmare than a fantasy. Richard meets The Girl when her falling tomato plant almost injures him, and he develops a psychosomatic thumb twitch after spending one night with her in the same apartment. Because *The Seven Year Itch* is, in Kevin Ferguson's words, "an oral film" replete with images of food—soya bean burgers, burnt cinnamon toast, and potato chips dipped in champagne—we can read The Girl as threatening to "consume" Richard. When she feels the cool air from the subway, according to Ferguson, "Her pleasured response 'Isn't that delicious?' is basically a question of taste. The idea that the Girl can 'taste' the air blowing up her skirt echoes the film's other scenes of consumption" (44). Thus, The Girl warns

Richard, and the viewers, not to mistake her good nature for uncomplicated availability. "At the moment over the subway grate," Ferguson
explains, "when she seems to be the most revealing, open, and sexualized,
she lets drop a disguised hint about her consuming nature" (45). While
Ferguson may be overstating the extent to which The Girl intends to "trap"
Richard, her interest in her own pleasure threatens to overwhelm—to
consume—Richard. She doesn't stand over the grating to please him, but
rather to feel the cool breeze—she squeals in delight when another train
approaches, and lingers on the grate despite Richard's prodding, demonstrating her focus on herself, rather than on him.

If The Girl's sex appeal threatens to consume Richard, it does so because
postwar men saw shifting sexual mores as a threat. The Girl isn't interested in marriage, as "nice girls" were supposed to be. "People keep falling desperately in love with me," she complains. "They start asking me to
marry them. All the time. I don't know why they do it." The shot from over
Richard's shoulder shows her smiling enthusiasm as she explains why she
is relieved when she finds out Richard is married: "I think it's wonderful
that you're married. I think it's just elegant. . . . I mean, I wouldn't be lying
on the floor in the middle of the night in some man's apartment drinking
champagne if he wasn't married." When she explains that marriage would
mean "I'd have to start getting in by one o'clock again. . . . That's the wonderful part about being with a married man: no matter what happens, he
can't possibly ask you to marry him, because he's married already, right?,"
her face beams with delight, and she raises her glass to toast her good fortune in finding a married man with whom to spend her time. The reverse-
shot shows Richard grinning like a Cheshire cat. He has misinterpreted
her statement as an invitation to an uncomplicated affair, so he cranks up
the Rachmaninoff and leans in for a kiss, which she rebuffs with a comment about liking Eddie Fisher.[26]

The Girl must repeatedly snub men's advances, thereby engaging in a
form of sexual brinkmanship. These scenes highlight the woman's ability
to refuse sex, but also that she can use sex as a tool to get what she wants

from men (which, for most postwar women, was a commitment).[27] Robert Moskin, in a vitriolic article in *Look* in 1958, complained, "Who controls this increased premarital sex activity? The young American female. . . . The boy is expected to 'get all he can,' and the girl is expected to regulate him" (77).[28] Nora Johnson presented the woman's perspective for the *Atlantic Monthly* in 1959 when she wrote about the men who divided girls into "good" and "bad," and expected "good" girls to have sex as soon as they were "pinned or engaged" (59). She explained that such a shift "would require the girl to be an angel of civilized and understanding behavior at first, pacifying her man by a gentle pat on the knee at just the right time and keeping him at bay—and yet interested—in a way both tactful and loving (the teen-age magazines devote a lot of space to this technique and recommend warding off unwise passes by asking about the latest football scores), and then, once the pin has been handed over, to shed her clothes and hop into bed with impassioned abandon" (59–60). In other words, while postwar men were accustomed to brinkmanship, when they committed to a long-term relationship, they expected restraint to give way to reveal a sexpot.

In contrast with Richard, who is unable to control himself around her, The Girl, like women who engaged in brinkmanship, controls both her and his desires. When Richard overpours her champagne, "the sexual metaphor is given an even more submissive twist," Albert Mobilio points out, "as [Richard] himself sips off the excess from her dribbling glass. The emasculated 'nice guy,' [Richard] not only can't control his glee in the presence of a sex goddess but he's more than willing to clean up afterward" (56). Although The Girl knows what Richard wants, she resists him. She seems to have stepped out of his Rachmaninoff fantasy when she claims to get "goose pimples" from "Chopsticks," but when he says, "Now I'm going to take you in my arms and kiss you, very quickly, and very hard," she stops him, blocking her body with her arms and pulling her face away. But when he asks her to leave after he has knocked her off the piano bench with this attempted embrace, she maintains his interest by telling him he's "being silly." She stops his sexual advances, but her reluctance to leave and the sweet way she says goodnight indicate that she wants to keep his fantasies alive.

But The Girl is too "hot" for Richard to resist, so "hot," in fact, that she has to keep her "undies in the icebox" and contemplates soaking her sheets in ice water. Director Billy Wilder's use of the term "icebox" (this scene is not in the play) puns on the site of female frigidity. In order to avoid sleeping with Richard, The Girl—directly reflecting Kinsey's data, which shows that "frigidity" is more feigned than real—goes to great lengths to create the (artificial) effect of frigidity. A female physician whose research was generally ignored by the medical community reported in the *Medical Woman's Journal* in 1950 that frigidity was a "normal" response to the "thoughtlessness" and "emotional hurts" caused by partners, not a psychological or gynecological disorder (qtd. in C. Lewis 53). Kinsey confirmed her finding: while physicians and psychologists conventionally believed that up to 75 percent of wives were frigid, Kinsey found that only 10 percent of women were, and only temporarily (Bergler and Kroger 159, Kinsey et al. 357).[29] In the context of Kinsey's findings, The Girl makes clear that it is simpler to sleep with a man than to employ extreme, and extremely flawed, measures to cool off her underpants and her bed. Nevertheless, she employs these extremes in order to maintain her control of the situation.

This false "cooling" of a "hot" woman also alludes to the problems of censorship. Because the Production Code stated: "Adultery and illicit sex, sometimes necessary plot material, shall not be explicitly treated, nor shall they be justified or made to seem right and permissible" (Association 3), Richard and The Girl could not consummate their relationship, a crucial difference between the film and the play.[30] Wilder regretted having to make the film under these terms. "On Broadway," he said, "the guy has an affair with the girl upstairs, but in the picture, he only gets to imagine how it would be to go to bed with Marilyn Monroe. And just the *idea* of going to bed with her has to terrify him, or it won't get past the censors" (qtd. in Chandler 178).[31] That is, Richard's neuroses are designed to echo those of the censors.

Wilder suggests Richard's guilt motivates the film's failure to consummate the relationship, pairing The Girl's brinkmanship with Richard's fear of cultural sanction. Richard proposes "a nice quiet, serious talk" about psychoanalysis while cutting and squeezing lemons for Tom Collinses. His soliloquy on psychoanalysis is crosscut with scenes of The Girl, her feet propped in front of the air conditioner, discussing with herself her useless fan and her need for sleep. By saying, "There are no accidents," Richard tries to blame The Girl for engendering his fantasies about her, saying they result from her seductions. Meanwhile, she's still thinking about solutions to her cooling problem, including sleeping in sheets soaked in ice water, but her shots no longer feature her outstretched legs—instead, we see her in close-up, really contemplating how she can get some sleep before a big day of television work. Richard tells The Girl, "There's nothing to be ashamed of. Under this thin veneer of civilization, we're all savage," his own speech seeming to suggest that their attraction to each other will inevitably result in consummation—until the train of her own thought leads her to say, "I'd like to stay here with you tonight." Her focus is on a cool apartment, but his own prurient fantasies lead him to interpret her statement as an invitation to an affair. The two-shot shows her smiling and earnest, while his eyes bug out in fear. He loses his nerve, and tells her, "This may be a little too savage." While Richard initially agrees that it should be acceptable for her to sleep in his apartment, he fears being caught: "There's such a thing as society you know, laws, rules, I don't mean I necessarily believe in them, but after all, no man's an island." When she explains that she'll just sleep in the chair, he agrees, until he thinks of the prurient fantasies of those in the building who might see her leaving his apartment in the morning, fantasies that are confirmed when Kruhulik arrives and, despite Richard's attempts to hide The Girl in a wingback chair, sees her bare feet stretching out from the chair to hook her sandal straps on her toes.

At the same time, film censorship depends on those prurient fantasies—the film is riddled with suggestive scenes that work only with the aid of the audience's imagination.[32] For example, while the inset shot of The Girl's "Textures" photo for *U.S. Camera* shows her in a bikini, the dialogue suggests that she is nude: "I was, uh, it was one of these, artistic pictures," she explains as she lifts the right shoulder of her shirt. "It was called 'Textures,' because you could see three different kinds of textures: the driftwood, the sand, and me," she tells Richard, whose bulging eyes indicate he sees more than her polka dot bikini.[33] Before we see the inset shot, we imagine a nude photo. In addition, the film clearly implies The Girl is sexually experienced, even though she is unmarried. Lucy Bolton calls attention to "the ubiquitous sexual references . . . ('Do you really think you can get it open?')" that "undermine any 'wholesomeness' about The Girl's sexuality that she herself might constitute" (117). But The Girl's wholesomeness seems to be apparent in the way she is not sex obsessed. When she descends from the boarded-up ceiling, romantic lighting and music suggest her casual attitude toward sex and nudity are a gift from the gods (in sharp contrast to Richard's association of them with transgression, evident in his twitching thumb). Because the censors focused on the affair and Richard's fantasies, Monroe's performance could communicate both postwar women's experience and their ability to control their own, and others', desires, if it served their purposes. This role paved the way for Monroe's next role, as the openly experienced Cherie of *Bus Stop*.

BUS STOP

Whereas *The Seven Year Itch* communicates The Girl's sexual experience through innuendo, *Bus Stop* openly accepts female sexual experience. *Bus Stop*, based on a William Inge play, was adapted by George Axelrod, the author of *The Seven Year Itch*, and directed by Joshua Logan.[34] In the film, Monroe plays Cherie, a world-weary "chanteuse" who works at a Phoenix nightclub. Bo Decker (Don Murray) is in Phoenix to participate in the rodeo. Bo's mentor, Virgil (Arthur O'Connell), tells him it is time to meet a woman, as he has been alone on the ranch throughout his adolescence. Bo takes this advice to heart when he sees Cherie singing and claims her as his "angel." While Cherie is initially attracted to Bo, his manner of courting her—charging into her bedroom in the morning and reciting the Gettysburg Address, lassoing her, abducting her, and loading her onto a bus to Montana—understandably cool her affections. Only at the eponymous bus stop during a snowstorm, when the bus driver (Robert Bray) beats some sense into him, does Bo recognize that his behavior has been offensive and selfish. Once he apologizes to Cherie, she willingly boards the bus to Montana to start a life with him while Virgil stays behind.

Monroe's performance as the sexy chanteuse Cherie both acknowledges and directly challenges expectations for a sexpot. Cherie is, in many respects, the opposite of *The Seven Year Itch*'s fantasy "Girl." We first see Cherie from Virgil's perspective as he watches her from his hotel window; her bare leg on the windowsill attracts his attention. But she is not deliberately being sexy; rather, tired and harangued, she is fanning herself during a much-needed break from the pawing and whistling of the saloon crowd. Because we first glimpse Cherie in this private moment, this sequence "is self-consciously cinematic and virtually voyeuristic in revealing the interior of her life" (Rollyson *Marilyn* 107). Her life, as viewers soon learn, consists of a series of assaults on her privacy. A group of saloon patrons barge into the room where she is resting, pawing at her until her boss ushers them back into the main saloon. She returns to the window and hangs her head, but her boss pushes her around and insists she return to work.

Although she is a showgirl, Cherie is neither as glamorous nor as sexy as the fantasy women Monroe had previously played. When her boss tells her to get into her showgirl costume, what might have been titillating is instead quite awkward. Rather than seductively sliding pantyhose up her outstretched legs or shimmying into a tight-fitting garment, Cherie covers herself with her robe, gracelessly stumbles as she shoves her legs into the costume, and reveals the inner foundation of the garment rather than her breasts. Her striptease in reverse establishes the discord between the way she is expected to behave and how she actually feels; this discord reflects Monroe's own frustrations with playing "Marilyn Monroe." Monroe's influence on this film, and on the portrayal of Cherie, is unmistakable. Monroe personally selected Cherie's costumes, and director Logan and screenwriter Axelrod insist that Monroe shaped her role as Cherie. She shaped the film through characteristic gestures, such as scratching her head, burying her face in her hands, or leaning her face against her palms or forearms, "defining," as Carl Rollyson writes, "Cherie's fatiguing searching for an identity" (*Marilyn* 108). Cherie is not searching for just any identity, though—she is desperate for an identity that doesn't involve being the sexpot.

Bus Stop's early episodes establish the pattern governing Cherie's life: while men have never treated her well, she maintains her self-respect by clinging to her dreams of completing her journey from, as she tells her coworker, "River Gulch [to] Hollywood and Vine," where, she claims with wide eyes, "You get discovered, you get tested with options and everything. And you get treated with a little respect, too!" These lines, delivered early in the film, unmistakably allude to Monroe's own battles with Hollywood. Everyone watching the film, knowing that Monroe had walked out on Hollywood because she was only given dumb blonde roles, and now seeing her in another at least superficially dumb blonde role, would certainly know that Cherie was more likely to get "treated with a little respect" by a rodeo cowboy than by Hollywood. They would also recognize the sexpot's desire for respect as a character trait drawn directly from the actress's persona.

As Monroe's first film after she studied at the Actors Studio, *Bus Stop* earned her praise, but not respect. According to the *Hollywood Reporter*, *Bus Stop* reveals that, contrary to the "knowing laughter about Miss Monroe's attempts to broaden her native talents by working at her acting . . . she now has the last and very triumphant laugh. . . . The celebrated

attractions are still happily there but they have been augmented by a sensitivity, a poignancy and an apparent understanding that Miss Monroe did
not display before" ("Bus" 3). Cherie's Ozark accent and stylized performance of "Old Black Magic," which is sung rather unpleasantly in the style
of a "hillbilly" "chanteuse" who also has to manage her own stage lighting
with her feet, demonstrate vividly Monroe's acting ability, of which even
the *New York Times* critic Bosley Crowther, who had lambasted Monroe
in her previous roles, approved.[35] But although Crowther and others recognized that she could act, they also noted her physique and attributed
her performance to Logan's directing. The film's narrative also makes
jokes at her expense, for example, when photographers from *Life* magazine take a picture of her bottom as she bends down to get her lipstick.
Thus, Monroe's own career demonstrates how difficult it was to gain
respect from Hollywood, a fact that makes Cherie's dream all the more
naive.

Cherie is not naive, however, in matters of sex; this character trait
derives from Monroe's status as a sexpot whose sexual liaisons didn't
detract from fans' admiration. *Bus Stop* participates in a gender role reversal in that Cherie is sexually experienced, but Bo is virginal. As the film's
trailer explains: "He didn't want her to know that when it came to women,
he knew nothing, but nothing. She didn't want him to know that when it
came to men, she knew plenty, but plenty." The film was marketed as "the
coming of age of Bo Decker . . . and the Woman who Made Him a Man!"
The trailer's joke works because it proclaims the opposite of the conventional scenario. But here the sexpot isn't a figure for censure. Instead, her
sexual experience is, albeit tongue-in-cheek, praised.

Initially, it seems that *Bus Stop* has set Cherie up as a woman for an
inexperienced man to "practice on," thereby chastising her for her experience. Virgil encourages Bo to explore his sexuality, telling him, "You're
twenty-one years old, and we're on our way to a big city, Phoenix, Arizona.
It's time you met up with a gal." He warns him, however, not to set his
sights on an "angel," as Bo intends, but on "some plain-looking little old

gal with a cooperative nature and a good personality."[36] Virge's advice suggests that "gal[s] with a cooperative nature," that is, sexually experienced women, aren't worthy of marriage. He even ribs Bo, telling him he knows he is attracted to the women in cheesecake magazines. (Here, the film alludes to Monroe's nude photos, which, as noted in chapter 2, were the first nude photos of a celebrity that most Americans saw, and thus she likely played a role in many a teenage boy's fantasies of "the woman who [would make] him a man.") Bo seems to corroborate Virge's opinion regarding "cooperative" women when he insists, "If I do find me a gal, it ain't gonna be a gal from all those magazines. I already decided. I'm gonna get me a angel." Although Bo insists that a pinup model could not be his angel, he changes his mind when he sees Cherie on stage in a burlesque costume, and later insists, "I don't want no schoolmarm! I want Cherry!" Bo's repeated mispronouncing of Cherie as Cherry hints at his desire for sex. Bo's angel is not a complacent "good" girl, but a woman uniquely equipped to provoke desire, a sexpot, but one he wants to marry.

Because Cherie desires respect, she was initially attracted to Bo when he quieted the crowd during her performance: "It was real nice the way you made everybody shut up in there. Like you had respect for me. You made them have respect too. I liked that." But Bo quickly contradicts her first impression by insisting that they are getting married when he hasn't properly asked her, and by repeatedly embarrassing Cherie at the rodeo, where he treats her as though she is his possession. Bo wants to bend Cherie to his will: "I'm just gonna pretend that little old calf is Cherry. I'm going after her, and I'm gonna get her, and when I get her, I'm gonna rope her." Cherie admits that she's attracted to Bo, but she isn't convinced to marry him because her understanding of love involves more than physical attraction. In one of the film's most melancholy moments, she admits to a fellow bus passenger that she's not sure if she will ever find a suitable man: "Maybe I don't know what love is. I want a guy I can look up to and admire, but I don't want him to browbeat me. I want a guy who'll be sweet with me, but I don't want him to baby me either." Monroe's performance in this relatively long take demonstrates her alternating desire and frustration, until finally she says, "I just gotta feel that whoever I marry has some real regard for me, aside from," and here she closes her eyes and clenches her jaw, "all that lovin' stuff, you know what I mean?" She admits that she'll bring "that lovin' stuff" to the relationship, but insists that she deserves respect. Cherie speaks for her worth despite being a sexpot, a worth to which women (who, according to the practice of brinkmanship, were told to be attractive to get a man, but not to have sex) could relate.

While Cherie insists on respect despite her sexual experience, Bo's inexperience is the film's central joke, a joke that calls attention to the absurdity of the double standard. Virge encourages Bo to gain experience, but he belittles Cherie for having it. Explaining that sexually experienced women aren't acceptable brides, Virge says, "I ain't sayin' this particular gal you picked out ain't a good one to practice on. But a fella can't go around marryin' the first gal he meets." When Virge explains to Cherie that he doesn't want Bo to marry her, she indignantly responds, "It's 'cause I ain't good enough for him, is that it? I suppose he's as pure as a bunch of driven snow." Confirming Bo's "purity" at the same time as he censures Cherie's impurity, Virge explains that Bo "spent his whole life pretty far out in the country." When Cherie questions Virge's logic, explaining, "I know what happens in the country, I'm from the country myself. I've been kissin' boys since I was knee high to a . . . ," Virge keeps her from detailing her experience, saying, "You're kind of sophisticated for Bo." "First time, huh?," Cherie asks, and the close-up, which shows her finger on her lips and her wistful eyes, makes clear that she regards this as a sign of respect for her: "Sure ain't never had that honor before." The scenario this exchange alludes to unmistakably reverses 1950s gender roles. In 1957, MD Lena Levine wrote that it was the husband's job to teach the inexperienced wife, who is "dismayed at feeling little or no sexual desires, which she had been sure would automatically come to her with marriage" (34). Cherie's perspective is perhaps more realistic—all those sexually experienced men had to have had partners.

While Levine argued that wives had no sexual desires, *Bus Stop* suggests that men must learn to satisfy women's sexual desires. Cherie is uniquely equipped to teach Bo what he needs to know about satisfying women, and as he learns, the film reflects the period's post-Kinsey emphasis on the need for men to engage in the proper techniques, both of seduction and sex. Bo's approach is wrong from the start; he corners her in the doorway, and the medium close-up two-shot shows him dominating her space as he starts his speech: "Now, I come down for the rodeo tomorrow with the idea in mind of findin' me an angel, and you're it. Now I don't have a lot of time for sweet talkin' around the bush, so I'd be much obliged to you if you'd just step outside with me into the fresh air." Bo's lack of "time for," as he confuses the metaphor, "sweet talkin' around the bush" can easily be interpreted as code for his reluctance to engage in foreplay, either conversational foreplay or the physical foreplay associated with the "bush."[37] As he claims that he has no time for foreplay, Bo represents the public resistance to Kinsey's unconventional finding that frigidity was not a psychological disorder but rather the result of ineffective sex techniques. According to *Sexual Behavior in the Human Female*, "The average female . . . does not begin to respond until there has been a considerable amount of physical stimulation" (626–627). In 1954, gynecologist and psychiatrist Arthur Mandy insisted that, if men read the report, they would understand "the importance of the male's stimulating the female, up to and *including* orgasm, by labial and clitoral manipulation, rather than by sole concentration on *coital* positions and techniques" (101–102). However, this advice rarely made it into the popular press; even when it did, authors themselves "beat around the bush" by only hinting that husbands should read the book to find out how "correct physical stimulation" could lead wives to "enjoy these relations" (Davidson and Mudd 115). Although Cherie agrees to go into the alley with Bo, we see her holding herself at a distance from him, giving him space to prove himself worthy of her attention, which he does by swinging from the rafters.

Figure 4.4. Bo's effective caresses. Frame enlargement from *Bus Stop*.

As a Code-approved film, *Bus Stop* could not go into detail regarding Bo's sexual technique, but his inadequacies at seducing women are reiterated throughout the film, clearly alluding to the prominent context of Kinsey's findings on female pleasure. Virge suggests that women sometimes like men for their minds, so Bo barges in on Cherie when she's asleep and encourages her to "get attracted to [his] mind" by listening to him recite the Gettysburg Address. The way the scene is shot, however, underscores that Virge doesn't know how best to seduce a woman. As Cherie insists that she has "no intention in the world of marryin'" Bo because, she says, "I know all about your mind I ever want to know," the camera is behind the headboard, so that the bedrails resemble cell bars across the characters' faces. This shot indicates that Bo's inept approach bars Cherie from becoming further involved with him. When Bo begins caressing her naked arm and hip, the camera moves to the side, so that it is clear when Cherie, aroused by his physical stimulation, acquiesces and turns toward Bo (Figure 4.4).

To seduce Cherie, Bo must learn to humble himself. The bus driver, acting as a surrogate for Virge, beats some sense into Bo, making a condition of Bo's loss that he must apologize to everyone he has annoyed on the bus ride, including Cherie. He finally admits, "Cherry, it wasn't right of me to do what I did to you. Treatin' you that way, dragging you on the bus, tryin' to make you marry me whether you wanted to or not. Do you think you could ever forgive me?" She replies, "I guess I been treated worse in my life." Although Cherie looks defeated throughout this scene, she also approaches Bo with the same kind of respect she seeks for herself. Closing the physical gap between them, Cherie crosses the room and sits beside Bo, beginning, "Bo, I just wanted to tell you something. It's kinda personal and embarrassing, too. But, I ain't the kind of girl you thought I was. . . . I guess a lot of people'd say I led a real wicked life, and I guess I have, too." When Cherie says she's had "quite a few" previous boyfriends, Bo admits, "I guess I just didn't know anything about women, 'cause they're different from men." Cherie's response, "Well, naturally," insists that Cherie knows about both women and men, making her an appropriate teacher of how men should respond to women.

Through Cherie, and by extension, Monroe's sexual but not wanton persona, *Bus Stop* bespeaks a cultural shift in which unmarried sexually active women deserved as much respect as virgins. "Seeing as how you had all them other boyfriends before me," Bo states, "and seeing as how I never had one single gal friend before you, well, Virge figures that between the two of us, it kinda averages out to things being proper, and right." Bo's stubborn desire to marry Cherie, despite her past, leads Virge to finally accept her, but Bo still relies on Virge's authority. Cherie avoids making eye contact with Bo as she waits for him to explain if he feels the same as Virge, but an extended close-up two-shot illustrates, through the shot composition and editing, how they come to a mutual understanding. "I've been thinking about them other fellas, Cherry," Bo says, his face dominating the frame such that only one of Cherie's eyes is visible as she glances hopefully up at him (Figure 4.5). "I like you the way you are, so what do I care how you got that way?," he continues, as the camera gradually tilts down to show her full face only when Bo has accepted her sexual experience. In this shared shot, "with Cherie's upper body lying along the bottom of the frame and [Bo] leaning above her," as Ana Salzberg points

Figure 4.5. Bo initially dominates Cherie. Frame enlargement from
Bus Stop.

Figure 4.6. As Bo acknowledges Cherie's past, the camera tilts down to
show her full face. Frame enlargement from *Bus Stop.*

out, "the two merge in a body-landscape, a panorama of passionate recognition" (142) (Figure 4.6). Cherie's eyes close in relief—for once, being
the sexpot has not diminished her worth in the eyes of another.

    After this, a series of shot/reverse-shot close-ups alternately isolates
each of their faces as they realize their affection for each other, and signals how Bo's acceptance of Cherie's past enables her to "go anywhere in
the world" with him. Bo's acceptance of Cherie's past is out of keeping with
the conventional attitude toward experienced women. Levine advised
women to keep their sexual experience a secret, because, according to a

marriage counselor, "It's a rare man . . . who can hear about his wife's pre-marital sex and completely condone and accept it" (60). The series of close-ups in this sequence, rather than two-shots, indicates that Bo and Cherie are individuals before they are a couple, and, contrary to the advice of postwar marriage counselors, that their past experiences must be accepted before they can begin a successful relationship.

But what does Cherie gain when she agrees to marry Bo? Most obviously, she gains a way out of the saloon circuit and a spouse, despite conventional warnings that men don't marry women who aren't virgins. As the couple stands outside the bus, saying goodbye to Virge, who refuses to accompany them, Bo recognizes that Cherie must be "freezing" in the thin coat she has been wearing since he forced her onto the bus to Montana, and offers his heavy coat. The shot lingers on her as she wraps herself in its luxury. While Rollyson reads Cherie's enjoyment at this moment as "recognition of what she has won," he doesn't say what that is, but implies it is the security of marriage (111).

If we focus on Cherie as a sexpot, a more significant gain for her is reciprocity—both in terms of sexual pleasure and respect. The film's final moments make clear that Cherie can expect more than the security of marriage in the form of the "deep freeze" Bo had promised, "or an electric washer, or any other major appliance you want." As Cherie wraps herself in the coat, she turns her head from left to right, lingering in the sensation of the coat's fur trim against her skin, displaying the closed eyes and open mouth associated with Monroe's signature expression of sexual pleasure (Figure 4.7). Cherie's visible pleasure indicates that Bo will work to satisfy her sexual needs, just as he does her more immediate physical needs. After this exchange, moreover, Cherie gives Bo her scarf, hinting at a reciprocal relationship, a gesture that makes him whoop as he considers her needs again and helps her board the bus ahead of him. In short, Bo finally makes Cherie "hot" for him by thinking of her needs, demonstrating that he has learned the lessons indicated by Kinsey's controversial findings regarding female sexual pleasure.

Figure 4.7. Cherie's pleasure. Frame enlargement from *Bus Stop*.

SOME LIKE IT HOT

Drawing on her sexually charged roles in *The Seven Year Itch* and *Bus Stop*, *Some Like It Hot* more openly asserts Monroe's sexuality. In *Some Like It Hot*, Joe (Tony Curtis) and Jerry (Jack Lemmon), two hard-up musicians who inadvertently witness the St. Valentine's massacre in Prohibition-era Chicago, escape the mobsters pursuing them by disguising themselves as women. Joe becomes Josephine and Jerry becomes Daphne in order to join an all-girl jazz band bound for Florida. After he spends some time with Sugar Kane Kowalczyk (Monroe), who tells him she hopes to meet a millionaire in glasses, Joe concocts a second disguise, as the bespectacled Shell Oil Jr. In a significant plot twist, Joe, as Shell Oil Jr., feigns impotence to allow Sugar to prove her aptitude for lovemaking. Meanwhile, Jerry as Daphne meets a real millionaire, Osgood Fielding (Joe E. Brown), whom, despite her initial impression that he is a "dirty old man," she agrees to marry. When the Chicago mobsters show up at the Florida hotel, the disguises unravel, but not before Josephine kisses Sugar goodbye. Despite learning that Joe is both Josephine and Shell Oil Jr., Sugar insists on beginning a relationship with him. Jerry, even after he confesses he is a man, remains unable to shake Osgood, who maintains they are getting married. *Some Like It Hot* presents a fluid view of gender roles and a less moralistic attitude toward sexual behavior than that which typified the 1950s, thereby capitalizing on both *Sexual Behavior in the Human Female* and Monroe's sexpot persona.

Some Like It Hot, more so than Monroe's other roles, illustrates her unique ability to defy conventional moral codes without appearing defiant. Although Wilder, who cowrote and directed *The Seven Year Itch*, also cowrote and directed this film, Sugar differs greatly from the fantasy figure of The Girl, who represents allure without consummation, and so avoids transgressing the conventions governing sexual behavior. Sugar is sexy and admits to being "not very bright," but she is much more assertive than The Girl; she seduces Shell Oil Jr. to get what she wants. In so doing, Sugar contradicts two pieces of conventional wisdom regarding sex that had proven restrictive to postwar relations: first, that the sex act for women should entail passivity, and, second, that sexually satisfying women interfered with men's pleasure. Sugar's sexuality is aggressive, but also aggressively focused on the man's pleasure, and as such it alleviates any anxiety about satisfying her, providing another reason to like the sexpot.

The film's Prohibition-era setting is adapted to the 1950s by virtue of Monroe and the meanings she brings to the film. "Dressing up the 1950s as the 1920s," as Gerd Gemünden sees it, "allows Wilder to contrast the stifling and confining Eisenhower years with an era that was known for its audaciousness and unlawfulness, its sexual liberties and progressive ideas, and its economic and political volatility" (102). But it also allows Wilder to call attention to the way sexual ideology in the 1950s was transforming by recognizing, through discourse about Kinsey's reports, the kinds of sexual behaviors in which Americans actually engaged. *Sexual Behavior in the Human Female* points out that the greatest changes in female sexual behavior occurred in the generation that was in their teens and twenties in the 1920s (244).[38] During the 1920s, sex was separated from procreation, and the period's "sexual liberalism," as John D'Emilio and Estelle Freedman write, "affirmed heterosexual pleasure as a value in itself, defined sexual satisfaction as a critical component of personal happiness and successful marriage, and weakened the connections between sexual expression and marriage by providing youth with room for some experimentation as preparation for adult status" (241). Sugar's nearly transparent dresses signal her freedom from the "buttoned-up" mores of the postwar period's cultural conservatives; her sheer dresses are as transgressive for the 1950s as the flapper look was for the 1920s.[39] Sugar and the film's other women are not stereotypically conservative 1950s women; Kinsey's findings regarding female sexual behavior evidently apply to them. Setting the film in the 1920s therefore contrasts the wild, immature sexual free-for-all of the flappers with the more mature partnering of sex with love in the transitional double standard of the 1950s.

The film uses any indications of homosexuality in a similar manner—that is, to show the harmlessness (relative to other sexual options) of sex outside of marriage. In *Some Like It Hot*'s famous final sequence, Daphne, in order to convince Osgood that they can't get married, cycles through typical excuses—"I'm not a natural blonde," "I smoke," "I've been living with a saxophone player," "I can't have children"—but finally, because Osgood doesn't care about any of these things, Jerry exclaims, "I'm a man" and removes his wig, to which Osgood replies, "Nobody's perfect." The film ends with a two-shot of them looking straight ahead, Osgood grinning, Jerry baffled, as they speed into the future. Writers Wilder and I.A.L. Diamond recognized that they could only push the boundaries so far. The final lines of the script read: "Jerry looks at Osgood, who is grinning from ear to ear, claps his hand to his forehead. How is he going to get himself out of this? But that's another story—and we're not quite sure the public is ready for it" (156).[40] While Wilder and Diamond suspected that the public was not ready for a fully realized homosexual relationship onscreen, the end of Sugar's story promises she will finally begin the sexual relationship she's been angling for (albeit with Joe rather than a millionaire).

The ease with which Sugar accepts Daphne and Josephine as women suggests that she's more comfortable with their new identities than they are, making her a model for accepting gender fluidity. Sugar befriends them as women; as they chat in the ladies' room, she confides in them

Figure 4.8. Two women in bed. Frame enlargement from *Some Like It Hot.*

about her past and her drinking. When Sugar climbs into Daphne's berth to avoid being caught drinking by the band leader, Sweet Sue, it is clear that the two of them have sexual chemistry despite the fact that Sugar thinks she's in bed with a woman. Sugar snuggles up to Daphne, but Jerry is uncomfortably titillated because he's supposed to be a woman. And the more Daphne trembles, the more physical Sugar gets: when she rubs Daphne's legs between her feet, Daphne has to remind herself, "I'm a girl" (Figure 4.8). Later, Sugar receives a tender kiss from Josephine, a kiss from which she does not pull away. Neil Sinyard and Adrian Turner note the "audacity" of this kiss: "Hollywood's supreme sex-symbol is given her most passionate screen kiss by another woman" (222). Sugar accepts that these men are women, and that women are sometimes attracted to other women, subversively hinting at a new era of sexual mores.[41]

A few details from public responses to *Some Like It Hot* will highlight just how remarkably Monroe disarmed the most subversive aspects of her role in the film. Crowther hinted at the possible homosexuality in the film, but did not recognize it as such, instead using the film to prove that film censorship was changing: "There's a scene in this Hollywood picture in which a lightly clad Marilyn Monroe does some rather voluptuous snuggling up with Jack Lemmon in the upper berth of a Pullman car. Even though it's true that Mr. Lemmon is impersonating a girl and Miss Monroe is taken in by the deception, it's a scene that would curl the hair of Will H. Hays, who used to have some rigid notions about scenes of gentlemen and ladies in bed. . . . Only it's done much more boldly and frankly than it could have been a few years ago" ("To Be" X1). Not only does this review call attention to the fact that Monroe is "rather voluptuous[ly] snuggling" someone she thinks is a woman, but it praises the film for it. Furthermore, clergymen complained to the censor, Shurlock, regarding the film's "clear inferences of homosexuality and lesbianism" (Little). Shurlock, however, responded that the film had received "nothing but praise" in reviews, and concluded his response with a parting shot: "We are of course not defending the two exaggerated costumes worn by the leading lady; but we gathered these were not your major concern" (Shurlock to Little). Although two of Sugar's scenes could signal homosexual desire, and although she admits to living with men outside of marriage, her costumes, at least in the eyes of the Production Code Administration, constitute the biggest threat to public morals associated with her character. This is a new era indeed.

Some Like It Hot is clearly infused with a 1950s context of anxiety about gender roles, which stemmed not only from shifting understandings of marriage (see chapter 3), but also from the pervasive publicity regarding the sex reassignment surgery of Christine Jorgensen in 1952.[42] Summarizing the anxieties surrounding gender fluidity raised by Jorgensen, Gobind Behari Lal writes for American Mercury: "How secure is anybody's sex? What is it to be a man or to be a woman? How much sex change is possible in a human being? Can a man and a wife walk into a hospital and come out roles reversed, Joe turned into Jane, Jane into Joe?" (39). Note that Lal is not only worried about biology—he's worried about gender roles.

Drawing on the opinions of scientists, Lal reports that "to be human means to be Man-with-a-touch-of-Woman, to be Woman-with-a-touch-of-Man" (42). *Some Like It Hot* dramatizes what it means "to be Man-with-a-touch-of-Woman," or the concept of gender performativity now foundational to feminist theory. According to poststructuralist feminist philosopher Judith Butler, gender is not essential, but rather "a performance that is *repeated*" (191).[43] Joe and Jerry do more than dress as women—they perform the identities of women. When Joe calls the agent Poliakoff (Billy Gray) to accept the gig in the all-girl band, he purses his lips and rolls his eyes up in an exaggerated performance of femininity. Wilder cuts from the scene of this phone call, when the two are still dressed as men, to two pairs of stocky legs stumbling in high heels across a train platform. But Jerry's high heel bends under him, and the look on his face indicates that he is not so sure his performance is accurate.

Sugar appears on the platform to serve as a model for the men-performing-women at the moment Jerry worries, "We're never going to get away with it." We first see Sugar from the shoulders up as she sashays down the platform. As Jerry comments that she "must have some sort of built in motor or something," he convincingly copies her shimmying shoulders (though viewers are spared any attempts on his part to copy her "Jello on springs" behind). "It is almost as if," argues Rebecca Bell-Metereau, "they admire femaleness to such an extent that they are eager to do as good a job as they can at actually becoming female" (57). Jerry reacts to Sugar's performance of femininity by declaring, "It's a whole different sex," a response Daniel Lieberfeld interprets as "gender essentialism." However, Wilder's focusing first on the men-as-women's legs and then showing Sugar from the shoulders up subverts the essentialism of the conventions associated with filming men and women.[44] Moreover, this joke's transgressive potential stems from the fact that, by adopting a few mannerisms, these men can successfully perform femininity, thereby rendering *inessential* many of the limiting characteristics associated with femininity, such as passivity, helplessness, and stupidity.[45]

Joe and Jerry, however, do not initially demonstrate that they accept women as their equals. Jerry refers to the women as "goodies" and wants "to borrow a cup of that Sugar." It takes the course of the film—and being treated the same way they have treated women—for their performances as women to transform Jerry and Joe from being stereotypical men. Their arrival in Florida removes them from the safer all-female (excepting Beinstock [Dave Barry], who is nearly blind) world on the train and places them in the direct path of lecherous men. The elderly Osgood Fielding immediately sets his sights on Daphne, pinching her in the elevator, and a diminutive bellboy hits on Josephine. While Daphne is surprised, because, as she says, she's "not even pretty," Josephine explains, "They don't care, just so long as you're wearing a skirt. It's like waving a red flag in front of a bull." These statements underscore the problems with how Joe and Jerry had treated women, including their bandmates, and indicate that they are learning, through their successful performances of femininity, how it feels to be a woman.[46]

Much has been written about the "drag" performances of Tony Curtis as Joe/Josephine/Shell Oil Jr. and Jack Lemmon as Jerry/Daphne, but fewer authors have attended to Monroe, who also, as *Newsweek* noted at the time, "is, as usual, an extremely effective female impersonator, herself" ("Wonderfully" 113). Referring to a biological female as a female impersonator underscores how much Monroe treated gender as a performance: her sexpot persona was a performance she excelled at by exaggerating the culture's conventional expressions of femininity, most notably through her prominent breasts (accentuated by her costuming), her childlike naivete, and her seeming vulnerability. As Susan Griffin insists, "Monroe must learn to impersonate not only a 'woman,' but she must impersonate culture's *ideal* of a 'sexual' woman. And if she is numb to her own feeling, she must imitate culture's dream of female sexuality" (212). However, Monroe's performance of femininity in this film is not as submissive as it initially seems. Whereas Sugar had once accepted that men would seduce her, then leave her, when she tells Junior she is a "society girl" who attended the

Sheboygan Conservatory of Music, she adopts the gold-digging persona associated with Monroe's earlier roles and goes after what she wants.

Sugar also informs Joe's understanding of how to perform masculinity. Bemoaning her past affairs with saxophone players who left her with nothing but "a pair of old socks and a tube of toothpaste, all squeezed out," Sugar tells Josephine that she intends to meet a millionaire in glasses while they're in Florida, because "men who wear glasses are so much more gentle and sweet and helpless." Monroe's previous films had built up to this moment, when audiences would criticize not Sugar for having sex with all these saxophone players, but the saxophone players for subjecting her to their ruthless "love 'em and leave 'em" standards. Acting as a "typical" saxophone player, Joe nuzzles up to Nellie (Barbara Drew) just to borrow her car. Therefore, to attract Sugar, he has to act out of character, as a helpless bespectacled millionaire reading the stock columns, to the point of feigning impotence.

Through Junior's impotence and Sugar's assertiveness, *Some Like It Hot* reflects a widely noted, and debated, shift in late 1950s sex roles. Throughout the 1950s, conservative writers countered Kinsey's findings by insisting that truly "feminine" women approached "the sexual act itself" with "receptiveness and a certain passivity" (Coughlan 109).[47] "Today's American male, if the experts are right," J. Robert Moskin writes in the year of the film's release, "has even lost much of his sexual initiative and control; some authorities believe that his capacity is being lowered. More women are taking charge of sex relations, and they now have three new weapons [brinkmanship, birth control, and female pleasure] to make their control effective" (78).[48] Complaining that a husband could "no longer concentrate on his own pleasure [because] he must concern himself primarily with satisfying his wife" (78), Moskin hints at a desire for male passivity even as he advocates for a passive wife. It is little wonder, then, that as these conversations dominated the postwar atmosphere, many films—*The Best Years of Our Lives* (1946, dir. William Wyler), *Sunset Boulevard* (1950, dir. Billy Wilder), *The Marrying Kind* (1952, dir. George Cukor), *Shane* (1953, dir. George Stevens), *The Country Girl* (1954, dir. George Seaton), *All that Heaven Allows* (1955, dir. Douglas Sirk), *Picnic* (1955, dir. Josh Logan)—dramatized how males might use a certain passivity to their advantage, allowing women to fawn over and chase after them. *Some Like It Hot* treats both the "receptive" man and the woman who takes charge as positive developments—after all, both get what they want.

Sugar is clearly an aggressive woman seducing a passive man, but she does so in a gentle, nurturing way. Her means of sexual persuasion first become apparent when Sugar and Junior take a motorboat to Osgood's yacht. Sugar leans back against the boat's seat, and the high-angle shot combined with her sheer dress with strategically placed rhinestones presents her nearly naked bosom to Joe, figuratively suggesting that she is offering herself to him "on a platter" (Figure 4.9).[49] Costume and lighting conspire to remind us that Sugar is a sexpot, but we also know that the sexpot gets "the fuzzy end of the lollipop" if she doesn't look out for herself. When Junior tells Sugar that they're alone on the yacht, she confesses, "You know I've never been completely alone with a man before . . . in the middle of the night . . . in the middle of the ocean." Her strategic pauses indicate that she's not a virgin. She practically offers to make love to him. She assures him that she knows he is a gentleman, but Junior confesses that he's "harmless" because women no longer do anything for him. He says, "If I ever found the girl that could, I'd marry her just like that" and snaps his fingers. After Junior tells her about his impotence, she pulls out all the stops—hands Junior a second glass of champagne after he drains the first one, dims the lights, turns on soft music, climbs on top of him, and kisses him, repeatedly, until his glasses begin to steam.

Yet *Some Like It Hot* does not portray the shift in sex roles as a threat, and Joe does not consummate the relationship just because a sexy woman is seducing him. In fact, Wilder intended Joe's passivity as a joke. Summarizing an interview with Wilder, Gene Phillips writes: "Wilder points out that, if Joe were the aggressor in this scene and overpowered Sugar, it would be dirty. But if she is the aggressor and seduces him because she

Figure 4.9. Sugar's nurturing bosom. Frame enlargement from *Some Like It Hot.*

thinks he is impotent, it is funny" (227). While postwar commentators argued that female sexual aggression was often the root cause of impotence, the scene in which Sugar "cures" Junior on the yacht makes female sexual aggression an enjoyable cure, thereby valorizing female assertiveness. In so doing, the film echoes controversial advice popularized in *Reader's Digest.* In an excerpt from her book *Help Your Husband Stay Alive* reprinted as "What Every Husband Needs," Hannah Lees explained, "It is essential to a man's well-being that he feel virile and physically attractive" (137). "The whole question is whether her want warms her husband or scares him," Lees elaborated. "It will scare him if she expects him to make love to her. Yet it can be the nourishment he has always needed if she is willing to make love to him" (139–140). The sexpot, with her experience, confidence, and attractiveness, offers just what is needed in this scenario. Sugar makes no demands on Junior, despite her sexual assertiveness. In so doing, she serves as a sexual fantasy at the same time as she advances the shifting sexual mores that made it acceptable for women to be assertive partners.[50]

This "reversed" sex scene transforms Joe. Although Joe tells Jerry, "It's going to break Sugar's heart when she finds out I'm not a millionaire. That's life. You can't make an omelet without breaking an egg," he isn't as callous as he seems, for he insists on saying goodbye to Sugar even though the Chicago mobsters have discovered them. When Jerry points out, "You usually walk out and leave 'em with nothing but a kick in the teeth," Joe replies, "That was when I was a saxophone player. Now I'm a millionaire." Although Joe refers to his false role, he also points out that Sugar's expectations for him have taught him how to perform masculinity. He demonstrates that he's a new man when he gives Sugar the diamond bracelet Osgood had given Daphne. Sugar confirms that, although he has left her to marry another woman, Junior is "the first nice guy I ever met in my life. The only one who ever gave me anything." Because of Joe's habit of taking money, cars, and time from Nellie and the girls in the band, we can assume that she's the first girl he's ever given anything to, and thus that his time living as a woman has transformed him into a more generous, considerate mate. When he hears Sugar singing, "I'm through with love, I'll never fall again," Joe can't resist the urge to console her. As she sits on the piano, dejected, eyes closed, he walks up to her, still in full Josephine costume, lifts her chin, kisses her sweetly, wipes away her tears, and says, "None of that Sugar, no guy is worth it."

Recognizing that Josephine is Junior (she has never met Joe), Sugar chases after him. Although Joe insists, "You don't want me Sugar. I'm a liar and a phony, a saxophone player. One of those no-goodniks you keep running away from," Sugar can't deny her attraction to him. Sugar accepts Joe's past as a saxophone player, as Josephine, and as Shell Oil Jr., perhaps because Joe knows about her past but nevertheless has treated her with some respect by admitting that "no guy is worth it." As she chases Josephine, Sugar reveals that she is not "through with love" entirely, but rather she is through with love based on deceptive behaviors and double standards. She and Joe ride off into the sunset, beginning a relationship built upon honesty about their pasts.

Those of Monroe's films that most blatantly capitalize on her sex appeal draw on the transgressive elements of her offscreen life. As The Girl in *The Seven Year Itch*, Monroe most clearly plays a version of herself—she has posed nude, she is single but not virginal, she is an actress. The Girl demonstrates how Monroe's offscreen transgressions embodied the kinds of female sexual behavior that Kinsey reported, the validity of which many Americans were debating at the time. Monroe's offscreen life also informs the role of Cherie in *Bus Stop*, who is eager to find "respect" on Hollywood and Vine, but who instead finds respect for her sexual experience. Finally, in *Some Like It Hot*, Sugar has been "used" like a tube of toothpaste, much like Monroe herself, whose affairs were gossip fodder, but she aggressively pursues a man and maintains her sex appeal. This series of films from Monroe's canon demonstrates her unique contribution to the postwar moment. Although Monroe was a sexpot, she credibly combined compliance and independence, seeming submissive while making her right to self-satisfaction axiomatic.

CHAPTER 5

THE ACTRESS AND
HER METHOD

RESISTING PLAYING "MARILYN MONROE"

In *All about Eve*, one of the first films to bring Monroe into the spotlight, Margo Channing (Bette Davis) criticizes her male director and playwright for thinking of actresses as bodies without minds. In the same film, Margo refers to her boyfriend Bill (Gary Merrill) as a Stanislavskian director. In *All about Eve*, Monroe played Miss Caswell, an actress with limited potential (see chapter 2), and she would remain associated with the untalented actress throughout her career. Although Monroe's role as Miss Caswell indicates that she was set up to be a body without a mind, and her subsequent roles encouraged conceiving of her as such, Monroe, as I have shown, resisted such oversimplification through her film performances. Playing "Marilyn Monroe" was in some respects playing a surface that reflected America's anxieties back to it, and these included anxieties about what it meant to be an actress. Monroe's acting training indicates not only her desire, but also her effort to transform herself into a serious actress. While much of the public may have never regarded Monroe as a serious actress, her film roles after 1955 were shaped by her Actors Studio training, and three of these films, *The Prince and the Showgirl* (1957, dir. Laurence Olivier), *Let's Make Love* (1960, dir. George Cukor), and *The Misfits* (1961, dir. John Huston), purposefully engage with what it meant to play, that is, perform, the role of "Marilyn Monroe" in postwar culture.

Figure 5.1. An awkward position. Frame enlargement from *River of No Return*.

After the major successes of 1953, Monroe found herself in roles that, rather than further develop her both as sexy and as a star, reduced her to the window dressing she had played back in 1952. For example, in *River of No Return* (1954, dir. Otto Preminger) she plays a saloon singer for whom the camera shows little respect (Laura Mulvey used this role to exemplify the gaze; see "Visual" 40). As she sits on a piano with her legs spread, her thighs frame the back of a spectator's head, and the gazing men who surround her make clear that she is there to be objectified (Figure 5.1).[1] Following this role, Monroe challenged the studio and refused to appear in *The Girl in Pink Tights*, because, she said, "If I keep on with parts like the ones [Fox] has been giving me, the public will soon tire of me" (qtd. in Spoto 259).[2] She recognized that playing "Marilyn Monroe" meant playing more than the sexpot.

Nevertheless, Monroe took a role as a hatcheck girl and aspiring performer, Vicky, in *There's No Business Like Show Business* (1954, dir. Walter Lang; hereafter referred to as *Business*) as part of her renegotiation with Fox after she refused to make *The Girl in Pink Tights*.[3] *Business*, despite being a film starring Ethel Merman, treats Monroe with little more respect than *River* had, but it does give viewers an opportunity to see Monroe in what Matthew Solomon has dubbed one of her many metaperformances, or roles in which she "embod[ies] characters who make their living as performers onstage, but who lead the rest of their lives offstage" (109). For example, viewers see Vicky as a performer even backstage, as she smoothly moves through various roles as she prepares to greet a producer in her dressing room. One of these performances involves stating "Charmed, I'm sure" with the same elocution deployed in Monroe's earlier performance as Lorelei in *Gentlemen Prefer Blondes* (1953, dir. Howard Hawks). When Tim Donahue (Donald O'Connor), rather than the producer she expects, knocks on her door, she performs the disinterested woman who sees through his pretense of interviewing her for *Variety*, with no hint of the Lorelei persona she had presented moments before. When the producer does knock on her door, she turns on the Lorelei act once again. This metaperformance calls attention to the varied performances of the actress both on- and offstage.

Nevertheless, if, as Solomon remarks, "Monroe's metaperformances often reflect on her own acting and the construction of her stardom" (109), what *Business*, and indeed many of her other roles, comment upon is the difficulty she faced in being recognized as more than a sexpot. Vicky's performance of "After You Get What You Want" resembles Lorelei's performances in *Gentlemen Prefer Blondes*—we hear the same deep singing voice, and see the same arm gestures and chest shimmy.[4] But whereas Lorelei maintained a professional distance from the audience, and only suggested her sex appeal, Vicky emphasizes her sex appeal by wrapping her leg around a pole at the ballroom entrance, sitting on the patrons' tables, and wearing a sheer, nude costume with strategically placed rhinestones and a slit up to her hip. Such suggestiveness is exacerbated in the later "Heat Wave" number. In this number, as Vicky discusses the temperature "down south" and "hot and humid nights," the low angle captures men's heads clustered near her groin, and the dance she performs suggests mock ecstasy (Figure 5.2). Ed Sullivan, with only a little exaggeration, called the performance "one of the most flagrant violations of good taste" he had ever seen (qtd. in Pullen 7). *Business*, and *River of No Return* before it, made the sexpot trashy rather than dignified, vulgar rather than

Figure 5.2. A suggestive "Heat Wave." Frame enlargement from *There's No Business Like Show Business.*

sensitive. These roles limited Monroe's chances to add complexity to the sexpot through her performances.

The films in which she was cast in 1954 asked Monroe to play the sexpot as joke more than star, but these roles, which caused her to break her studio contract and travel to New York, also led her to an acting style that would give her the tools she needed to imbue the sexpot with humanity and vulnerability. As chapter 4 showed, although Monroe never completely distanced herself from her initial persona as a sexpot, she always complicated sexy roles through her performances. Nevertheless, stardom itself, as Karen Hollinger explains, "encourages the acting mode of personification, with the star just doing what she or he has become famous for doing or just being the way fans expect the star to be," and these kinds of roles "render [the star's] talent suspect" (52). Although Monroe worked to improve her acting throughout her career, debates about whether she could, or should, act also dogged her throughout her career. In the films made after she began working with Lee Strasberg of the Actors Studio in 1955, she played showgirls who knew that others viewed them as sexpots, but who also resisted the jokes others made of them. Her performances demonstrate that the sexpot recognized when she was being objectified and often resisted that objectification by asserting her subjectivity. While Monroe's performances were certainly mediated by elements of filmmaking that include directing, editing, and mise-en-scène, as Cynthia Baron and Sharon Marie Carnicke point out, "the bank of knowledge and experience that actors draw on to produce the gestures, expressions, and intonations . . . collaborate and combine with other cinematic elements to create meaning in film" (17). Monroe's acting is always mediated by aspects of film form that stem from the collaborative nature of filmmaking, but her agency in creating her performances is apparent in the many scenes that depend on how she uses her body and voice for meaning. Monroe drew on her own experiences in Hollywood to create, through her gestures and expressions, performances that challenged the stereotypes associated with playing the sexpot, and thereby challenged the stereotypes associated with playing "Marilyn Monroe."

But Can She Act?

Monroe's sex appeal led to questions about whether she was a talented actress or just a body. The innocence that tempered her sex appeal seemed to indicate that she lacked the intellect necessary to craft dramatic performances—thus her desire to play Grushenka in *The Brothers Karamazov* could never be more than a joke.[5] But because she was part of the studio system, Monroe received acting training throughout her career. According to Baron, synchronized sound films produced demands for voice and actor training programs such that "by 1939 all of the major studios had actor training programmes" (34). Such training programs remained in place throughout the studio era. Fredda Dudley, for example, noted in a special series for *Photoplay* in 1950 that newcomers who passed the screen test would then participate in "private work" with a drama coach "twice a week," as well as classes in "acting, diction, dancing, riding, and gymnasium" in addition to "casting auditions and tests" (November 1950, 92). The first installment of the series, in September 1950, featured Monroe as one of the newborn stars and so associated her with this extensive training. Monroe participated in conventional studio actor training, and she also took acting lessons with the Stanislavskian acting teacher Michael Chekhov at the Actors Lab in Hollywood at the beginning of her career.

Nevertheless, critics accused Monroe of simply "playing herself" throughout her career. This was, as Baron and Carnicke point out, typical of popular magazines, which "equated Hollywood actresses with models . . . into the early 1950s" (22), crediting their directors with the achievement of actresses' performances. Not only was Monroe a former model, but also her physical appearance typically was the primary component used to evaluate her film performances. For example, "The more she tries, the less she accomplishes," writes critic Archer Winsten. "Like a flower, she has always been at her best simply by being," he adds, negating the labor behind Monroe's film performances. Likewise, reviewer Bosley Crowther notes, "We hope it will not seem too ungallant if we make so bold as to observe that Marilyn Monroe does not perform as a great actress; she performs as a great physique" ("Look" X1), and *Time* quotes one of her directors as saying, "That blonde can't act her way out of a Whirlpool bra" ("To Aristophanes" 74; see also Zolotow 260). Acknowledging that Monroe could act would mean acknowledging that the conspicuous sex appeal associated with the sexpot was also an act, and thereby undermine the myth of availability surrounding Monroe's star persona. Early in her career, publicity agents used details of Monroe's behind-the-scenes labor to temper the sexpot image, but it did not result in her being taken seriously as an actress.[6] Instead, she spent her career insisting that she was more than a sexpot, that she was, in fact, an actress.

Critics were more likely to recognize the labor that Monroe put into attracting attention offscreen. In 1952, defending Monroe against detractors, Isabel Moore writes, "To the oft-repeated charge that Marilyn is stupid, the answer is that no one can be stupid and get to the top in one of the toughest cities in the world" (70). When Monroe very publicly made Twentieth Century-Fox executive Darryl Zanuck wait ninety minutes for her to appear at a Hollywood dinner, she inspired columnist Sheilah Graham to comment on her power: "Though a lot of people had her tagged as dumb, she knew enough to learn to use what heaven had seen fit to give her. The wisecracks, the cleavage, the never being on time (the studio actually has to employ a maid just to awaken Marilyn in the morning!)," according to Graham, "didn't just happen accidentally. It's all been carefully planned and expertly executed to make Marilyn what she is today—the most exciting star in Hollywood. If people talk, who cares? Not Marilyn. Not while she's riding on high, at least" ("Why" 97). If she was a poor actress, she was at least a talented celebrity.

It's important to remember that, as a celebrity, she was playing "Marilyn Monroe." Stars are uniquely positioned, it seems, to be accused of playing themselves. Baron traces the idea that actors played themselves to 1930s and 1940s studio publicity, which "focused the public's attention on stars' personalities rather than their craftsmanship" (31). This is part of what contributed to the stars becoming stars, according to Virginia Wright Wexman, who argues that "movie stars are not just 'actors'—in some sense they always play 'themselves'" (x; see also Dyer *Stars* 154–162, Hollinger 10, Pullen 8). Barry King refers to this as "personification" ("Articulating" 168). According to King, the star is at the mercy of her extrafilmic persona when building a character; stars are those actors "whose narrative agency or 'character' rests on an extra-diegetically preserved persona" ("Embodying" 48). Viewers identify with the persona and the "type."[7] Stars of the studio era were pushed into types in order to capitalize on previous successes, but, as Jeanine Basinger notes, performing to type required the talent and labor necessary to convince audiences to believe it (*Star* 73–74). The star "type" needed to reflect the star's persona as created in publicity. This is why stars seemed to be playing themselves—they were playing the selves they also played in publicity.[8] Contrary to the belief that this meant she couldn't act, then, Monroe gave a performance so convincing in all realms of her public existence that her ability to maintain this type in her film roles was believed to be not a performance at all.

Fans, of course, wanted the stars to "play themselves" so they could experience greater access to the "authentic" star persona. However, in Monroe's case, film critics treat "playing herself" as not acting. "Her myth-making publicity, while helping to fabricate mass madness for her," explains Maurice Zolotow in his 1960 biography of Monroe, "also disposed the critics to see her film performances as a form of strip-teasing rather than as deliberately contrived acting performances" (289). When critics see Monroe's performances as "strip-teasing," they are criticizing Monroe for tantalizingly revealing all that the public wants to see of her—the well-known aspects of her persona, including her austere childhood, her lack of formal education, her sex appeal, and her naivete—in place of true talent. Monroe is one of the "spectacular performers" noted by Kristen Pullen, actresses whose physical appearance makes it difficult to recognize the work that goes into their performances (11). Monroe's appearance, and her sexpot persona, made it difficult for audiences to recognize her performances *as* performances, but Monroe's late-career film roles consciously reflected on the labor of acting, as well as the labor involved in performing the sexpot.

Despite her successes in 1953, the story persisted that Monroe could not act; this persistent narrative, along with her 1954 roles, seemed to be another joke of which Monroe was the butt. Monroe proactively dealt with criticism of her acting ability when she abandoned Hollywood in late 1954, bargaining for the improved contract she signed over a year later, on December 31, 1955.[9] This contract gave her $100,000 per film, required her to make only four films (instead of the previous fourteen) in seven years, allowed her to make films outside of Twentieth Century-Fox, and gave her director approval on all her films and cameraman approval on two of the four (Leaming 192). What Monroe did not win, however, was the ability to approve scripts, so the studio continued to offer her "dumb blonde" roles. Nonetheless, industry insiders considered the outcome of Monroe's battle with the studio a success. According to an industry veteran, Monroe's "new $400,000 contract for four pictures in seven years is one of the greatest single triumphs ever won by an actress against a powerfully entrenched major studio. No one believed she'd get away with it, but she won virtually everything she demanded. And, remember this, the money is paid to Marilyn Monroe Productions and so she'll get to keep far more than a salaried actress. Marilyn Monroe may turn out to be not only the sexiest but the smartest blond of our time" (qtd. in Manning 96).

The press agents spun Monroe's victory to their advantage: Rogers, Cowan and Jacobs characterized her as fighting a "constant fight to find herself," one that endears her to "every lover of every underdog" (5, 6).[10] Nevertheless, Monroe wasn't satisfied by this "compromise on both sides"; she explained, "I do not have story approval, but I do have director approval. That's important. I have certain directors I'll work for and I have trust in them and will do about anything they say. I know they won't let me do a bad story. Because, you know, you can have a wonderful story and a lousy director and hurt yourself" (qtd. in Wilson 94). At this midpoint of her career, Monroe recognized, and demanded, the supports she needed to produce a strong performance.

Monroe's physical appearance, as well as her biography, overshadowed her dedication to her craft. As biographer Donald Spoto notes, in contrast to the first eight years of her career (1947–1954), when Monroe appeared in twenty-four films, during the second half of her career, she appeared in only five. Spoto points out that this shift in her productivity has been attributed "to laziness, alcohol and drug addiction and psychological problems" (256), but he argues that we should instead read into this second half of her career a greater sense of purpose and determination. Monroe was undeniably a huge star, not just arm candy, who resonated with the public in a way few Hollywood blondes had done before (see chapter 1). She turned to Lee Strasberg and his acting style, the Method, during her break from Hollywood to demonstrate her serious desire to improve as an actress.

THE METHOD

The acting style known as the Method derives from the theories Constantin Stanislavsky developed with the Moscow Art Theater in 1898 in order to help actors develop a practicable craft, rather than rely on intuition. Foster Hirsch notes that, rather than invent a practice, Stanislavsky recorded "a vast unwritten body of knowledge," producing a "reference and a guide" (37). In the 1930s, two former Moscow Art Theater members, Richard Boleslavsky and Maria Ouspenskaya, began the American Laboratory Theatre (ALT) in New York with Stanislavsky's permission, and here, the man who represents the American Method enters the picture, for Lee Strasberg studied at the ALT (Enelow 8–9). Strasberg formed the Group Theatre with Cheryl Crawford in 1931, but Strasberg's strong personality soon led to rifts within the group, and Strasberg found himself on the outs. In 1947, Crawford, Elia Kazan, and Robert Lewis started the Actors Studio, and, despite reservations held by many, Strasberg became its artistic director in 1951, holding that place until he retired in 1981, just a few months before his 1982 death.

From the earliest days of the Group Theatre, Strasberg was, and continues to be, a polarizing figure. Stella Adler famously said that, when she studied with Stanislavsky in Paris in 1934, Stanislavsky emphasized the play's "given circumstances," or context, over the actor's emotions, which she felt Strasberg emphasized to the point of exploitation, leading her to split from the Group (qtd. in Hirsch 78). Articles of the 1950s and 1960s refer to Strasberg as a "high priest" (Rogoff 132) and "Lord over a small temple" (132), and call members of the Actors Studio "worshippers" (Zolotow "Stars" 84), calling attention to Strasberg's cult-like proceedings at the Actors Studio. Contemporary writers also recognize Strasberg's polarizing nature. In the edited collection *Method Acting Reconsidered*, David Krasner titles his chapter, which actually defends the Method against its critics, "I Hate Strasberg." Rosemary Malague refers to Strasberg as an "unlicensed analyst" who often diagnosed the professional problems of actresses as particularly gendered problems (33). In his defense, Strasberg admitted that his Method differed from Stanislavsky's and claimed that his purpose was only to help actors produce their best, most believable, work.

Even Strasberg's staunchest critics recognize that he did contribute something valuable to actor training. "Many of his foundational principles— relaxation; concentration; sensory, physical, and emotional awareness—," notes Malague, "surely hold potential benefit for any actor" (71). Colin Counsell highlights the main components of the Method style as "behavioural detail, 'plausibility', a sense of profound psychological depth, a marked linearity or smoothness to the performance as a whole" (25). The Method's emphasis on plausibility and coherence encouraged the actor to consider the character's psyche. Because "the Method insists that the actor discover an 'inner justification' for everything he or she performs and that all theatrical action be 'logical, coherent, and real,'" explains David Savran, the Method also shores up "the much-desired stability of the individual," making it uniquely suited to the postwar context (33). For Method performances to successfully dramatize the split between private and public, they have to first establish that a coherent private self exists, and in Method performances, the private self is often one that is painfully affected by the demands of conforming to public life.[11]

Strasberg trained actors to make the tension between their inner selves and public presentations known through relaxation exercises, sensory exercises with significant objects, and "private moment" exercises, among others. Strasberg said he often began work by asking actors to relax onstage, invariably finding that when they thought they were relaxed, they were still "blocking" their emotions from being released (*Dream* 104). He also asked actors to interact with objects onstage as a way of calling up their emotions, and would ask them to perform "private moments," things they would only do alone, such as shower, onstage. These exercises are designed to help actors appear more "natural" on stage, and to allow them to experience real, remembered emotions, rather than to fake reactions.

Affective memory (sometimes called emotional memory) is one of Strasberg's most controversial contributions to actor training, but understanding it is crucial to understanding Monroe's late-1950s roles. The alternating difficulty in expressing oneself and emotional outbursts that often characterize Method performances have led critics to call the Method performer "neurotic" (Naremore 18; Wexman 166). But whereas Strasberg's Method encouraged actors to express "genuine" emotions onstage, it discouraged emotional outbursts and insisted that actors maintain control over their emotions at all times. Strasberg stresses the difference between relived emotions, which are likely to reach beyond the actor's control, and remembered emotions, which can be used to re-create a controlled emotional experience onstage. He says, "The actor's emotion on the stage should never be really real. It always should be only *remembered* emotion. An emotion that happens right now spontaneously is out of control. . . . Remembered emotion is something that the actor can create and repeat" ("Working" 132). Strasberg placed greatest emphasis on recalling a few select past emotional experiences, "like a conditioning factor" (qtd. in Hirsch 141, from tapes of sessions on file). The actor then calls on her own past experiences to re-create the appropriate emotion in response to the play's text, and so the actor remembers her own emotional experiences during the performance in order to create an emotion that is accurate to the character.[12] Strasberg often encouraged his actors to engage in psychotherapy, but the training he provided at the Actors Studio was designed to give actors tools to re-create carefully controlled, genuine emotion in their performances.

Affective memory is one of the main components of the Method that has resulted in its consistently being misunderstood and maligned, and it also seems to be the reason that very few female Method actors are taken seriously. For example, Hirsch discusses Marlon Brando, James Dean, and Robert De Niro at length, then says no women have had the same status as Method actors: "In American movies, to be sensitive, high-strung, unusual, defiant, maybe even a little crazy, and female doesn't get you as far as to be all those things and male" (319). The emotional outbursts associated with male actors were credited with creating a new form of expression; female actors doing the same were perceived as hysterical or unfeminine. Director Billy Wilder told Zolotow that the Method was acting training from "people who don't believe in under-arm deodorants" who "want to make every actress ugly and dirty. This they think is being true to life" ("Stars" 83). Wilder implies that the Method strips actresses of their physical appeal, and thus makes them unmarketable—probably a somewhat just critique. In the same vein, however, Hirsch has suggested that being a sexpot might have made Monroe more acceptable as a Method actress, because "beauty . . . protected her from seeming truly crazy and therefore subversive. It helped to contain the public's view of her, so that she didn't seem seriously unhinged, the way a plainer-looking woman who had many of the same symptoms might have" (329). At the same time, Strasberg's training in particular has been associated with exploiting actresses, both psychologically and sexually. Malague points out that, while male Method actors are praised for their "tough" performances, female Method actors are praised for "risk-taking" and "vulnerability," keywords that signal caution to most feminists. She continues, "The woman who offered herself as a victim or sexual object surely was (and sadly, might still be) the most marketable actress" (5). What this makes clear is that Method acting always presents a double bind for women.

Strasberg's Method certainly has its strengths and weaknesses, but a particular strength we should acknowledge is that Method acting, and theorizing on it, provides one of a still limited number of theoretical paradigms through which to discuss acting.[13] The acting training that was common within the Hollywood studio system, paradoxically, became both more and less visible with the Method's takeover in Hollywood: more visible in that awareness of Hollywood actors' training came to the fore; less visible in that the Method became associated with nonacting—with the mumbling and playing oneself that the idea of acting training resists. It is important to note, as George Kouvaros does, that the Method's performance style "strives to erase the conditions of its own existence" (41). Thus, if a Method performer is doing it right, it is difficult for audiences to "read" the labor of acting in the performance, instead leading audiences to think of the actor as, at best, translating herself into the character, and, at worst, playing herself.

Although Method training has its downsides, many of the problems associated with it become benefits when applied to film acting. Carnicke argues that Strasberg made Stanislavsky's Method suitable for film actors by shifting the role of authorship of a performance from the actor to the director. The Method encourages emotional immersion in the role rather than controlled distance, the acting coach often manipulates actors into such immersion and praises breakdowns, and the director's commands ultimately dictate the actor's performance—and all of these translate well on film. Strasberg said in a Studio session, "When the actor is capable of giving to the director anything that he wants, then I consider the acting problem solved" (qtd. in Carnicke 79; Strasberg session 165, December 5, 1961). Why does this solve the acting problem? Because, when making a film, the actor often creates a performance out of order, and so reacting to a scene that hasn't occurred yet becomes more difficult. The actor still must produce the appropriate emotional response, but, using Strasberg's Method, the actor produces that response to a cue from the director, and from her training in using her emotional memories. The relationship between these emotional memories and the content of the play or script is irrelevant under Strasberg, Carnicke explains, because "the content of the thought [is] less important than how it is read by the camera" (82). The widescreen cinematography that became popular in 1953—at the height of Monroe's success—called for more expressive acting, and, as Hollinger argues, "renovated the Hollywood studio style from actors simply playing roles tailored to their star images to the cultivation of performances that rendered complex, emotionally rich characterizations" (14). When an actor is capable of acting not in response to other actors but in response to a director's commands, she is able to perform piece by piece, out of order, without an audience, and to the camera. The problems with the Method were also the reasons that so many film actors took to it; what remains to be seen is evidence of an actress successfully using the Method in her films. Marilyn Monroe provides that evidence.

MONROE AND THE METHOD

When Monroe walked out on her studio contract, her desire to improve as an actress became yet another joke of which she was the butt. Zolotow, for example, insists that all she "had to do was part her lips, breathe heavily and heave her bosom for the twelve weeks it takes to finish a movie" ("Stars" 44).[14] His intensely sexual description of what could serve as "acting" for Monroe exemplifies how opposed Monroe the sexpot was to Monroe the serious actress. Monroe's Method performances acknowledge her status as simultaneously a sexpot and working actress, and in so doing complicate the sexpot behaviors present in the scripts with some vulnerability, but more resistance. While it becomes clear, especially in *Let's Make Love*'s "My Heart Belongs to Daddy," that Monroe could not escape being infantilized in her roles, it also becomes clear that she used her Method performances to intimate that she, and other women experiencing similar situations, could resist the men who tried to objectify them by asserting their subjectivity.

Before Monroe attended her first Actors Studio sessions in the spring of 1955, Strasberg distanced the Method from Hollywood. Jack Garfein, artistic director of the Harold Clurman Theatre, states that "Lee persuaded them [his pupils] that they owed it to their artistic development to stay in New York and study, rather than go off to make movies" (qtd. in Hirsch 160). Nevertheless, Strasberg enthusiastically welcomed Monroe to Actors Studio classes, seemingly contradicting himself. He gave Monroe special treatment: she didn't have to audition, as others had, to become a member. According to Hirsch, Strasberg responded to those who accused him of lusting after fame by clarifying that "the Method was useful to film acting, . . . but acting in films should not be seen as its goal or as the highest embodiment of its lessons" (162). Although Monroe clearly gave Strasberg a clout he could not achieve with other actors, it also seems likely that he genuinely believed she could improve as an actress—for if she demonstrated that she couldn't, it would be more detrimental to his reputation than it would to hers.

Critics of the Method tend to see it as exploiting Monroe's sexpot persona. Although she was not an official member of the Actors Studio, Monroe both received individual training from Strasberg and participated in group sessions. One famous exercise in which Monroe participated was the animal exercise, in which an actress studies an animal's mannerisms and then performs as if she were that animal. Monroe was assigned to "play" a kitten. While Rollyson says this exercise allowed Monroe to "she[d] adult inhibitions in order to recover a primordial spontaneity free from stereotyping" and therefore contributed to her "ease of movement" (104), Malague disagrees, insisting that asking a "sex kitten" to "pla[y] a *kitten*" draws on the stereotypes already associated with her and "reinforce[s] her limitations, reducing her to a habitual (i.e., manufactured) self" (65). Monroe performed the kitten well, but both critics see this as a result of her innate characteristics rather than as the result of her acting training. Monroe also performed several scenes for the Studio actors, but Malague points out that even the "serious" roles Monroe chose to play—Lorna Moon, Anna Christie, Blanche Dubois—are sexually charged roles that draw on their "resemblance . . . to her own life" (65). Malague wants to make Monroe's experience with the Method "a cautionary tale" (62), and therefore finds it difficult to see how Monroe could have benefited from training with Strasberg. But perhaps Monroe chose these scenes because they featured sexpots like her, and she felt she could bring an emotional depth to the stereotypes. As Hirsch points out, "'Use yourself,' Studio actors are continually admonished. 'Use your past, use your pain.' Monroe understood instinctively how to do this" (327). Other actors who witnessed Monroe's performances, including Kim Stanley and Strasberg's daughter Susan, praise Monroe's scenes at the Studio (see S. Strasberg 85, 101; Rollyson 105–107). Perhaps she used her vulnerability and the stereotyping that dogged her entire career to complicate the sexpots she played at the Studio.

Although Monroe had turned to the Method to enhance her acting ability, her training only raised more doubts about it; so many, in fact, that Pete Martin titled his 1956 biography *Will Acting Spoil Marilyn Monroe?* Martin concludes that, despite whatever she might have learned from the Actors Studio, Monroe's sex appeal would still draw fans to the theaters (128). *Bus Stop* (1956, dir. Josh Logan), a film I discussed in chapter 4, was the first film Monroe made after she began training with Strasberg. Monroe took an interest in the entirety of her role in *Bus Stop*, and especially influenced the mise-en-scène by choosing her own costumes—a moth-eaten green dress and ripped tights for a down-on-her-luck chanteuse—and designing her own makeup—a ghastly white for a woman who works all night and sleeps all day. Her performance in the film, too, is clearly a performance—the chanteuse is a terrible singer who has to manage her own stage lighting with her feet—and Hirsch reads her deliberate pauses in conversations about the nature of love as "rippl[ing] with affective memories" (328). Monroe used her training and her past experiences to effectively portray a character who wanted respect more than anything but kept finding herself performing in cheap saloons.

Contemporary reviewers recognized Monroe's skillful acting in *Bus Stop*, but also continued to associate her with the sexpot. Reviewer Crowther, who, just a year before, had doubted Monroe's acting ability, gave her credit for her performance: "In one light, she is foolish and funny, but in another she is dignified and sad. It takes playing to catch all her facets, including the tawdry, the ridiculous and the banal. And Miss Monroe gives her that playing, with a flat Ozark accent and all" ("Proof" X1; see also "Screen" F19). According to *Life*, *Bus Stop* demonstrates that at her Actors Studio classes, Monroe "has learned a great deal about her trade, developing a sure satiric touch as a comedienne" while also maintaining her appeal when she "dances in daring costumes, wiggles in and out of tight dresses, lolls lusciously and uses a baby voice to set off an unbaby-like figure" ("Unveiling" 79). Despite Monroe's attempts to use her acting to distract viewers and reviewers from her body, her sexpot appeal still colored reactions to her performances. "While Monroe's interest in Method conformed to changing trends in Hollywood performance," Mulvey argues, "it was also a gesture towards contradictions at the heart of a studio's control over its contracted stars: once an image had proved itself valuable at the box office, it would be (almost always) frozen, immutable in perpetuity" ("Thoughts" 207). But perhaps, as Mulvey speculates, Monroe was also "beginning to perform the showgirl dilemma" as a "'theoretical' reflection on the lived nature of 'to-be-looked-at-ness'" ("Thoughts" 208). That is, if Monroe was going to continue to receive sexpot roles, she could nevertheless use her Method training to imbue her performances with commentary on what it means to be viewed continually as a sexpot. In fact, Monroe's Method performances reflect on acting, insist that the sexpot is a performance, and challenge the sexpot's presumed availability and good nature.

The Prince and the Showgirl

The second film Monroe made after participating in Actors Studio training was *The Prince and the Showgirl*. This was also the first (and only) film made by Marilyn Monroe Productions, Inc., and the title demonstrates how unlikely a choice this film was for a woman trying to resist the sexpot stereotype. However, Monroe chose Laurence Olivier as her costar and director for this adaptation of a Terence Rattigan play written for the 1953 coronation, and clearly hoped to acquire some credence from working with a renowned repertory actor. Although the studios would not give her the opportunity to prove her acting skill, Marilyn Monroe Productions, Inc. allowed her to create the opportunity for herself by hiring Olivier, whom many thought to be one of the greatest actors of the period, and demonstrating her ability to act beside him. *The Prince and the Showgirl* is the story of a Carpathian Regent (Olivier) in London for the coronation of King George V in 1911. The Regent butts heads with his teenage son, Nicky (Jeremy Spenser), who will soon be king and wants to overthrow his father. The Regent, a reputed womanizer, visits a production of *The Coconut Girl* to take his mind off political conflicts, and, while he is there, picks out an American actress, Elsie Marina (Monroe), to invite to dine at his embassy. She agrees to go to what she thinks is a dinner party, but when she discovers he has planned to seduce her after a private meal, she tries to leave, and, when that doesn't work, drawing on her experience with similar situations, she evades his advances while still taking advantage of his hospitality.

The Prince and the Showgirl demonstrates not only the clash of European and American, royalty and working class, but also the conflict between two styles of acting, with Olivier as the Regent signifying repertory training and Monroe as the Showgirl signifying the Method. The making of the film was highly publicized, and audiences would have likely read Monroe's Method training into her performance (and Olivier's expertise as a repertory actor into his). Monroe's performance confronts the jokes made of her as a sexpot and actress, but also the jokes made about her production company, about middlebrow entertainment, and about the value of American culture abroad.

Characters use performance language throughout the film, suggesting that Elsie treats everyday life as a performance. When the head of the Foreign Office, Northbrook (Richard Wattis), tells Elsie she should only speak after being directly addressed, Elsie's fellow actor Fanny (Daphne Anderson) translates his advice into actors' terms: "Wait for the cue before speaking the line, dear." As Northbrook describes the members of the royal family and escorts Elsie to the drawing room upstairs, the moving camera captures both the length of the journey and Elsie as she glances at her surroundings. The overwhelming environment, combined with the overwhelming information, causes her to exclaim, "I'm shaking! This is worse than the first night." And, although she recognizes her "cue" to exit after the Regent has said goodbye, *deus ex machina*-type devices keep pulling her back into the scene, extending her performance—first, the Queen Dowager makes her a lady-in-waiting for the coronation, and then Nicky invites her as his date for the coronation ball. The performance language used throughout the film underscores the similarities between acting and political maneuvering, while also reminding us that Elsie is always performing, and that her performance at the embassy is just another role she, as a sexpot, is forced to play.

Because she has had to beat off men like the Regent before, Elsie is well versed in both the words and the moves of seduction. When Northbrook asks, "Why this panic over a harmless little tête-à-tête supper?," Elsie indignantly turns to face him and then, nearly pushing her body against him in rage, tells him all she knows about the moves that characterize such suppers: "champagne . . . and something cold to follow because we really don't want the servants around, do we? . . . and after supper, . . . you must be *very* tired, why don't you put your feet up on this nice sofa?" Elsie can't escape, however, because Northbrook, in his desperation to not upset the Regent, has argued so long that, when she opens the door to leave, she is face to face with the Regent. She finds herself in a similar position several times during the cold supper that the Regent arranges, but every time the Regent comes too close, the moving camera captures how swiftly she turns and walks the other direction, never missing a beat in the conversation. Elsie makes evident that her sex appeal has given her the requisite experience to avoid sex. This places Elsie in control of the scene; despite the Regent's political status, she resists his advances.

By contrasting Elsie's seeming artlessness with the Regent's stuffiness, the film consciously showcases the difference between the American Method and the British repertory style of acting. Hirsch discusses the differences between Studio and British acting thus: "British acting" is "external, cultivated, and manicured, like a well-tended English garden; . . . it is set and rigid, with no room for the adjustments and improvisations that the Studio actor prizes; and . . . as a result of its meticulous attention to form, it leaves you cold. At the Studio, British acting seems just that: acting—behavior that has been trimmed and arranged for public display" (220). On the other hand, "the Studio style is rough-and-ready, instinctive, improvisatory, proletarian, physically active, and defiantly emotional," says Hirsch (220). Olivier exacerbated these distinctions in his costuming: he donned a false "nose, mustache, monocle, [and . . .] accent" for the role (S. Strasberg 117).[15] But Olivier's obvious distancing of the role from himself calls attention to his acting and makes it easy to efface the labor that went into Monroe's performance, as Hirsch does when he says, "Olivier seems to be playing a role, while Monroe seems to be playing herself; Olivier is knocking himself out doing a turn while Monroe sails through the movie without any visible acting effort" (328). We should challenge the notion that if acting doesn't appear to be difficult work, it must not be work, as well as the idea that playing a character similar to oneself makes it easy to do so.

At times Elsie resists being the sexpot; at other times she consciously gives a sexpot performance, even seeming to perform "Marilyn Monroe." Elsie's shoulder strap breaks when she shakes the Regent's hand, repurposing a stunt Monroe had used when greeting the press to announce that she was making this film with Olivier. Within the film, this move draws the same reaction it drew at the press conference—the stuffy British react with glee to her American "charm." Elsie's smile in the aftermath is warm and winning, while the actress next to her in line clenches her teeth in a tight smile and side-eyes her. That is, Elsie's costars recognize the performance she is giving, but she disarms their critiques with a gentle smile. Elsie is not cowed by the embassy's formalities; Northbrook repeatedly corrects her address of the Regent, until she says under her breath, in one of the most casual and "real" moments of the film, "Oh, to hell with it." Her relaxed attitude sweeps into the embassy like a breath of fresh air, forcing the stuffy diplomats to relax a little. Elsie also performs the sexpot to have a little fun for herself. When the Regent ignores Elsie to make

Figure 5.3. Elsie playing "Marilyn Monroe." Frame enlargement from *The Prince and the Showgirl*.

some phone calls, the shot foregrounds her as she grabs the champagne bottle and turns on a performance of "Marilyn Monroe," heaving her bosom, squealing, and putting her hand on her cheek as she asks, "Do you really think I ought?" (Figure 5.3). The Regent remains oblivious in the background, until she squeals again after she fills her glass, finally attracting his attention. When Elsie plays "Marilyn Monroe," she makes evident that "Marilyn Monroe" is a performance controlled by the actress; the sexpot is a performance controlled by the woman.

This film focused on performance also comments on the Regent's performance. The Regent tries to seduce Elsie using, it should be noted, all the lines she predicted he would, finally declaring, "What are words, when deeds can say *so* much more," as he swiftly rises from the stool at her feet and leans over her for a kiss. She knocks him to the side and laughs at what she calls "that performance of yours," criticizing it as "terrible." She expected more "fire and passion" from a womanizing Regent, and says, "If I had known this was all that was going to happen, I wouldn't have even been nervous." He pouts, so she both tells and shows him how to really seduce her. Strolling across the room as the camera tracks her, she tells of "gypsy violins" and "strange, seductive perfume," caressing her own face and décolletage before turning to face him. As Kristen Pullen points out, while "actors' physical bodies" are "indicative of authentic emotion within naturalist discourses of acting," the "beautiful, sexual, and active as well as specifically raced and classed body destabilizes the naturalist illusion," pulling focus from the performance to the body (25). Nevertheless, we must recognize this scene as a performance. Her work of attracting the Regent's attention has a definite starting and ending point, and is entirely under her control.

Even the British director, Olivier, when compiling the final cut, directed viewers to identify with Elsie's wonder and ease, and her emotional responses. Dale Silvina sees Elsie as "the viewer's surrogate in the film. . . . Each of the wonders Elsie encounters, from the magically disappearing servants and the sumptuous meal to the expected marvels of the coronation and coronation ball, is something calculated for the viewer's own wonder and delight" (34). Elsie enters the embassy, for example, and stops, as the camera, in medium close-up, registers her widening eyes and her lower jaw circling in astonishment as she breathes, "*Gosh*" (Figure 5.4). We register her reaction prior to seeing the inside of the embassy, which, we see in the following shot, is ornate and expansive. In fact, in several of the most confusing or awe-inspiring moments of the film, the camera tracks forward to register in medium close-up or close-up Elsie's widening eyes and slightly open mouth. Elsie's wonder at the coronation parade is one of the actions that begins to soften the Regent's tough exterior—she covers her mouth in embarrassment after Northbrook stops her from waving at her friends in the crowd, but the lingering reaction shot of the Regent

Figure 5.4. "Gosh." Frame enlargement from *The Prince and the Showgirl.*

shows his lower lip turning ever-so-slightly upward into a smile. Viewers are meant to identify with Elsie's perspective, to wonder at what she sees, but also to admire her wonder.

Although Elsie successfully carries the film's emotional center, Olivier tried to discredit Monroe's performance. He famously butted heads with Monroe over the difference between their acting approaches—he wanted weeks of rehearsals; she didn't know what to do in rehearsal; he was demanding; she was petulant. According to Olivier, in the coronation scene, he commanded her performance: "Now, catch sight of that stained glass window—it's the most beautiful picture you can imagine. Let some tears well into your eyes, Marilyn . . .'" (Olivier 210). As a testament to his directing prowess, Olivier writes, "As if by magic, submissive and scrupulously obedient, she followed every instruction exactly and at once and, what is most important, quite perfectly. I had cause to reflect once more, this time with gratitude, 'Of course, she's a model'" (210). But, given

Carnicke's argument that Strasberg's Method is an ideal means of training a film actor, Monroe's success here cannot just be attributed to her
modeling work. Her Method training equips her to, as Olivier instructed,
"let some tears well into [her] eyes." Whether she was thinking of this
beautiful window is hard to say, but she was thinking of something that
would produce the requested tears—she used the Method to create this,
one of the most highly praised moments of her performance in this film.
(She used a similar technique, it is said, to convincingly perform her love
for the Regent—she thought of Frank Sinatra and Coca-Cola when looking at him [see S. Strasberg 118].) In this case, Olivier's remarks, meant to
demonstrate his skill, have the effect of demonstrating hers.

Monroe's use of the Method also becomes clear in the film's politically
charged scenes, in which she demonstrates how Method actors interacted
with objects to express the feelings they hid behind a more collected exterior. When the Regent admits to not being "able to think up a charge" for
a political radical he has just arrested, Elsie's eyes widen, but she does not
speak. When he mentions "Un-Carpathian activities," she turns to look
at him, but his back is turned to her. She rises and goes to the buffet, then
turns again to look at him when he mentions the "*stupid* Americans" who
are protesting the arrest. Elsie makes her reaction to the Regent's words
known through her reaction to the food, as she angrily scoops it onto her
plate, then only moves it around her plate as she gets more disgusted with
his comments about American democracy, mocks his laughter at the
"crazy Americans," and holds her champagne disdainfully at a distance.
Elsie's interaction with the food in the Regent's stateroom hasn't been compared to Terry Malloy's (Marlon Brando) handling of Edie's (Eva Marie
Saint) glove in *On the Waterfront* (1954, dir. Elia Kazan), but surely it captures what Wexman calls "a Method-inspired use of objects," too (175).[16]
Method acting expresses "a tension between an outer mask of stoic strength
and self-control and an inner emotional core constantly on the verge of
breaking through in the form of a violent outburst," explains Hollinger
(15). Rather than a hysterical outburst, Elsie's interaction with the objects

in this scene allows her to physically express her emotions in a relatively constrained way.

In these moments, the Method also shows its political usefulness. Of course, there can be no mistaking the joke about "un-Carpathian activities," especially in the immediate context of the making of the film.[17] In June 1956, just before Monroe traveled to London to begin shooting, Arthur Miller testified before the House Committee on Un-American Activities about his involvement with Communist organizations, although he refused to name names. During a recess in the testimony, as the *New York Times* reported the next day, Miller announced his plans, of which she was not yet aware, to marry Monroe: "Arthur Miller, playwright, disclosed today a past filled with Communist-front associations and a future filled with Marilyn Monroe" (Drury 1).[18] Monroe never wavered in her commitment to Miller and to political freedom, just as Elsie's unabashed patriotism in *The Prince and the Showgirl* begs us to read her as fiercely honest and fiercely loyal. When the Regent comments on "stupid Americans," she toasts "to President Taft," once in an exhortatory voice, then more insistently, and finally, in a close-up, whispering. She mutters under her breath, "I should darn well think they would protest, arresting people that way," meaning on phony charges. She later finds herself in the position of a "spy," listening in on a conversation in German between Nicky and an ambassador. The medium close-up shows that she is doing more than overhearing—she is attentively listening to his conversation, despite her friends shouting at her from the street. When she tells Nicky what she has heard, she scoffs at his warnings, "Dangerous! Don't give me that. I'm an American citizen; nobody can do anything to me." (These lines, it should be noted, echo something Monroe is supposed to have said when the studio executives were telling her not to support Miller in public: "This is America, and I'm standing with the Constitution and Jefferson" [qtd. in S. Strasberg 102–103].) Elsie does not reveal Nicky's plan, though she does encourage him to rethink it. Through her Method performance in this film, Monroe not only demonstrated her control of her performance, but also spoke for an American identity that expressed loyalty to one's fellow citizens.

In the end, the American style, and American politics, triumph, for, while the Regent looks ridiculous as a mooning, lovestruck man, Elsie can both play lovestruck and demonstrate her maturity. When she has finally convinced the Regent of the power of love at the end of the film, in the "morning," as she says, "it's up to me to be the grownup one." He has planned special passports and romantic trips; she underscores the importance of his role in politics, and points out that, when he is relieved of his regency, she will be relieved of her acting contract. When he says, "You do not realize what can happen in this world in eighteen months," she plaintively answers, "Yes, I think I do. I really think I do." Despite the Regent in the foreground in this shot, Elsie's subtly thoughtful face in the background captures the honesty and maturity of her response to the situation. Although she leaves the film without love, she collects her various "orders," gifts to her from members of the royal family, significantly handling the one from the Regent, then walks confidently out of the palace and out of the frame. As viewers, we are glad she has maintained her American integrity and natural ease, and that she has not been seduced by the stuffy diplomat.

LET'S MAKE LOVE

Monroe's next film would also pit the so-called naturalness of the Method against the stiltedness of a European performer. *Let's Make Love* is the story of performer Amanda Dell (Monroe), who is acting in a show that mocks the tycoon and international playboy Jean-Marc Clement (Yves Montand). When Clement attends a performance to gauge the offensiveness of its mockery of him, Amanda catches his eye. He introduces himself as Clement, but the director mistakes this for a performance and casts him in the show. To spend more time with Amanda, he claims to be a novice actor named Alexander Dumas. Montand's stilted performance, his

first in English, and the fact that Monroe once again found herself com-
bating her own sexpot persona, make it difficult to get many laughs out of
this musical comedy. The show within the film draws on Monroe's sexpot
image in its seductive musical numbers and skimpy costumes. Although
the plot is trite and the show within the show somewhat schizophrenic in
nature, this film nevertheless warrants some examination as a film that
discusses the work of acting.

Amanda complains that Clement has "watch[ed her] make a fool of herself" at the end of the film, but the film itself insists on making a fool of
Amanda from her first appearance, which is hypersexualized and infantilized at the same time. When Clement and his companion Coffman
(Tony Randall) come to see the show, they enter a theater which, because
of the blue and red stage lights, resembles a strip club. The resemblance
continues as the framing objectifies Amanda from her first appearance: viewers see a pair of legs, which turn out to be Amanda's, enter the
shot from the top—and, after a cut to Clement's reaction, we see a second shot of just the legs on the pole before they spread-eagle and then
slide down the pole. When she dismounts from the pole, Amanda, an
obviously mature woman, pouts, "My name is Lolita, and uh, I'm not
supposed to . . . play . . . with boys!" Although Amanda pouts and shim-
mies her way through this introduction, her indignation becomes apparent later in the number (Figure 5.5). The song's lyrics, "My heart belongs
to daddy, da da da da da da da da da," signify that Amanda is the infantilized sexpot, but other aspects of the performance, such as her expressions, indicate that she is tired of playing that role.

Perhaps Amanda is tired of playing the sexpot role because she has been
trying to become educated, and because she is dedicated to acting as a
craft. Because the film makes it clear that Amanda is, to some extent playing "Marilyn Monroe" (like Monroe, she's in night school classes to earn
her diploma because she "got tired of being ignorant"), it is not a stretch
to think we are supposed to read the film in the context of Method acting. In fact, Amanda frequently plays the role of acting teacher, echoing

Figure 5.5. The indignant sexpot. Frame enlargement from *Let's Make Love*.

instructions associated with the Method. For example, she tells Clement/
Dumas to "try acting with more assurance. By that I mean, he doesn't have
your sensitivity." She also uses Method fundamentals, such as relaxation
exercises and emotional memory, to help Clement/Dumas get into character, stating, "First, relax" as she visibly drops her shoulders and softens
her face. Then she tells him, "Keep telling yourself, 'I'm a louse. I'm a louse.
I'm a louse,'" presumably asking him to think about how a louse would
behave and to use his own emotional memories to play that part. The shot/
reverse-shot pattern focuses on her face, and her eyes express the rage she
would feel at encountering a louse. Clement/Dumas seems convinced by
what she says, as he starts to repeat, "I'm a . . ." but stops himself and objects
to her characterization. She praises his performance as just the kind of
thing Clement would do.[19] Later, she encourages him to imagine that
he, like Clement, gets any woman he wants—but when he says, "not any
girl"—meaning not her—she praises him for thinking of a unique cir-
cumstance for the character. Relaxation, imagining oneself in the character's unique circumstances, and using emotions to create the performance:
Amanda gives Clement/Dumas pointers in Method acting.

Amanda seems earnest and committed to her acting training in the
film, and repeatedly takes the position of an acting teacher. When Clem-
ent/Dumas tells her she shouldn't work so hard, she exclaims, "Dear man!

You've got a whole wrong idea. You'll never get anywhere in the theater unless you work. Right now, when you walk home, work." She then gives him an imagining exercise to help him get into character. Shot from over Clement's shoulder, we see her earnest and somewhat incredulous face, framed by her light hair and tan jacket against the dark background of the city street—her commitment to work seems to be validated as a light in the darkness. Later, when Clement/Dumas performs a comedy act designed by Milton Berle for the company, Amanda, rather than sitting with the other actors in the doorways, or with the director and Clement's entourage in the chairs at the front of the stage, sits alone in the center of some chairs at the back of the stage (it is a theater in the round). Here, she takes the position of the acting teacher (Strasberg customarily sat alone at the front of the group to watch performances at the Actors Studio). Clement/Dumas repeatedly looks for her reaction to his performance (although initially bewildered, she claps enthusiastically at the end of the performance). Amanda confidently explains her approach to acting throughout the film, and Clement/Dumas values her opinion of his performance.

Although many assume Monroe used the Method incorrectly by simply playing herself, in *Let's Make Love*, as in *The Prince and the Showgirl*, it becomes clear that she is using Method techniques to bring emotional depth to her characters and critique the sexpot roles she was given. In the "Let's Make Love" number, for example, Amanda undresses and seduces a man on a bed onstage. But she does this consciously as a performance, looking at the camera/audience at strategic moments, and thereby calling attention to the voyeuristic spectators looking in on this "private moment." When she has to sing "Incurably Romantic" with Clement/Dumas, it becomes clear that her seeming sexual availability is a performance—the sound mix takes Clement's/Dumas's singing down, and the director's commands to Amanda to "drape yourself over him" and "nuzzle him" dominate the soundtrack. She visibly takes direction here, demonstrating how the Method has made her attuned to the director's commands. These directions, by contrast, make Clement freeze, and the director cuts, while she shrugs and says, "Just relax." Not only does this scene demonstrate her ability to act on command, but it also demonstrates that the sexpot is a performance that she can turn on and off on command, and thus demonstrates the performing that constitutes playing "Marilyn Monroe."

Monroe's Method performance encourages audiences to read her star persona, and therefore her personal emotions, into the character of Amanda. For example, Amanda asks Tony (Frankie Vaughan), her costar, "How do you get out? You say I quit? That's not out. Tony, you're an actor, so wherever you go, whatever you do, how do you leave it behind?" The pleading look on her face suggests that this applies to Amanda as well. Later, when Amanda dines with Clement/Dumas so Tony can steal his number, her shots in the shot/reverse-shot pattern show her looking down at the table, then back up at Clement/Dumas, as she oscillates between her private thoughts and an attempt to be a cheerful dining partner. As she admits, "I've done some things in my life that are very painful to talk about," her brow furrows, her hand tightly clenches her glass, and her thumb rests against her lip—every gesture here is in service of remembering, but not speaking, those painful experiences. We see the pain cross her face, but we also see her strive to not relive those feelings but to just, as Strasberg advised, remember them.[20] Her eyes remain cast downward as she confesses the "awful dirty trick" she is playing on Clement/Dumas, but she looks him in the eye as she explains herself—and her arm, which the frame captures moving back and forth across her lap, registers her anxiety and guilt.

Amanda also has a chance to voice her outrage at being made a fool. Backstage, Clement continues to insist on his identity, and Amanda grows increasingly angry, as she demonstrates by turning away from him and brushing her hair rapidly with fierce, hard strokes. But her anger lasts only for a brief moment, and soon she covers her face, brush still in hand, and whines, "I can't stand anyone who makes fun of me!" (Figure 5.6). Expressing the frustrated agony of one who has been made fun of many times

Figure 5.6. The sexpot's pain. Frame enlargement from *Let's Make Love*.

before, Amanda soon grows angry again and storms out of the room, refusing to continue to be the butt of this joke. Clement's mistaken identity is only resolved when he lures her to his offices, where he can play himself in the right context to convince her of his identity. She faints when she realizes she has been speaking to Clement all along, and when she comes to, she shakes her fists, shouts, "Shame on you!," and rises to her feet. As he continues to explain himself, she shakes her arms free of his grasp and hides her face in the doorframe. When she declares, "I've never been so humiliated in all my life!," audiences hear and see the reaction of someone who has been humiliated many times.

Amanda is the butt of the joke, but she eventually recognizes that she has been mocked and voices her complaints about it. Although she asks him again, "How could you bear watching me make a fool of myself?," her indignation is easily overcome by his singing "Let's Make Love." She turns away from Clement as he sings in her ear, and Amanda's performance shines once more as we see her thinking through the implications of being the object of Clement's affections. A smile slowly crosses her face as she admits it was silly that she thought he had the same name as the author of *The Three Musketeers*, then her face turns sour as she calls him a "faker," softens when she pleads, "Why do I like you?," and she finally melts and succumbs to his embraces. She walks to the back of the elevator, where she faces the camera as Clement kisses her shoulders, and her face lights up with her two final punchlines: "Should I still get my diploma?" and "Will they be surprised at night school!" Although the end of the film still makes her a joke, she now seems to be in on it.[21]

THE MISFITS

In the final film she completed, *The Misfits*, Monroe found herself playing not just the sexpot, but actually playing "Marilyn Monroe" and, once again, she used her Method training to demonstrate that although she might look the part of the sexpot, the sexpot could challenge what men expected of her. Montgomery Clift wrote the following exchange between his character, Perce, and Monroe's character, Roslyn, in his script notes for *The Misfits*: "You know what—what—I could swear you were M. Monroe" (qtd. in Girelli 194). Clift's imagined conversation also underscores that this time, the script, written for Monroe by her husband Arthur Miller, in fact asked Monroe to play herself. By asking her to play herself, however, this film gives Monroe the chance to demonstrate to audiences that "Marilyn Monroe" was a performance. When Roslyn visibly moves from sadness to cheerfulness, when she resists male advances and the expectations associated with her reputation as a nightclub dancer, and when she insists on being heard, Roslyn does things Monroe had been doing for years, encouraging audiences to see Monroe as more than a sexpot.

The Misfits has become notorious for the number of drafts it went through as it became a chronicle of the hurts leading up to Monroe's divorce from Miller, for the delays and costs associated with the production (the most expensive black and white film made at the time), and for being the final completed film of both Monroe (who died in August of 1962 without having finished *Something's Got to Give*) and Clark Gable (who died in November of 1960, just two weeks after completing shooting). *The Misfits* tells the story of Roslyn, a woman who, after securing her Reno divorce, finds herself unable to shake off the advances of a number of men, including Guido (Eli Wallach), a mechanic and pilot, and his friend Gay (Gable), an aging cowboy. Guido invites Gay, Roslyn, and Roslyn's friend and landlady, Isabelle (Thelma Ritter), to his unfinished house in the desert, where, after a night of drinking, Roslyn decides to stay and experiment with "just living" with Gay as her guide. Guido later tells Gay about some mustangs he has seen in the mountains, and Gay agrees to round them up and sell them to be turned into dog food. At the rodeo, they find a third man, Perce (Clift), who has chosen to become a rodeo cowboy rather than submit to wage labor. After Perce is injured in the rodeo, the three men and Roslyn drink heavily, then drive back to the house in the desert. The next day, they all go up to the mountains to catch the mustangs. Roslyn is opposed to the killing of defenseless animals; Gay is opposed to what he considers to be demeaning work for "wages"—but in the end Roslyn convinces Gay to free the few mustangs they have captured. Roslyn and Gay agree, in the film's final moments, to establish a more permanent life together, perhaps even to have a child.

Publicity underscored that Marilyn Monroe was playing "Marilyn Monroe" in this film.[22] Before the film's release, *Time* explicitly enumerated the similarities between the character Roslyn and the actress Monroe: "Like Marilyn, Roslyn is a fractured, manhandled woman always 'searching for relationships,' full of hurtful memories about parents who 'disappeared all the time.' Helpless, yet flush with appetite, she is a compulsive time killer, shows a disturbing skill at batting a paddle ball on a string—which Marilyn does constantly" ("Marilyn" 57). Reviews of the film after its release also recognize Monroe playing herself in the film; *Time* emphasized that it was "above all, a long . . . , fatuously embarrassing psychoanalysis of Marilyn Monroe, Arthur Miller, and what went wrong with their famous marriage" ("New" 68).[23] And yet, insiders insisted that it took real skill to perform oneself.[24] According to Sidney Skolsky, a Hollywood columnist and close friend of Monroe's, "Marilyn, I believe, turns in her best dramatic performance. She is more of a large part of the genuine Marilyn than she has been in any movie. I can understand her being nervous and uncomfortable during the filming; she revealed plenty of herself, and I don't mean flesh and the wiggle" (14).[25] Skolsky unites "performance" and "the genuine Marilyn" here, calling attention to how even "playing herself" was a carefully crafted role.

The script's multiple drafts (rewritten on the set during filming, but also rewritten several times from 1957 to 1960) initially bespeak an attempt to idealize Monroe as a princess or homemaker, but, in the end, show how the sexpot was inescapable despite her resistance to it. For example, Roslyn's first appearance in the first draft of the script, from October 1957, reads: "She is dressed in jeans and a blouse, with a beige bandana holding her hair. The reins of the horse are draped over its neck; she is holding open a homemaking magazine like *House and Garden*, and is absorbed in it as the horse takes her faithfully up the steep trail" (Miller, *The Misfits* 1957, 1). The article she is reading is "Tips for the Woman Who Lives Alone," and, a fairy-tale princess, she says good morning to a grasshopper that lands on the page, whistles to a bird, says hello to nature, and praises the horse (Miller, *The Misfits* 1957, 1). By the time *The Misfits* began production, in July 1960, Miller introduced Roslyn very differently: as a woman whose car is dented because, as her friend Isabelle explains, "the darn men in this town . . . keep running into her just to start a conversation." No longer one with nature, and no longer able to have a private moment to herself, Roslyn is harassed by those who cannot resist her.

Throughout the film, point-of-view shots encourage viewers to gaze at Roslyn's enticing figure. Gay and Guido frequently watch Roslyn—as she dances, as she hits a paddle ball, as she rides a horse—and their point-of-view shots highlight that they serve as surrogates for the audience members who have come to ogle the star. Reviewer Stanley Kaufman points out that Huston's "camera occasionally peers lubriciously down the girl's bodice or elsewhere to remind us that Roslyn is really Marilyn Monroe" (26). Roslyn's sexual availability seems a foregone conclusion: moments after Guido meets Roslyn, he asks her to go out with him after her divorce hearing. However, Roslyn recognizes that, to most men, she is one in a long line of women, and thus, when Guido offers to let her use his house, she asks, "Last woman's gone?" Similarly, when Gay cooks her breakfast after they have spent the night together, she asks, "You do this often?" Although both men say they have never done these things before, as Elisabetta Girelli points out, Guido's and Gay's behavior, and Roslyn's response to it, establish a pattern for "'normal' masculinity" (188–189). Normal masculinity in this context depends upon the sexpot as an available person through which to demonstrate one's normalcy.

The pinup photos of Monroe taped to Roslyn's closet door directly allude to the sexpot's inability to escape her past.[26] The July 1960 version of the script refers to these as "photos for the doorway of a second-class nightclub" (Miller, *The Misfits* 1960, 49). The photos attract Guido's gaze when Roslyn shows him how she has redecorated the house, and Roslyn is forced to speak the cruel lines, "Oh, don't look at those, they're nothing. Gay just hung 'em up for a joke." When Guido insists on opening the closet door again, she pushes it closed and pushes him out of the room, looking both annoyed and angered when she passes before the camera (Figure 5.7). Roslyn thus represents Monroe's own experience—eight years after her nude photos were made public, her past still haunted her.

The Misfits suggests that Monroe isn't the glamorous sexpot of the past, but no one can forget that woman and see her for who she is now. The experience of shooting the film demonstrated that Monroe could not escape her sexpot persona—one extra "told Marilyn she recognized her from the famous calendar picture" (Goode 103). The pinups within the film ensure that audiences associate Roslyn with the sexpot's past. As Ana Salzberg writes about the shots of the taped pinups, "Featured in her most clichéd poses of female stardom, the pinned-up Monroe recalls the Mulveyan object 'cut to the measure' of the male gaze . . . a one-dimensional figure existing on screen to satisfy a desirous perspective." However, in this scene, "with her hair in braids and dressed in jeans with little make-up," Monroe is, as Salzberg notes, "nearly unrecognizable as the woman in the pin-ups" (145). Not only has she changed her appearance, but she also

Figure 5.7. Roslyn closes the door on Marilyn Monroe. Frame enlargement from *The Misfits*.

forbids Guido's ogling the photos, demonstrating that she is not that available woman anymore. Thus, Roslyn challenges the understanding of Monroe as nothing more than a pinup; when Roslyn closes the door on Marilyn Monroe, she prompts viewers to interrogate the relationship between the actress and the sexpot.

Roslyn clearly confronts the expectations others have for the sexpot by resisting the men's sexual advances. She says to Gay, "I don't feel that way about you, Gay," and although this statement seems a bit unreliable because they end up in bed together shortly thereafter, it also makes clear that the relationship is consummated on her terms. When Perce tells her, "I trust you, Roslyn. I think I love you," she says, "No, you don't know me." When Guido tries to kiss her, she pushes him away; later, he offers to stop the mustang hunt if she's "through with Gay now" and if she "give[s] [him] a reason." Instead of jumping into his arms, Roslyn tells him off, and the efforts she makes throughout the film to gain her voice culminate with her impassioned speech: "A reason? You, a sensitive fellow. So sad for his wife. Crying to me about the bombs you've dropped and the people you

killed. You have to get something to be human? You never felt sad for anybody in your life. All you know is the sad words. You could blow up the
world and all you would feel is sorry for yourself." Roslyn insists that she
be treated as a person with complex emotions, not as a sexpot just waiting to be propositioned. And, although Roslyn lives with Gay outside of
marriage, the film does not take this as evidence of her sexual availability
to all men. In fact, because Gay "condone[s] her sexuality," according to
Miller (McIntyre 78), the film succeeds in making her less of a sex symbol
and more of a modern woman who is comfortable having a sexual relationship without marriage but unwilling to have sex with just anyone who
comes along.

Roslyn also resists through her sensitivity, demonstrating how Monroe used the Method to create this role in which she deftly moves between
melancholy and cheerfulness. Audiences likely would have read her acting
training into this role; it was advertised as "the first time" that audiences
would see "the character she has always sought as an actress" (qtd. in
Kouvaros 57). Roslyn recognizes what people want from her and tries to
turn in good performances despite the melancholy that colors most of
her interactions.[27] For example, when Isabelle mentions a cowboy she
once knew, Roslyn hopefully suggests that Gay and Guido might know
him and could help her find him again, but Isabelle and the cowboys
mock her for "thinking [she] can change things." In this scene, Roslyn's
face tells the story, as her expression morphs from anger to helpless
despair, but finally, she resigns herself to cheerfulness and stands up and
asks for music. The low-angle shot when Roslyn returns to her performance of cheerfulness makes her loom large over the other characters,
visually signaling that her power is in her cheerfulness. A similar sequence
is repeated a few minutes later. Gay encourages Roslyn and Guido to "put
on a show" because they are both good dancers, and, while Roslyn cheerfully complies for one song, when the music changes, she asks Guido why
he never taught his now dead wife to dance. Guido doesn't want to

discuss it, but Roslyn continues to express her feeling that husbands and wives don't "[teach] each other what we really know." Sensing the shift in the mood, however, she begins snapping her fingers and returns to cheerfulness, chiding him with a line similar to one she surely had heard herself, "Guido, you're a nice man, smile!" Roslyn receives positive reinforcement from the other characters when she performs in ways that meet their expectations for a "happy girl." When she provides a paddle ball show at the local bar, winning money and entertaining the crowd, her upbeat display, and the crowd's reaction to it, prompts Isabelle to declare, "That girl can do anything," and Gay to whisper in her ear, "I'd marry you." Roslyn responds, "Thanks for saying it, but you don't have to do that"—she knows the proposal is to the performed happy girl, not Roslyn. While Roslyn is often the voice of reason in the film, when it is clear that she has dampened the mood or disappointed the men, she strives to rekindle the cheerful mood. In this way, she makes evident that the sexpot is not the happy girl of men's fantasies while also demonstrating that she cannot escape being thought of that way.

Roslyn also challenges the idea of the sexpot as compliant and uncomplaining. When Guido praises his deceased wife for being as "uncomplaining as a tree," Roslyn responds, "Maybe that's what killed her. I mean, a little complaining helps sometimes, maybe." Roslyn shifts restlessly within the frame, but never looks directly at Guido, and swallows hard as she says these lines, before calling out to Isabelle. Her expressions and gestures tell us that she feels his pain, but she feels more for his wife and herself, women who might benefit from complaining. In the 1957 draft, Roslyn more eloquently explains her perspective: "A person should never get mad, or even say something they really mean. People laugh at you if you do that. Especially a woman. And I never did, I never got mad. Not 'til the last year or so. Soon as I started to say what I thought I lost my husband. That's the truth. You know why girls lie to you? Because that's what you want. You can't stand the other thing. Nobody can. And it's alright, unless you want to be a freak. Whereas nobody wants to be that" (Miller, *The Misfits* 1957, 100).

Roslyn consistently insists on being heard, even if it might make her a "freak"—and a freak, in this film, seems to be any woman who complains, who stands up for herself. She insists on driving her own car out to the desert house in order to be in control of her movement, argues with Gay about killing a rabbit, and struggles to convince the men not to capture and sell the horses. Basing their understanding of her simply on how she looks, the men expect Roslyn to be "as uncomplaining as a tree," but she refuses to let them tell her what to do and what to think.

The film suggests, however, that a woman not defined by the needs of men is formless, impenetrable, and incomprehensible. Indeed, the back-lighting and soft focus make Roslyn appear slightly hazy (Figure 5.8), underscoring how Guido and Gay perceive her. According to Guido, "She's kinda hard to figure out, you know. One minute she looks kinda dumb, brand new like a kid, and the next minute she . . . she sure moves, though, doesn't she?" When Roslyn comments that Gay looks at her like she's "crazy," he reassures her, "I just look that way 'cause I can't make you out." What these men can't "make out," it seems, is how she can appear so "prime," as Gay puts it, and yet not act like the sexpot she appears to be.

When Roslyn dances aimlessly across the yard, self-absorbed, spinning and hugging herself, she demonstrates her unavailability. With her back to the camera, her straps fall from her shoulders, and she finally embraces a tree. Roslyn's self-motivated dance acknowledges her sexpot appearance and subverts it by making it possible that her body exists for herself rather than for men: she controls her sexuality. As Richard Dyer notes, *The Misfits* breaks with the rest of Monroe's oeuvre in that it "begins to hint at a for-itself female sexuality as formlessness. The men in the film look on, unable to comprehend her sensuality; grasping a tree she looks out at them/us with a hollow expression of beatitude, straining to express what is already defined as inexpressible" (*Heavenly* 61). Thus, Roslyn's dance, as

Figure 5.8. Soft focus Roslyn. Frame enlargement from *The Misfits*.

J. M. Coetzee explains, allegorizes Monroe's "resistance to the highly focused and even regimented models of sexuality purveyed not only by Hollywood and the media but by academic sexology. Roslyn is dancing out a diffuse and—in the light of the rest of the film—forlorn sensuality to which neither Guido's sexual predatoriness nor [Gay's] old-fashioned suave courtliness is an adequate response" (65). This dance makes Roslyn "less of a sex symbol than a nature symbol," as Alexander Walker notes, "a species that offers few handholds for a determined man of action" (311).[28] In other words, in *The Misfits* the sexpot, unattainable and self-driven, rather than male-driven, is thus not really a sexpot.

Rather than make her succumb, the men's physical and emotional demands on her as the available sexpot inspire her to speak her mind. Roslyn is a mercurial force—although she causes the men's unraveling, they also look to her for healing.[29] Following the rodeo and a night of drinking, Guido, who is drunk, drives Roslyn home. She sits in the backseat with Perce's bandaged head on her lap and her hand on Gay's shoulder as he lies passed out in the back. Guido, staring straight ahead, begins a rant about wanting someone to "say hello," and he accelerates as he grows increasingly frustrated. When they finally reach the cabin, Roslyn has to clean up these messes—she apologizes to Guido to stop him from hammering at the house in the dark, she keeps Perce from unraveling the bandage around his head, and she comforts Gay as he complains about her helping the other men. She's supposed to fix everyone, to heal everyone, and they'll endanger themselves and her until she does so.

While within the film everyone expects Roslyn to fix them, it is evident to viewers that she needs to be relieved of their demands. Finally achieving a moment of peace after putting all three men to bed, Roslyn, who had been leaning inside the doorframe with her back to the camera, turns around, leans against the house, looks to the heavens, and whispers, "Help." Because the men expect her to heal them, to make them whole, she herself is in danger. Her plea for help builds on the most enduring of the symbolic legacies of Monroe—the need for aid. However, at this point in the film, Roslyn makes this call so quietly that no one comes. Only Alex North, who composed the music for the film, has remarked on what Roslyn's plea for help adds to the development of her character: "I felt there a need to write a piece—the only piece in the whole score that uses a jazz idiom. There I found the use of jazz most expressive in conveying her feeling of being the mother of three children, singing the blues. It was the height of her despondency and frustration" (qtd. in Goode 320). Because the men are three overgrown children (Perce, when half-asleep, even calls her "Ma"), they do not consider how they might help her, or that she is an independent person, not someone defined by or bound to a man.

Finally, to stop the men from killing the mustangs, Roslyn accuses them of being murderers; this outburst demonstrates how she challenges the sexpot persona by insisting on being heard. When Gay refuses her offer to buy the horses, Roslyn runs off into the distance, screaming, "Killers! Killers! Murderers! You liars! All of you, liars! You're only happy when you can see something die! Why don't you kill yourselves and be happy? You and your God's country, freedom. I pity you! You're three dear, sweet, dead men!"[30] This outburst allows Roslyn to criticize these men, their lifestyles, and the demands they place on others. Roslyn is anything but uncomplaining in this scene, and, as Counsell notes about the Method, "Emotion, and particularly unpredictable emotion, implies spontaneity," making the performance more plausible (58). The spontaneous expression of emotion associated with the Method here allows her to speak for the defenseless animals; it also allows her to use her feelings against those who would see her complexity and dynamism killed in roles as an uncomplaining sexpot. Her prior unanswered plea for help also lends some psychological consistency to this later outburst—she cannot continue to allow her surroundings to envelop her if she wants to be heard.

Huston films Roslyn's screaming in a long shot, rather than in a series of close-ups, and thereby helps her distance herself from the sexpot. Although Kouvaros argues that "the environment" "mock[s]" this outburst by dwarfing it in "the vast expanse of empty space" (180),[31] it seems that her rage becomes all the more palpable because it is seen from a distance (Figure 5.9). Dwarfed by the landscape, she no longer appears as the sexpot objectified by close-ups of jiggling body parts. Dwarfed by the landscape, we register her effort to be heard, not seen. Georgiana Banita notes that the film ends with Roslyn's "empowerment" (94), and Savran claims this is Miller's "first—and only—work . . . to offer a radical critique of the conventions of male heroism and to clear a site of female resistance" (43). In the end, Roslyn's voice is heard, suggesting that this distance and this scene were necessary to make the men see Roslyn as a thoughtful person with a valid perspective, not as an incoherent mystery. Her complaining saves the horses' lives and puts her on an equal footing with Gay, allowing them to form what might be a stable relationship.

Roslyn's outburst brings us full circle, back to the film's first scene in which Roslyn insisted on speaking her experience in her own words. In her first scene, Roslyn is practicing (and forgetting) her lines: "He persistently [*sigh*] how does that go again? . . . Well, do I have to say that? Why can't I just say that he wasn't there? I mean, you could touch him, but he

Figure 5.9. The sexpot's rage at a distance. Frame enlargement from *The Misfits*.

wasn't there."[32] This scene represents Monroe's Method approach to acting, as well as the pervasive criticisms of her acting abilities. Her supposed inability to remember lines should be read in the context of her Method training, however. Method actors were known for resisting or rejecting the script. As Shonni Enelow explains, "The script represents more than the play at hand; it stands for 'scriptedness' in general; social rules and conventions, authoritarian directives, and repressive cultural norms, as well as the conformity that seemed to attend mass cultural production and shackled free expression" (12). Monroe embraces the Method's resistance to the script, saying: "If you happen to invert a phrase—YOW! I've told Arthur it doesn't make any difference as long as the meaning is there. . . . I can't memorize the words by themselves. I have to memorize the feeling" (qtd. in Goode 200). Roslyn gives a similar reason for why she can't remember what she's supposed to say at her divorce hearing: "I can't memorize this. It's not the way it was."[33] This desire to speak the words she feels rather than recite what has been written represents a challenge to conformity—Roslyn refuses to conform to the standard divorce script. This scene allegorically calls attention to how Monroe resisted the script's control over her performance but also, significantly in the McCarthy-era context and at a time when her husband was under investigation, to her inability to speak a party line, to say other than she feels, and to hide latent Communism. Paradoxically, however, her refusal to say what others tell her to also hints at her control over her performance—her performance expresses her feeling, rather than another's words.

Although Roslyn resists those who would have her behave as an uncomplaining sexpot, film reviewers agreed that Monroe was still playing "Marilyn Monroe." Ruth Waterbury reviewed Monroe's performance in a way that all but calls her a sexpot: "Marilyn was the new acting Monroe. Don't ask me if I think this acting is necessary. I'll tell you I don't. She has plenty enough for stardom just naturally" (9). A *Cue* reviewer comments on what he saw as a new stiltedness in her performance: "The wonderful intuition of her earlier career has gone; and the cerebral Method has now taken over. You can see the wheels working behind those wide eyes and furrowed brow" ("New Films"). Arthur Knight writes that Monroe's performance "leaves the impression that an earlier Monroe, with or without Miller and Method, was funnier, lusher, smarter" (94). Monroe in her more "natural," pre-Actors Studio state, a state previously criticized as talentless, was now considered superior to the Monroe whom audiences knew worked at acting. In 1961, Alice McIntyre confirms, "Her talent is for responding to the lens, for registering herself as a purely visual phenomenon, and, in the face of this, it is meaningless to wonder, *can she act*? (Of course she can act. What do you *think* she is doing?)" (78). While McIntyre indicates that Monroe's talent for "appearing" is the result of effort, and not just showing up, few authors understood that even "playing herself" was a performance for Monroe.

Resisting the sexpot persona, in the end, demonstrated how the sexpot persona had become an inescapable part of playing "Marilyn Monroe."

Miller writes that his attempts to help her break away from doing this "had apparently proved the opposite"—that she had no home in the world as anyone other than "Marilyn Monroe" (*Timebends* 474). Monroe complained, "When I married [Miller], one of the fantasies I had in my mind was that I could get away from Marilyn Monroe through him, and here I find myself back doing the same thing [in *The Misfits*], and I just couldn't take it" (qtd. in Meyers *Genius* 105, 223). Monroe and Miller acknowledge the sexpot persona within the character of Roslyn, but the advantage of hindsight allows us to recognize how Roslyn resisted doing what was expected of the sexpot. According to Sarah Churchwell, "Roslyn is just an older, sadder and wiser version of The Girl" from *The Seven Year Itch* (1955, dir. Billy Wilder) (66). But she is not *just* The Girl—what would The Girl be as older, sadder, wiser? Monroe, playing Roslyn, suggests that an older and wiser version of The Girl would at least be aware of the effect of her persona on others.

The sexpot makes a big impact, but the extent to which the sexpot is a performance, and to which the skill it takes to create what she created goes unnoticed, makes her life more difficult. What producer Frank Taylor wrote in his script notes applies with striking aptness to Monroe as much as to the character she played: "Roslyn: She's the hero, she alone has enough courage to venture in a land that will always be foreign and hostile to her: the world of those who need her. That includes the men, all the men, of course. . . . They may forget her, but what she brought them will stay with them. That's her victory, a victory she never will be able to enjoy, and that's the price she has to pay for being what she is. She's every thing that's right and good, she's life as it should be, she's what stays with us when the clamor and the noise and the lies and the dust have settled. But she always will be recognized too late" (1–2). And so it is fitting to close this chapter with the fans who expressed a great deal of confidence in Monroe's acting abilities. "She is a real delight on the screen and becomes better in each picture," one wrote to *Photoplay* in 1959 (Wickland 10). After Monroe's death, Hedda Hopper received a letter from a member of the Actors Studio, who wrote,

"I think she was truly loved by most New York actors and certainly respected. This is not usual for New York actors who have a different sense of theater from the screen actor" (Holland). We will never know Marilyn Monroe, but we can marvel at how she played "Marilyn Monroe," a role that she could act out, resist, and subvert, one that made her a star, and one that, from some circuits, garnered her respect as an actress.

CHAPTER 6

CONCLUSION

A "MARILYN MONROE" TYPE

Marilyn Monroe combined the sexpot and star in a way that made her the frequent subject of imitation; however, these imitations underscore that she was truly inimitable. Several dramatic representations of the 1950s seemed to make Monroe into a fictional character even while she was alive. An episode of *I Love Lucy*, which aired on November 8, 1954, alluded to the actress when Lucy performed "a Marilyn Monroe type" by wearing a tight, strapless dress, mincing her steps, sashaying, blinking frequently, tossing her hair, and opening and closing her mouth, saying about Monroe, "She has a way of carrying herself, and smiling just so" (Figure 6.1). George Axelrod's 1955 play, *Will Success Spoil Rock Hunter?*, and the subsequent filmic adaptation (1957, dir. Frank Tashlin) starring Jayne Mansfield as Rita Marlowe, the vapid, sexy, blonde actress resembling Monroe, demonstrate how pervasively Monroe had become the quintessential sexpot to the wider culture.[1] In addition to her allusions to Monroe's appearance, Rita Marlowe utters lines that resemble Monroeisms, for example, "I have no romance. All my lovers and I are just friends." In 1958, a film loosely based on Monroe's life called *The Goddess* (dir. John Cromwell) drew on Monroe's biography, emphasizing how the actress Emily Ann's (Kim Stanley) loveless childhood, mental instability, and promiscuity shaped her path to becoming adored by millions. Monroe the sexpot was the butt

Figure 6.1. Lucy as a "Marilyn Monroe type." Frame enlargement from *I Love Lucy.*

of many jokes, but careful attention to her film performances elucidates what separates Monroe from these impersonations. Monroe was an act, and in some senses it was easy to "play" her for a few moments; but to truly play "Marilyn Monroe," to truly resonate with audiences, these performances needed the mix of humor, vulnerability, and cultural relevance that only Monroe succeeded in bringing to the sexpot.

Monroe resisted the sexpot, but she never abandoned it. In fact, the roles she most desperately wanted demonstrate that she recognized the sexpot's central place in her persona—a persona that consisted of using the sexpot to challenge postwar mores and to confront the expectations associated with the attractive woman. Perhaps nothing makes clearer the important meanings Monroe brought to a film than considering how we would have understood *Breakfast at Tiffany's* (1961, dir. Blake Edwards) had Monroe—who was under serious consideration for the part—been chosen over Audrey Hepburn for the lead. Truman Capote, author of the novella on which the film was loosely based, said, "Marilyn was my first choice to play the girl, Holly Golightly. . . . Holly had to have something touching about her . . . unfinished. Marilyn had that. . . . Audrey was not what I had in mind when I wrote that part" (qtd. in Inge 317). Capote calls attention to the vulnerability and sensitivity that were central to Monroe's sexpot persona.

Capote's Holly had much in common with Monroe. Like Monroe, she had "a face beyond childhood, yet this side of belonging to a woman" (Capote 12). Capote's Holly is blatant about sex. When she finds out the narrator is a writer, she says, "I've never been to bed with a writer. No, wait . . . ," and mentions a writer with whom she has been to bed (19). Holly asks her friend Mag Wildwood if her lover bites in bed; Mag says she doesn't remember: "I don't d-d-dwell on these things. The way you seem to. They go out of my head like a dream. I'm sure that's the n-n-normal attitude." "It may be normal, darling; but I'd rather be natural," Holly replies, echoing Monroe's own statements about sex.[2] "Listen. If you can't remember, try leaving the lights on," Holly advises (50). Finally, the Holly of the novella, echoing sentiments Monroe made famous at the end of *Gentlemen Prefer Blondes* (1953, dir. Howard Hawks), insists that sleeping with men for money has its own moral code: "I haven't anything *against* whores. Except this: some of them may have an honest tongue but they all have dishonest hearts. I mean, you can't bang the guy and cash his checks and at least not *try* to believe you love him" (82). As Capote wrote her, Holly is openly sexual but uses humor and honesty to disarm her critics.

Even the screen version of Holly—heavily modified to accommodate the censors—would have been an apt vehicle for Monroe. Holly stuffs the telephone in the suitcase, she says, "'cause it muffles the sound"; this silly gesture seems typical of Monroe's characters, who read books upside down (*Millionaire* [1953, dir. Jean Negulesco]) or keep their "undies in the icebox" (*The Seven Year Itch* [1955, dir. Billy Wilder]). Holly describes what she calls the "mean reds": "suddenly you're afraid and you don't know what you're afraid of." Had Monroe played the part, this statement would allude to her well-known mental disturbances; her suicide attempts became public knowledge thanks to a *Time* profile in 1956.[3] Holly comments that "it's useful being top banana in the shock department," and Monroe was certainly known for being daring; that she admitted to posing nude because she needed money made her shocking behavior endearing, or, as Holly puts it, "useful." When in Tiffany's jewelry store, Holly comments, "It isn't that I give a hoot about jewelry, except diamonds of course," but she also doesn't plan to wear diamonds until she's over forty—these lines seem like they could have been spoken by Monroe's Lorelei Lee (*Gentlemen*). Finally, when Paul calls Holly "a girl who can't help anyone—not even herself," he echoes a number of writers who thought of Monroe as helpless and in need of male protection.[4]

Monroe longed to play the part of Holly Golightly, the hillbilly turned New York playgirl, but Audrey Hepburn received the role. Although Monroe and Hepburn became big stars in the same period, their personae were on opposing ends of the spectrum of female sexuality. At the same time that Hepburn was a Cinderella whose transformation unleashed her sophisticated and lovable self, Monroe evoked associations with women so sexual that they had to fight off men's advances. Hepburn's films were coming-of-age romances; Monroe's were sex comedies in which she was often the butt of the joke. Hepburn's dignified persona brought a touch of class to the role; Monroe's sexpot persona might have been considered too risqué in a film that already challenged the censors.

Holly's forthright attitude about sex prevented the film from being faithful to Capote's novel. That Holly was a call girl made Paramount executives worry about getting the film past the censors. Screenwriter George Axelrod (who had written the play *The Seven Year Itch* and adapted the Monroe film *Bus Stop* [1956, dir. Josh Logan]) solved the problem by displacing Holly's over-the-top sexuality onto Paul, with whom Holly refuses to form a relationship because he, like she, is a gigolo. Even after this change, production documents indicate that the filmmakers needed to eliminate the overt sex. In his summary of the screenplay, Geoffrey Shurlock, head of the Production Code Administration, crossed out even happy-ending sex between Holly and Paul, leaving a document that looked like this: "Paul's novel, which has Holly for its heroine, is accepted and he and Holly celebrate. ~~They end up spending the night together.~~ Paul realizes he has fallen in love with Holly and breaks with 2E" (qtd. in Wasson 95, line crossed out in the summary). *Breakfast at Tiffany's* does not have any sex scenes, but, had Monroe been its star, it seems likely that it would have, since in both *Some Like It Hot* (1959, dir. Billy Wilder) and *The Misfits* (1961, dir. John Huston) she played characters who had sex outside of marriage.

Casting Hepburn against type as Holly was the final step in asserting the film's "decency." Hepburn had become a star in the 1950s playing innocents who underwent dramatic transformations and gained the love of older men—Hepburn as Holly was, as Sam Wasson puts it, a "cockeyed dreamer á la Princess Ann in *Roman Holiday* and Sabrina in *Sabrina*" (89). Hepburn shaped Holly in a way that made Capote's story acceptable in early 1960s Hollywood: Hepburn's Holly is sophisticated and independent. Holly constantly runs out on men before any sex occurs, something audiences would have been unlikely to believe of Monroe. When Hepburn as Holly watches a stripper perform, her sophisticated elegance distances her from the scene, so that her queries about whether the performer is "talented" or "handsomely paid" seem wholesome. "Do you think you own me?" Holly says. "That's what everybody always thinks, but everybody happens to be wrong." Although many of Monroe's characters might have uttered those lines, none would have convincingly conveyed Hepburn's sense of sophisticated independence.

In short, Hepburn made the film an escape from reality, another Cinderella story, while Monroe would have made it an engagement with the sexual realities of postwar America, fully capitalizing on her unique ability to combine the role of sexpot with major Hollywood stardom. Considering how Monroe would have shaped *Breakfast at Tiffany's*, had she been given the role, illustrates what I have been arguing throughout this book: Monroe's sexpot persona inflected each of her film roles, but she also found ways to complicate and resist what was expected of the sexpot, making her a star.

The final line of *Some Like It Hot* summarizes the basis of Monroe's appeal: "Nobody's perfect." From her earliest work as a model, when she created the images that would undergird her status as an icon, Monroe worked with her imperfections. Her first modeling agent and coach, Emmeline Snively, told her to smile differently because her gumline was too high, and critics commented on her fluctuating weight. Nevertheless, postwar Americans seemed unable to get enough images of Monroe. Her pinup poses became so iconic that they inflected her film roles, such that she was a former pinup model in *The Seven Year Itch* and *The Misfits*. The publicity image of her white dress for *The Seven Year Itch* appeared on the front pages of many major American newspapers. Monroe became a star in an era when a movie star's picture was front-page news.

Monroe's offscreen life inflected the meanings of her films. Monroe certainly was an imperfect wife. Offscreen, she divorced three men— James Dougherty (after four years), Joe DiMaggio (after nine months), and Arthur Miller (after five years). Her imperfections, however, endeared her to postwar men and women, who were also struggling with the radically reconfigured social landscape of the postwar period. Monroe's films engaged with the period's proliferating marital advice. Onscreen, she played a working pageant queen wife in *We're Not Married!* (1952, dir. Edmund Goulding), a murderess in *Niagara* (1953, dir. Henry Hathaway), and gold diggers in *Gentlemen Prefer Blondes* and *How to Marry a Millionaire*. Her personal life colored these roles, such that they seemed to reflect her own struggles to choose between marriage and her career. Monroe's films reflected the unacknowledged pitfalls of marriage and the problems with a cultural discourse that encouraged women to be housewives.

Monroe communicated sex appeal through her body and a lack of sala-
ciousness through her wide-eyed, smiling face, thereby serving as a perfectly imperfect sexpot. She was not an over-the-top insinuator in the style
of Mae West nor a hardened go-getter like Jean Harlow—rather, her double entendres were always delivered as though she didn't know what she
was saying. Monroe's delivery mode made it seem unlikely that she was
consciously using her sex appeal to manipulate others. She made frank discussion of sex acceptable, and thereby ushered in the sexual revolution of
the 1960s. Her roles in *The Seven Year Itch*, *Bus Stop*, and *Some Like It Hot*
attest to the changing understanding of female sexuality in the postwar
period. By playing women not interested in marriage, but interested in
pleasure, Monroe reflected Kinsey's findings in *Sexual Behavior in the
Human Female* that about half of women engaged in sex outside of marriage. What's more, while in these roles her desire for pleasure is apparent, the films received Production Code Administration approval. Monroe
thereby contributed to the weakening of that body's power.

Throughout her career, Monroe's star persona demonstrated a desire
for privacy and power over one's own life that is dramatized in *The Misfits*.
Four times Roslyn obsessively chants, "I can go in, and I can come out" as
she jumps up and down the house's makeshift concrete block step, indicating how much she wants control over the direction of her life. George
Kouvaros reads this scene as affirming Roslyn's "confiden[ce]" in her
"ability to negotiate the threshold between home and world" (187). The
threshold between home and world in the film allegorizes a similar threshold between the star's private life and public persona. When Roslyn finds
the concrete block and proudly places it beneath the doorway, she demonstrates her mastery of the threshold, and implicitly indicates the possibility that a star might control her privacy. Roslyn's final line, "How do
you find your way back in the dark?," however, expresses doubts about that
control, that is, about the possibility of a star's existing outside of stardom.

Although she resisted playing "Marilyn Monroe" in her final films, it
is also apparent that playing her became inescapable. "One had to face the

inbuilt paranoid opening in the ups and downs of her standing with her public," Miller said of Monroe's state when he was writing *The Misfits*. He explains, "She, the woman, could not send herself out to perform and make appearances while remaining at home to create a life. Having to look at herself with two pairs of eyes, her own and a hypothetical public's, was as inescapable as it was enervating in the end" (*Timebends* 459). Monroe continually enacted a double life, both offscreen and onscreen—but her film performances allowed her to acknowledge and resist the sexpot that writers, directors, and audiences wanted her to be. *The Misfits* also unites Monroe's screen persona and offscreen life in resistance to conventional values: her character embraces divorce, lives with a man who is not her husband, and openly criticizes men who betray trust. How Monroe embodied the contradictions inherent in both postwar culture and Hollywood stardom, fittingly, becomes most apparent in her final film.

Reflecting on the climactic horse-roping scene in *The Misfits*, J. M. Coetzee writes, "The horses are real, the stuntmen are real, the actors are real; they are all, at this moment, involved in a terrible fight in which the men want to subjugate the horses to their purpose and the horses want to get away; every now and again the blonde woman screams and shouts; it all really happened; and here it is, to be relived for the ten-thousandth time before our eyes. Who would dare to say it is just a story?" (67). Although Coetzee's point is to disparage "all the cleverness that has been exercised in film theory since the 1950s to bring film into line as just another system of signs" in favor of underscoring that "there remains something irreducibly different about the photographic image, namely that it bears in or with itself an element of the real" (67), his doing so illustrates, although he does not intend it to, the extent to which film is a system of signs. For what he calls "an element of the real" is only partly real; the rest—including Monroe's star persona—is mediated fiction; "Marilyn Monroe" is a role an actress plays.

The role Monroe created has resonated far beyond the 1950s context; S. Paige Baty, among others, has enumerated what she means to contemporary audiences.[5] Baty theorizes that Monroe has become a "representative character" (8), "a body on which contestations over gender, the political character of culture, processes of simulation in contemporary America, current regimes of knowledge and power, and the forms of mass-mediated historical consciousness have been and continue to be written" (20). And while Baty speaks for how we use Monroe in the present to remember and perhaps advocate for prior ways of being American, I argue that Monroe represented many of the same things to her contemporaries.

The last line of Monroe's final interview is "please don't make me a joke" (Levy 77). While I can think of a number of works that seem to make her a joke, many writers have exercised caution and restraint in telling Monroe's story. This project, I hope, satisfies her wish by demonstrating that, far from being a joke, she was central to postwar American culture. I have deliberately avoided speculating about Monroe's personal life. Much of the evidence I use is the evidence the average fan of the 1950s would have had—what was printed in fan magazines and gossip columns. Although her persona certainly contained elements that were already working to make Monroe into a joke in the 1950s, it also contained much that demonstrates how she challenged the sexpot role with sensitivity and humor. Many people felt, and still feel, as though Monroe speaks to their concerns: as women negotiating between homemaking and careers, as lonely individuals who long to feel attractive and witty, as victims of exploitive labor conditions, as inwardly fragile beings with tough exteriors. Monroe believed her films would reveal her significance as a public figure. She told James Goode, on the set of her final completed film, "To really say what's in my heart, I'd rather show than to say. Even though I want people to understand, I'd much rather they understand on the screen" (qtd. in Goode 199). Through her performances, Monroe dramatized the conflicts inherent in performing the sexpot, as well as the tensions within postwar culture. She resisted the sexpot by being "some kind of mirror," reflecting, as I have shown, the tension for women between independence and marriage, between financial freedom and marriage, and between sex and marriage; the tension for women between brinkmanship and sexual desire, between attractiveness and insisting on their own pleasure, and between strict gender roles and the increasing fluidity of gender presentation; and, finally, between availability and resistance, and between appearance and performance.

ACKNOWLEDGMENTS

Many years ago, when I began working on a dissertation on Marilyn Monroe, I received a Marilyn Monroe magnetic dress-up set. I stored it away over the course of several moves, but my five-year-old daughter discovered it anew last summer, initially referring to her as "the dress-up girl" (now she knows plenty about Marilyn Monroe). This is a form of "playing Marilyn Monroe," one that persists in our contemporary culture. Monroe's popularity has not waned in the more than fifty-six years since her death, and I am grateful for the work done over the years by biographers, critics, and filmmakers, which I build on here. Through exploring the ways in which Monroe's humor, vulnerability, acting skill, and cultural relevance made her more than a sexpot, I hope to contribute my part to our understanding of why Monroe was one of the most popular stars of the 1950s, which I think will go some way toward explaining her enduring legacy.

Many people have helped me develop my analysis of Monroe, and I am honored to have this chance to thank them. Alan Nadel encouraged this project from my first semester as a doctoral student at the University of Kentucky, and taught me invaluable lessons about research, writing, and friendship. I am also grateful to Virginia Blum, Randall Roorda, and Diane Negra for their guidance as I completed the dissertation out of which this book grew. My graduate work on this project was supported by a Presidential Fellowship, a Dissertation Year Fellowship, and a Kentucky

Women's Club Research Grant. The Bonnie Cox Graduate Research Award, the Dissertation Enhancement Award, and the Ben Wathen Black Memorial Graduate Scholarship funded two weeks of research at the Margaret Herrick Library of the Academy of Motion Picture Arts and Sciences; the Cinematic Arts Library at the University of Southern California; and the Warner Bros. Archives, School of Cinematic Arts, University of Southern California. I am grateful to the dedicated and helpful librarians and archivists at these institutions.

I also extend my gratitude to those people who have supported me as I transformed my previous work into this book. My colleagues and students at Georgia Southern University's Armstrong Campus have provided valuable encouragement and conversation; I would especially like to thank Karen Hollinger, Beth Howells, and my student research assistant, Ben Cela. My students in a summer course at The Learning Center of Senior Citizens, Inc., in Savannah provided passionate insights that helped me see this project anew. A Languages, Literature, and Philosophy Summer Research Grant supported an intense summer of drafting and revising. I am also indebted to Leslie Mitchner and Lisa Banning of Rutgers University Press and the anonymous reviewers of my manuscript, who contributed much to the final project's shape.

My greatest debt is owed to those who have seen me through this project from start to finish and are still by my side. To my late father, Don, and my mother, Sandy Wischmeier, who have instilled in me an unflagging work ethic and enthusiastically cheered for my accomplishments, I am forever grateful. My husband, Wes, has done more than his share of chores, and has heard more than he wanted to about Monroe; and my daughter, Avalee, has not yet known life without me working on this book, and both of them love me anyway. This book would not exist without the love of these people.

Portions of chapter 3 have been published in a different form as "How to (Marry a Woman Who Wants to) Marry a Millionaire," *Quarterly Review of Film and Video* 31.4 (2014): 364–383.

FILMOGRAPHY

99 River Street. Dir. Phil Karlson. Edward Small Productions, 1953.

A Blueprint for Murder. Dir. Andrew Stone. Andrew L. Stone Productions, 1953.

All about Eve. Dir. Joseph Mankiewicz. Twentieth Century-Fox, 1950.

All That Heaven Allows. Dir. Douglas Sirk. Universal International Pictures, 1955.

An American in Paris. Dir. Vincente Minnelli. Metro-Goldwyn-Mayer, 1951.

Anne of the Indies. Dir. Jacques Tourneur. Twentieth Century-Fox, 1951.

The Asphalt Jungle. Dir. John Huston. Metro-Goldwyn-Mayer, 1950.

As Young as You Feel. Dir. Harmon Jones. Twentieth Century-Fox, 1951.

The Best Years of Our Lives. Dir. William Wyler. The Samuel Goldwyn Company, 1946.

The Bigamist. Dir. Ida Lupino. The Filmakers, 1952.

The Big Heat. Dir. Fritz Lang. Columbia Pictures, 1953.

Breakfast at Tiffany's. Dir. Blake Edwards. Paramount Pictures, 1961.

Bus Stop. Dir. Joshua Logan. Twentieth Century-Fox, 1956.

Cinderella. Dirs. Clyde Geronimi and Wilfred Jackson. Walt Disney Productions, 1950.

Clash by Night. Dir. Fritz Lang. RKO Radio Pictures, 1952.

The Country Girl. Dir. George Seaton. Paramount Pictures, 1954.

Criss Cross. Dir. Robert Siodmak. Universal International Pictures, 1949.

Designing Woman. Dir. Vincente Minnelli. Metro-Goldwyn-Mayer, 1957.

Don't Bother to Knock. Dir. Roy Baker. Twentieth Century-Fox, 1952.

Don't Change Your Husband. Dir. Cecil B. DeMille. Artcraft Pictures Corporation, 1919.

From Here to Eternity. Dir. Fred Zinnemann. Columbia Pictures, 1953.

Funny Face. Dir. Stanley Donen. Paramount Pictures, 1957.

Gentlemen Prefer Blondes. Dir. Howard Hawks. Twentieth Century-Fox, 1953.

The Goddess. Dir. John Cromwell. Columbia Pictures, 1958.

Home Town Story. Dir. Arthur Pierson. Metro-Goldwyn Mayer, 1951.

How to Marry a Millionaire. Dir. Jean Negulesco. Twentieth Century-Fox, 1953.

Insignificance. Dir. Nicolas Roeg. Recorded Picture Company, 1985.

King Kong. Dirs. Merian Cooper and Ernest Schoedsack. RKO Radio Pictures, 1933.

Kiss Me Deadly. Dir. Robert Aldrich. Parklane Pictures Inc., 1955.

Ladies of the Chorus. Dir. Phil Karlson. Columbia Pictures, 1948.

Let's Make It Legal. Dir. Richard Sale. Twentieth Century-Fox, 1951.

Let's Make Love. Dir. George Cukor. Twentieth Century-Fox, 1960.

Love Happy. Dir. David Miller. Artists Alliance, 1949.

Love, Marilyn. Dir. Liz Garbus. Diamond Girl Productions, 2012.

Love Nest. Dir. Joseph Newman. Twentieth Century-Fox, 1951.

The Marrying Kind. Dir. George Cukor. Columbia Pictures, 1952.

The Misfits. Dir. John Huston. Seven Arts Pictures, 1961.

Monkey Business. Dir. Howard Hawks. Twentieth Century-Fox, 1952.

My Week with Marilyn. Dir. Simon Curtis. The Weinstein Company, 2011.

Niagara. Dir. Henry Hathaway. Twentieth Century-Fox, 1953.

Now, Voyager. Dir. Irving Rapper. Warner Bros., 1942.

O'Henry's Full House. Dirs. Henry Hathaway, Howard Hawks, Henry King, Henry Koster, and Jean Negulesco. Twentieth Century-Fox, 1952.

The Outlaw. Dir. Howard Hughes. Howard Hughes Productions, 1943.

Picnic. Dir. Joshua Logan. Columbia Pictures, 1955.

Pickup on South Street. Dir. Samuel Fuller. Twentieth Century-Fox, 1953.

The Postman Always Rings Twice. Dir. Tay Garnett. Metro-Goldwyn-Mayer, 1946.

The Prince and the Showgirl. Dir. Laurence Olivier. Warner Bros., Marilyn Monroe Productions, 1957.

Rear Window. Dir. Alfred Hitchcock. Alfred J. Hitchcock Productions, 1954.

"Ricky's Movie Offer." *I Love Lucy*. Season 4, Nov. 8, 1954.

The Robe. Dir. Henry Koster. Twentieth Century-Fox, 1953.

Scudda Hoo! Scudda Hay! Dir. F. Hugh Herbert. Twentieth Century-Fox, 1948.

The Seven Year Itch. Dir. Billy Wilder. Twentieth Century-Fox, 1955.

Shane. Dir. George Stevens. Paramount Pictures, 1953.

Singin' in the Rain. Dirs. Stanley Donen and Gene Kelly. Metro-Goldwyn-Mayer, 1952.

Some Like It Hot. Dir. Billy Wilder. United Artists, 1959.

Strangers on a Train. Dir. Alfred Hitchcock. Warner Bros., 1951.

Sunset Blvd. Dir. Billy Wilder. Paramount Pictures, 1950.

Tarzan and His Mate. Dir. Cedric Gibbons. Metro-Goldwyn-Mayer, 1934.

That Touch of Mink. Dir. Delbert Mann. Granley Company, 1962.

There's No Business Like Show Business. Dir. Walter Lang. Twentieth Century-Fox, 1954.

This Charming Couple. Dir. Willard Van Dyke. McGraw-Hill Text Films, 1950.

A Ticket to Tomahawk. Dir. Richard Sale. Twentieth Century-Fox, 1950.

Vicki. Dir. Harry Horner. Twentieth Century-Fox, 1953.

Viva Zapata. Dir. Elia Kazan. Twentieth Century-Fox, 1952.

We're Not Married! Dir. Edmund Goulding. Twentieth Century-Fox, 1953.

Why Change Your Wife? Dir. Cecil B. DeMille. Famous Players-Lasky Corporation, 1920.

Will Success Spoil Rock Hunter? Dir. Frank Tashlin. Twentieth Century-Fox, 1957.

NOTES

CHAPTER 1 — INTRODUCTION

1. Monroe and screenwriter Ben Hecht coauthored this autobiography. Although it is difficult to determine its truthfulness, the autobiography is important because it contributes to Monroe's star persona, revealing, despite being published after her death, what its writers wanted others to think about her. See Spoto 268–270, who questions whether Hecht or his agent, Jacques Chambrun, wrote the manuscript. Regardless of its authorship, as Churchwell points out, "in the end its very doubtfulness, its collaborative authorship, its alternate disparagement and aggrandizement, its endless recycling in further accounts, does make *My Story* look, colloquially speaking, like the story of Marilyn Monroe's life" (107).

2. See Bode on the role film screenings play in keeping Valentino's image alive.

3. On the stability of dead stars' images and their usefulness to advertising, see Patti 189, 194; and McDonald, *Hollywood Stardom*, 36.

4. See Levitt on "Hollywood's Dark Tourism" for a discussion of the business of dead celebrity tourism.

5. Marchant discusses the meanings various kinds of star photography, including publicity stills, behind-the-scenes stills, and portrait photographs, add to a star's image.

6. Readers interested in Monroe's biography have several fine options and should be prepared to compare texts. I recommend biographies by Spoto; Leaming; and Banner; and Churchwell's analysis of the biographies.

7. See also Manning 58.

8. Studies of stars in their social and historical contexts are subject to being charged with reflectionism. Although it is impossible to be completely objective, by thinking of the films as indices to a larger cultural context (which leaves its

traces in narrative situations and dialogue), we can at least be certain that we are considering elements of the cultural context with which Monroe's contemporaries would have been familiar. These same contextual materials resonate in Monroe's publicity as well as in audience commentary on the films and fan letters. While there are certainly additional topics that were important to postwar Americans, then, Monroe's films provide a reliable indication of the issues that overlapped with her stardom and generated her appeal for fans.

9. I am aware that Morin called Monroe "the *good-bad girl*" (22) and "a remarkable synthesis of star and pin-up" (43), dubbing her unique in being a pinup who is not anonymous. I will go into more depth than Morin, detailing how Monroe synthesized those extremes.

10. In an article published in 2017, Mulvey sees Monroe differently, as perhaps challenging "to-be-looked-at-ness" ("Thoughts" 208).

11. To discuss the workings of scopophilia, Mulvey posits three separate "gazes": the camera recording the woman, the audience watching the film, and the characters looking at each other within the film ("Visual" 46–47).

12. For example, do the viewers submit to the images of the star flooding them by becoming passive spectators, as in a masochistic relation to the star (Studlar "Masochism" 211, 215)? Or do the viewers revel in the images of (particularly female) stars that flaunt the trappings of gender performativity in order to destabilize gender hierarchies (Doane *Femmes* 26)? Mulvey revised her theory in "Afterthoughts" in 1981.

13. See Cowie 71, 114. Mayne likewise recognizes the ambivalence inherent in ever-changing film narratives, and suggests "the cinema functions both to legitimatize the patriarchal status quo and, if not necessarily to challenge it, then at the very least to suggest its weak limits, its own losses of mastery, within which may be found possibilities or hypotheses of alternative positions" (25).

14. For example, Affron studies the work of Lillian Gish, Greta Garbo, and Bette Davis, but insists that the stellar performances of these actresses were attributable to the directors, not the actresses. In contrast, Pomerance's *Johnny Depp Starts Here* focuses with great alacrity on Depp's "theatricality" as an acting style, and traces the way that "theatricality" influences the meaning of particular films. Naremore's study on *Acting in the Cinema* provides the necessary vocabulary for discussing star performances. Naremore addresses what sets something apart as acting—the performance space, the way the actor addresses the audience, mannerisms, the fit between character and persona, and mise-en-scène (3–4). Other significant studies of star acting include Hollinger's *The Actress: Hollywood Acting and the Female Star* and Lovell's and Krämer's collection *Screen Acting*.

15. Cole's affiliates note the (uncharacteristic) patience he had with Monroe: vocal coach Hal Schaefer called him *"very* patient," contrary to his attitude toward professional dancers, and Jane Russell said, "He was darling with her" (Loney 203).

16. Stacey's study of British audiences has usefully elaborated on the ways audiences respond to stars with "'devotion', 'adoration' and 'worship,'" as well as imitation (138, 162). Other studies engaging an ethnographic approach to studying Hollywood stars include Hansen's *Babel and Babylon: Spectatorship in American Silent Film* and Moseley's *Growing Up with Audrey Hepburn: Text, Audience, Resonance.*

17. Monroe's 1951 contract with Fox gave her $750 a week, with a raise every six months until her salary capped at $3,250 per week (Banner 176).

18. Grosses for other years are as follows: $3.8 million (1954), $4.9 million (1955), $4.2 million (1956), $1.5 million (1957), $0 (1958), $7 million (1959), $1.8 million (1960), and $3.9 million (1961) (tallies by Higashi 18).

19. *Photoplay*'s "annual circulation figures hovered around 1 million in the 1950s and even increased slightly, while weekly box-office receipts dropped 50 percent due to television viewing" (Higashi 1–2). Despite box office declines, "newsstand sales . . . shot up 45 percent in the first half of the decade [1950s]. And *Photoplay* was one of two national magazines that enhanced its advertising revenue during a recession in 1954" (Higashi 2).

20. Monroe has a life beyond her film performances as a commodity and celebrity, and continues to generate revenue through a variety of magazine articles, films (DVD releases of her films, biopics, and documentaries), and consumer goods. This aspect of her significance has been studied in great detail by Baty and the contributors to *Fan Phenomena: Marilyn Monroe.*

21. Dyer's foundational work, *Stars*, discusses stars' ideological significance at length. See also Studlar's *Mad Masquerade*, Gledhill's "Signs," and J. Ellis, among many others.

22. Different members of the same audience will, inevitably, interpret the star's behavior differently; thus, what is acceptable to some may be unacceptable for others. Nevertheless, gossip about stars' behavior helps establish the mores of a community. See Hermes; and van Krieken 95.

23. See also Mobilio. Because Monroe's appeal to males is rarely questioned, I'm not addressing it in detail here. Monroe received a number of letters from grateful soldiers during the Korean War, and she had an ongoing friendly correspondence with James Haspiel, a member of the small group known as The Monroe Six, which is documented in Haspiel's book *Marilyn: The Ultimate Look at the Legend.* A few letters from male fans will be mentioned, but the overwhelming majority of those sympathizing with Monroe are from female fans.

24. I've asked both male and female students of mine who were adults in the 1950s what they thought of her at the time—some register indifference, some say they thought of her as sensitive more than sexy. Of course, hindsight is likely to have influenced these opinions.

25. Steinem points out that women in the 1970s and 1980s related to Monroe as someone with similar stories of sexual assault, overmedication, and heartbreak (28–29). Intimacy with Monroe's sufferings is part of what undergirds her lasting legacy.

26. "The problem that has no name," aptly named by Friedan in *The Second Sex*, is part of this silence.

27. Other writers praised the psychological exposé, including a Dr. Howard McIntyre, who wrote that the "character portrait" is "of great value to the psychiatrist in the character analysis of his own patients. Marilyn's success in the tawdry roles to which she has been assigned is not due to her anatomic structure, but is to be explained in that life force which cannot be concealed in any medium" (6). A letter from Bob Hoig gives the magazine "orchids" "for taking that candid stroll down the old id road" (4).

28. Hundreds of fan letters to Monroe still exist; Julien's Auction House in Beverly Hills auctioned three lots in December 2014. However, many of these letters, for whatever reason, are secreted away by their owners.

29. See Jordan, chap. 1, for an overview of Harlow's gold-digging roles, and Ohmer for an overview of Harlow's tough persona.

30. By the late 1940s, as she aged and had less "oomph," Sheridan became known for her roles in melodramas such as *Nora Prentiss* and *The Unfaithful* (both 1947, dir. Vincent Sherman).

31. See Solomon on the "Reflexivity and Metaperformance" that Monroe, Mansfield, and Novak had in common. Kim Stanley, another blonde actress of the 1950s, is also sometimes included in this grouping; she played a version of Monroe in *The Goddess* (1958, dir. John Cromwell). Stanley was a Method actress, more entrenched in the Actors Studio lessons than Monroe, but Vineberg argues that Stanley never succeeded as a Method actress because she could not play "'Normal' emotional states," but rather was "the embodiment of the actress as neurotic" (210).

32. Lane's article warns that Novak might be undone by her "love of love," Mansfield by her "love of publicity," and Monroe by her "love of art and the arty" (40–41).

33. Novak was named *Boxoffice*'s "Number One Star" in 1956, but she does not have the enduring legacy or the repeated successes of Monroe. See also Byars, who argues that Novak never became a huge star because her roles "foregrounded

conflicting constructions of femininity and . . . her performances heightened conflict and exhibited the difficulty of being a young, unmarried woman in the America of that time" (202), "rather than masking" the "tensions over gender construction" (198), as she alleges Monroe did. As I will argue in more detail in subsequent chapters, Monroe's films did not "mask" the contradictions within postwar culture. In fact, if we are aware of the discourses surrounding these tensions in the postwar period, we can argue that Monroe, too, embodied these struggles in her films.

34. See also Tom Ewell's interview with Charles Higham for *Australian TV Times* (qtd. in Tomlinson 169) and Saxton 48.

35. Contemporary reviewers also noted that other of Mansfield's roles bore a striking resemblance to Monroe's roles: a *New York Times* review of Mansfield's *Illegal* (1955, dir. Lewis Allen) said, "*Illegal* tries to blueprint *The Asphalt Jungle*'s Marilyn Monroe" (qtd. in Farris 64), and *The Wayward Bus* (1957, dir. Victor Vicas), in name and plot, was a take on Monroe's *Bus Stop*.

36. See McLean, *Being Rita Hayworth*.

CHAPTER 2 — BECOMING A STAR

1. See chapter 1, as well as Pullen; Salzberg; and Solomon.

2. See Baron for details on the pervasiveness of acting training in Hollywood.

3. Banner ("Creature") and Mobilio provide interesting insight on this image. The *New York Times* has recently released video footage of Monroe shooting this scene: https://www.nytimes.com/2017/01/13/nyregion/marilyn-monroe-skirt-blowing-new-york-film.html?_r=0.

4. Grable's pinup photo became the top promotional photo of the World War II era, a popularity she dramatized when she starred in 1944's *Pin-Up Girl* (dir. H. Bruce Humberstone) (Buszek 223).

5. See both Westbrook and Buszek for more on pinups, including pinups created by ordinary American women, which emulated those created by models.

6. These photos appear in photographer Andre de Dienes's book *Marilyn*. Spoto includes a photo of Monroe posing for pinup artist Earl Moran, and Mailer and Guiles include photos from Monroe's early modeling work and some studio cheesecake photos.

7. See, in particular, the memoirs of her photographers George Barris and Sam Shaw (with text by Norman Rosten). Stern's *Marilyn Monroe: The Last Sitting* documents Monroe's habit of crossing through photos she disliked. Banner's biography discusses Monroe's modeling work in detail in chap. 4. Goode provides a lengthy description of the process through which Monroe approved publicity

shots for *The Misfits* (1961, dir. John Huston) which went through five different agents before Monroe marked through the ones she disliked (118).

8. Agent Jim Byron had encouraged Jayne Mansfield to do something similar to "graduat[e] from the sexpot stuff and . . . evolv[e] with public approval after establishing their affection" (qtd. in Saxton 51). Mansfield, however, wanted to maintain her appeal as a personality, while Monroe was determined to be recognized as an actress.

9. Perhaps Monroe's nude photos are associated with exploitation because they became the first *Playboy* centerfold in 1953, with Monroe having no say in the role her nude body played in launching the new magazine. Hugh Hefner acquired the "Golden Dreams" photo for $500 and used the promise of reprinting it to secure advance orders of the first issue (Fraterrigo 20). Carpozi reports that the John Baumgarth Company sold six million copies of the *Golden Dreams* calendar (36).

10. Perhaps this explains, in part, the enduring iconicity of Andy Warhol's silkscreened *Marilyns*, which transform a close-up drawn from a publicity image for *Niagara* into a series of reflections on the surfaces of Monroe's face. Warhol's silk screens capitalize on how frequently Monroe's (ambiguous) face was printed on magazine covers throughout her career.

11. Similarly, Heath thinks of stars as operating "in the mode of presence in absence" (114); see both J. Ellis and Mulvey, *Death*, 161. See also Dyer, "Star" 136; de Cordova 140, 145; and van Krieken 10 for elaborations of the role of sexual secrets in star personae.

12. Theoretical understandings of how fans form intimate relationships with classical stars are underdeveloped if not entirely absent. I have turned to celebrity theory, which analyzes fan relationships with contemporary celebrities, in cases, such as that of gossip magazines, where the findings seem to apply. In addition to celebrity theorists cited in the text of this chapter, see, for example, Grossberg; Leets et al.; and Stever.

13. While stars' lifestyles were depicted as largely inaccessible to ordinary people during the Depression (because they were), establishing that the star is an ordinary person became a goal of publicity machinery in the 1950s (see Morin). Stories of stars' "ordinariness," argues Gamson, "promoted a greater sense of connection and intimacy between the famous and their admirers" (29). See both Burr and Dyer, *Stars*, and also Hermes for the role of gossip magazines in star publicity.

14. Monroe's upbringing frequently appeared in publicity. See "The Truth about Me" by Marilyn Monroe as told to Liza Wilson, in two parts, for the *American Weekly*, a Sunday newspaper supplement. The first part, appearing November 16,

1952, recounts Monroe's tough childhood and tells the story of her Hollywood name; part 2, appearing November 23, 1952, discusses Monroe's early film roles and her relationship with Joe DiMaggio. Monroe's former sister-in-law, Elyda Nelson, tried to debunk the Monroe mythology in "The True Life Story of Marilyn Monroe" in *Modern Screen* in 1952; Monroe responded to Nelson's claims in *Photoplay* in January 1953's "Marilyn Monroe Tells the Truth to Hedda Hopper." This is just a sampling of the nearly ubiquitous coverage of Monroe's childhood in early publicity. Every Monroe biography explores these details, and nearly every biography reaches a different conclusion regarding how bad it really was.

15. See also Corwin 106 and Graham, "Hollywood's Lost," 53.

16. Similarly, the fictional "Cal York" wrote in a 1952 *Photoplay* gossip column that Monroe was diligently studying acting (32), and in 1954 a *Movieland* writer praised Monroe's ambition and ability to ask others for advice ("Too" 60).

17. See also Corwin. At this early point in her career, this double life was not pathologized. *Time* magazine reported on Monroe's suicide attempts in 1956 ("To"), and Levy speculated about them in 1962. Because stories about Monroe's mental and physical illnesses were not part of her transition from sexpot to star, I do not discuss them here, but these stories certainly maintained public interest in Monroe as something other than a sexpot, and likely contribute to the public's continuing fascination with Monroe's life and death.

18. In 1952, *Time* reported that Monroe received "more than 5,000 letters a week from smitten admirers" ("Something" 88).

19. Many film scholars have recently challenged the idea that directors and editors create film actors' performances; see, for example, the essays in Lovell's and Krämer's *Screen Acting*, Hollinger's *The Actress: Hollywood Acting and the Female Star*, and Baron's and Carnicke's *Reframing Screen Performance*.

20. The Hollywood Production Code, established in 1934, provided guidelines for how to depict sex and crime, among other things. See Doherty, *Hollywood's Censor*, and Jacobs.

21. This theme also resonates in *Niagara* (1953, dir. Henry Hathaway), a film Monroe made the next year.

22. Earl's unfunny humor has been a theme throughout: Earl's Chinese imitation, which once had been funny to Jerry but no one else, becomes the thing Jerry asks Earl to do right before he starts strangling Earl.

23. Not an uncommon Hollywood strategy—it was used to great effect, for example, when introducing Bette Davis in both *Now, Voyager* (1942, dir. Irving Rapper) and *All about Eve*.

CHAPTER 3 — MRS. AMERICA

This chapter is derived in part from "How to (Marry a Woman Who Wants to) Marry a Millionaire," *Quarterly Review of Film and Video* 31.4: 364–383.

1. Much of the anxiety surrounding unmarried individuals was related to the homosexual panic that accompanied McCarthyism; see Corber. *Gentlemen Prefer Blondes* may reflect anxiety about homosexuality: critics have discussed the homoerotics of the disinterested Olympic swim team (see Rushing). These areas are ripe for investigation, but they are beyond the scope of this chapter.

2. Within the postwar context, even anthropologist Margaret Mead recognized that "the only truly acceptable pattern in American life is marriage, and both husband and wife are supposed to share its pleasures and its burdens. Bachelors and spinsters are both disapproved of and discriminated against" (27). See also Burgess and Wallin 218.

3. Burgess and Locke first identified this shift in their 1945 book *The Family: From Institution to Companionship*, which was reprinted in 1950.

4. Some postwar commentators were more extreme in their estimates of the divorce rate, which exacerbated the panic regarding marriage. For example, in 1953 Montaigne said that three out of five couples divorced (87). The soaring divorce rate in the 1950s echoes a similar pattern in the 1920s. In *Great Expectations,* May notes that the rising divorce rate in the 1920s (a 2,000 percent increase) was accompanied by an increase in the number of marriages, and reflected the increasing expectation that marriage would provide personal fulfillment. "The marriage crisis was relegated to textbooks during the 1950s," Shumway explains, but became headline-grabbing in the 1970s, when the divorce rate of 50 percent threatened to make marriage a short-term arrangement, and resulted in an emphasis on psychoanalysis as a possible corrective (135).

5. Marriage preparation courses had been taught in colleges since the 1930s, but in the 1950s they also entered the high school curriculum (Celello 88). On experts in the postwar period, see May, *Homeward Bound,* 29–32. Also see Ball, who analyzes the relationship between the social sciences and the government that developed in the postwar period. Biskind suggests that postwar culture "valued experts, but experts who would join the team and play ball"; in other words, experts in line with the Cold War consensus (54).

6. One of these manuals, Bowman's *Marriage for Moderns,* was made into an educational film, *This Charming Couple* (1950, dir. Willard Van Dyke). The film dramatizes in a more blatant manner than Hollywood fare the importance of choosing the right mate.

7. Regular marriage columns include: "The Companion Marriage Clinic" in *Woman's Home Companion* beginning in the mid-1940s; "Making Marriage Work" in *Ladies' Home Journal* starting in December 1947; "Can This Marriage Be Saved?" also in *Ladies' Home Journal* beginning in January 1953; "Why Marriages Fail" in *McCall's* in 1953 and 1954; and "Marriage Is a Private Affair" in *McCall's* in the late 1950s (see Celello 92–93).

8. E. Duvall and Hill call choosing a mate out of love "folly" (42), and Christensen insists that ideas of "the 'soul-mate' and 'love at first sight'" are "immature" (224, 252).

9. For example, the article "How to Be Marriageable" tells women "it is to the advantage of society, as well as themselves, that they conquer . . . barriers [to getting married, such as being too picky] in order to live fully and happily and make their maximum contribution to our society" (46).

10. Other manuals with chapters on adjustment include Judson and Mary Landis's collection of essays entitled *Readings in Marriage and the Family*; Mudd's and Krich's collection of essays entitled *Man and Wife: A Source Book of Family Attitudes, Sexual Behavior and Marriage Counseling*; Butterfield's *Planning for Marriage*; Cavan's *American Marriage: A Way of Life*; Himes's *Your Marriage*; and Christensen's *Marriage Analysis: Foundations for Successful Family Life*. Many of these manuals include the "Schedule for the Prediction of Marriage Adjustment" developed by Ernest Burgess, Leonard Cottrell, Paul Wallin, and Harvey Locke; see both Himes and Christensen.

11. While *We're Not Married!* in some ways participates in the long tradition of what Cavell calls "the comedy of remarriage" (dating back to Cecil B. DeMille's comedies *Don't Change Your Husband* [1919] and *Why Change Your Wife?* [1920]), the film does not feature the isolation of the couples or the playfulness Cavell associates with these comedies. Rather than rekindling their romances, these couples jump through bureaucratic hoops to obtain legal rights. The couples in *We're Not Married!* frequently bicker, and the film's attitude toward marriage is often cynical.

12. The press called Monroe "Mrs. America" when she married DiMaggio in 1954 (Meyers 155). A character named "Mrs. America" (with no resemblance to Monroe) also dances in the 1953 burlesque film *Striporama*.

13. Postwar marital advisors stressed the importance of children to "successful" marriages: Christensen reminds his readers, "Many people consider reproduction as the central or primary purpose of marriage" (449, see also 438). See also Das 5.

14. See also Butterfield 63 and Adams 23.

15. *Niagara* resembles a number of films from the period with a dark perspective on marriage, including *Rear Window* (1954, dir. Alfred Hitchcock), and films noirs such as *The Postman Always Rings Twice* (1946, dir. Tay Garnett), *Strangers on a Train* (1951, dir. Alfred Hitchcock), or *99 River Street* (1953, dir. Phil Karlson).

16. Brégent-Heald cites *Niagara* as an example of the border noir. Although Silver and Ward include *Niagara* in their *Film Noir: An Encyclopedic Reference to the American Style*, critics generally suggest the noir style was waning by the time *Niagara* was made. Both Spicer and Tuska argue that the style peaked by 1952, and *Kiss Me Deadly* (1955, dir. Robert Aldrich) is generally cited as the last noir of this "classical" period. Although Naremore's *More Than Night* asserts that noirs are "stylistically heterogeneous" (168), critics agree on several aspects of the noir style. For catalogues of noir's stylistic elements, see Silver and Ward 3; Naremore *More Than Night* 167; Place and Peterson 68; and Spicer 4.

17. On the postwar masculinity crisis, see both Maltby and Krutnik. On femme fatales and domesticity, see Haskell; Grossman; Spicer; and Boozer.

18. See also both Dimendberg and Tuska. The relationship between marriage and noir films has been addressed by a number of scholars, including S. Harvey, whose article "Woman's Place: The Absent Family of Film Noir" has become the definitive statement on family in noir. See also Dyer ("Postscript") and Spicer for analyses that engage with Harvey. More recently, Gates has noted how the female detective often becomes a wife by the end of what she calls "maritorious melodramas," and Renzi has discussed the surprising similarities between noirs and screwball comedies. These analyses, however, do not situate the marriages in these films within their cultural context and therefore miss the nuances that differentiate these troubled marriages from one another (e.g., whether the marriages are doomed because of a nagging wife, rich in-laws, or a career woman).

19. See also *McCall's* eight-part series "Why Marriages Fail," which ended in November 1954.

20. Sheen was a well-known figure in postwar America. In 1952, he won an Emmy for "Outstanding Television Personality." His television show, *Life Is Worth Living*, claimed to be "sponsored by God," and had ratings nearly as high as *I Love Lucy's*. Sheen also published several books and hosted *The Catholic Hour* radio show from 1930 to 1952.

21. The relationship between romance and murder is also highlighted in a *Saturday Evening Post* cartoon reprinted in *Building a Successful Marriage*. The cartoon features two boys leaving a noir film with the caption: "I shut my eyes during the kissing scene and make believe he's choking her" (Landis and Landis 41).

22. Monroe was on a weekly salary and would earn around $10,500 for the film.

23. See also Levine 20 and Christensen 172.

24. For a secondary summary of this issue, see May 126.

25. Adams provides just one voice in the extensive chorus on female frigidity in the postwar period, a topic that will be explored in more detail in chapter 4.

26. Others also noted the period's changing sexual mores and their impact on marriage; see Butterfield, *Sexual Harmony*, and Kelly.

27. Although the Production Code limited explicit portrayal of sexually suggestive material—"excessive and lustful kissing, lustful embraces, suggestive postures and gestures are not to be shown" (Association 4)—and forbade "nudity in fact or in silhouette, or any licentious notice thereof by other characters in the pictures" (Association 5), Rose is obviously naked beneath the white sheet that covers her to mid-chest, and her nudity is later suggested in the shower. The Production Code was adopted in 1930 (but not enforced until 1934), in response to complaints about the morality of movies. It remained in effect until the ratings system was implemented in 1968, but its power had already begun eroding by 1953. See Doherty (*Hollywood's Censor* and *Pre-Code Hollywood*); Jacobs; and Leff and Simmons.

28. In the September 1951 version of the script, Rose's motivation is George's trust fund (16–17), and in the final shooting script, Rose's motivation is the $400 a month she could get from George's sheep ranch (47), but both motivations are omitted from the film.

29. Chapter 4 discusses sexual expectations for women in more detail.

30. The star personae of the two female stars further complicate the film's conflicted position on female sexuality. Outside of *Niagara*, Peters made a career of playing sexy or exotic women, including Zapata's (Marlon Brando) wife in *Viva Zapata* (1952, dir. Elia Kazan) and a female pirate captain in *Anne of the Indies* (1951, dir. Jacques Tourneur). Immediately after *Niagara*, Peters played a prostitute in *Pickup on South Street* (1953, dir. Samuel Fuller), a murderess in *A Blueprint for Murder* (1953, dir. Andrew Stone), and a hard-living supermodel in *Vicki* (1953, dir. Harry Horner). In addition, Peters was the longtime mistress and subsequent wife of Howard Hughes. Peters and Hughes met in 1947, at which time there were rumors of marriage, but the couple did not wed until 1957, after Peters had married and divorced another man. Peters's developing screen persona as a sultry woman colors Polly's role in that audiences would have suspected, just as George did, that there was a sexual woman beneath Polly's demure surface.

31. See also Kaplan's edited collection *Women in Film Noir*; Oliver and Trigo; and Wager.

32. For others criticizing Monroe's sex appeal at this time, see Moore; Paul; Egleston et al.; and letters to the editors of *Life* magazine on June 15, 1953.

33. The film updates Anita Loos's 1925 novel in a number of ways. Although the Broadway adaptation of the novella maintained the 1920s setting, the film placed the story in a contemporary setting. In the novella, men strive to educate Lorelei; in the film, Lorelei assumes the role of the marriage expert.

34. See Ellen Wright for background on Russell's sexpot persona; she underscores that Russell was more famous for the salacious publicity for *The Outlaw* (1943, dir. Howard Hughes), which emphasized her breasts, than she was for any film role (129).

35. See also Christensen 256, Butterfield 4, and Das 63.

36. Pullen discusses the "female friendship, camaraderie, and intimacy" between Monroe and Russell that is apparent in publicity shots taken, but not used, in *Life* magazine's photo spread on the making of the film (50).

37. Landis and Landis (75) and S. Duvall (21) explicitly warn against "gold digging."

38. See Arbuthnot and Seneca 116, and Barton 127.

39. Many critics have commented on the juxtaposition of Russell's large frame with Monroe's small one, noting that Dorothy "virtually never moves in the constrained fashion of the 'lady'; she strides, arms swinging at her sides, shoulders erect and head thrown back" (Arbuthnot and Seneca 117) and that she "look[s] like a butch partner for Lorelei" (Banner 201). See also Wood (171) and T. McCarthy (509), who comment on the weak men in the film.

40. Banner notes that these women "evoke Bettie Page, the innocent girl with black hair and white skin who starred in the day's underground sadomasochist films" (253).

41. "Diamonds Are a Girl's Best Friend" was written in 1949 by Jule Styne and Leo Robin for Carol Channing's performance in the Broadway production of *Gentlemen Prefer Blondes*, and thus represents the concerns of the postwar period (rather than the 1920s, when Loos wrote the original story).

42. The Breen office of the Production Code Administration deemed these two lines, along with some additional verses elaborating on situations where women should cautiously protect their finances, acceptable according to the Code; they were removed for some unknown reason. (By way of comparison, the Breen office rejected the lines "But if you are busty / Your trustee gets lusty" ["Diamonds"].)

43. See Rowe.

44. The film reflects competing versions of the period's Cinderella narrative. One narrative, made famous by Disney's *Cinderella* (1950, dirs. Geronimi and Jackson), suggests that good-hearted, hard-working women deserve to "marry up," as long as they do so for love, while the other, advanced adamantly by Wylie, suggests

that women use the fantasy of "true love" to disguise their motivations to marry for money. I have discussed this in more detail in Konkle, "How."

45. Most advice books included chapters on money's role in successful marriages; see, "Finances and Adjustment in Marriage" and "Getting Your Money's Worth" (Landis and Landis), and "Money Matters in Marriage" (E. Duvall and Hill), as well as Christensen 146–167, Cavan 329–351, S. Duvall 76–92, LeMasters 401–483, and Himes 193–259.

46. *Harper's Bazaar* represented a high-end consumer lifestyle, featuring garments such as a 1954 advertisement for a "Southwest African Persian Lamb Coat," which retailed for $997. Even lower-end fashions, such as "Cashmere twosomes by Heatherton," sold for between $27.95 and $49.95, somewhere between half or all of a middle-class weekly income.

47. For examples of the fashion show scene in postwar films, see *An American in Paris* (1951, dir. Vincente Minnelli), *Singin' in the Rain* (1952, dirs. Donen and Kelly), *Funny Face* (1957, dir. Stanley Donen), *Designing Woman* (1957, dir. Vincente Minnelli), and *That Touch of Mink* (1962, dir. Delbert Mann).

48. *Millionaire* was the second film released in Fox's new CinemaScope format. Although filmed after *Millionaire*, the biblical epic *The Robe* (1953, dir. Henry Koster) was the first film released in CinemaScope because the studio thought its content better suited the medium's first appearance—presumably because it was about three men in a biblical story, rather than three women in a domestic plot (Cohen 276). CinemaScope was the most successful of the 1950s technological innovations aimed at revitalizing a film industry endangered by the 1948 Paramount Decree and the increasing domination of television. For an overview of CinemaScope and other technological developments, see Lev 107–126 and Belton.

49. *Playboy* magazine conveyed a similar message to its male readers: they didn't have to be millionaires to acquire at least some of the items the magazine contained (including, presumably, the women). See Nadel's *Containment Culture* on sex, class, and *Playboy*.

50. Monroe's marriage films are, after all, also about perpetuating racial "whiteness": thus, the most desirable wife is the whitest—from skin to hair to costumes. See Dyer's *White* and Banner's "Creature from the Black Lagoon" for more on Monroe's whiteness.

51. Presumably, Zanuck's well-known distaste for Monroe made him imagine Bacall, as opposed to Monroe, stretched out on sofas in the film.

52. See also H. Johnson, "3-D." CinemaScope was sold as a form of 3-D. An ad for *Millionaire* appearing in December 1953's *Photoplay* calls the film as "big as life and just as fun" and notes, "you see it without glasses." In this ad, the women pop out of the screen to beckon the viewer, and Monroe is the biggest and

foremost of the three. Widescreen, however, was not universally discussed in terms of its appeal—many feared that the intimacy offered by the view could also threaten audiences. The *New York Herald Tribune* characterizes the feeling as like "being smothered in baked Alaska," a decadent but nonetheless suffocating experience (qtd. in Buskin 154). As Rogers puts it, "Widescreen, in short, offered moviegoers an experience portrayed as both empowering and overpowering, at once rendering the human body on a gigantic scale and threatening to smother it" (75).

53. In fact, the image of Monroe's legs stretched across the screen is often used to demonstrate the difference between the CinemaScope aspect ratio and its predecessors; see Belton 144.

54. *Playboy* magazine, the first issue of which would be published the month after *Millionaire*'s release, draws on the interest in looking at spreads of women and capitalizes on the excess associated with Monroe's persona by featuring her in its first centerfold.

55. Marilyn Monroe's mates, onscreen and off, were often "ordinary" men. In *Some Like It Hot*, in a parody of this trend, she says, "Men who wear glasses are so gentle, weak, and helpless," and thus preferable. See Mobilio for a discussion of this phenomenon in *The Seven Year Itch*.

56. Monroe's other two husbands did not escape that role. Just after Monroe and DiMaggio married, the Japanese press referred to Joe DiMaggio as "Mr. Marilyn Monroe" (Charyn 87). Similarly, during the making of *The Prince and the Showgirl*, just two weeks after her marriage to Arthur Miller, the British tabloids referred to Miller as "Mr. Monroe" and "Marilyn's Boy" (Meyers 160).

57. Even though Cherie in *Bus Stop* (1956, dir. Josh Logan) ends up engaged, she resists this engagement for most of the film.

CHAPTER 4 — "IT'S KINDA PERSONAL AND EMBARRASSING, TOO"

1. *Playboy*'s upscale audience rivaled that of the *New Yorker* and *U.S. News and World Report*. In chap. 5 of *Containment Culture*, Nadel elucidates how *Playboy* established itself as a sophisticated men's magazine.

2. Without commenting on the irony of the story about Monroe's nude poses that ran just after her death, a tribute to her in the November 1962 issue points out that "it was neither friend nor lover, but a doctor who wrapped her nude body in a blanket and carried it to the mortuary in the back seat of his station wagon" (Meltsir 78).

3. See, for example, "Did Yves Cause Marilyn's Collapse?"; Lyle; and Tracy.

4. Rosenthal summarizes the studies (written during the 1920s and 1930s) of Katharine Davis, Lewis Terman, Marie Kopp, G. V. Hamilton, Dr. Robert

Dickinson and Lura Beam, and Dorothy Dunbar Bromley and Florence Haxton Britten. Fritz Wittels's *The Sex Habits of American Women* (1951) and Christopher Gerould's *Sexual Practices of American Women* (1953) were Kinsey's more immediate predecessors. (Gerould entered his copyright September 11, 1953; Kinsey's findings appeared in the news on August 20, 1953 and the book was released on September 14, 1953.)

5. In *Sexual Behavior in the Human Male*, Kinsey reported that "about 6.3 per cent of the total number of [male] orgasms is derived from homosexual contacts" (610), but the more surprising statistic was "that at least 37 per cent of the male population has some homosexual experience between the beginning of adolescence and old age" (623). Kinsey's first report became a bestseller fifteen weeks after its publication; see "Behavior, after Kinsey."

6. According to Freedgood, nearly 100 publications sent journalists to Kinsey's retreats (22). The Catholic publication *America* reported "that 72 per cent of the evening papers and 77 per cent of the morning papers gave the story space ranging from a few paragraphs to multiple-column spreads" ("Kinsey" 30).

7. Similarly, I. Williams, in his 1957 *Playboy* article "The Pious Pornographers," argues that mid-1950s women's magazines were sex-obsessed; they exclusively focused on sexual problems rather than pleasures.

8. Articles by Rosenthal; Havemann; Davidson; and an article in *Newsweek* entitled "All about Eve," among others, summarize Kinsey's findings in similar ways.

9. Among authors praising Kinsey, see Hurst; Freeman; *Time*'s cover story on Kinsey: "5,940 Women"; and Ditzion. Even some of the writers who criticized Kinsey noted that "a great public service has been done in this report and in the one on male sexual behavior by tearing away the puritanical camouflage which has surrounded the problem of the place of sexuality in our society" (Simpson 66–67). Scheinfeld both praises and criticizes Kinsey in *Cosmopolitan*'s "What's Wrong with Sex Studies."

10. See Freedgood; Davidson and Mudd; A. Ellis's introduction to *Sex Life of the American Woman and the Kinsey Report*, and, from the same volume, essays by Wylie and Freeman, as well as psychologist Giedt's study of "Changes in Sexual Behavior and Attitudes Following Class Study of the Kinsey Report."

11. Others who criticized Kinsey for disregarding love include Cantril; Bergler and Kroger; and Montagu. On Kinsey's subjects as liars, see both Banning and Norris.

12. See, for example, Chapple's editorial in the *Ashland Press* and Sorokin's *The American Sex Revolution*. Reumann analyzes the relationship between American sexual character and communist subversion in detail.

13. Bliven also encourages Americans to compare their behavior to that of Kinsey's subjects in order to alleviate any guilt they might feel about disregarding publicly professed sexual morals. Melody and Peterson reflect on the pivotal role printed discussions of sex played in forming private morals.

14. Other writers also associated Kinsey's work with the feminist movement; see, for example, both Batdorff and Groves.

15. Others who wrote about the eroding double standard include Batdorff; Freedgood; Freeman; and Wylie. For similar findings that women's sexual behaviors were becoming "looser," see articles by Bender and Widdener released prior to Kinsey's report.

16. For other assessments from the social sciences of the nation's sexual standards, see Christensen; McPartland; Wittels; and Gerould.

17. For Monroe as a fantasy sexual partner, see Kidd; Banning also aligns Kinsey with erotic B movies.

18. Others criticizing Monroe's sex appeal include Egelston et al. Moore; Paul; Scannell, "Letters: Bosomy Babes"; and letters to the editors of *Life* magazine on June 15, 1953, March 22, 1954, and January 19, 1959.

19. See, for example, "Did Yves Cause Marilyn's Collapse?"; and Lyle.

20. *Photoplay* explains Monroe's success in *How to Marry a Millionaire* (1953, dir. Jean Negulesco): she "combined sex and saucy comedy to entertain both masculine and feminine moviegoers" ("Announcing" 21).

21. Brubaker studied 18,000 subjects; Kinsey reported statistics on 5,940 women in his second report.

22. Kinsey's team found that 26 percent of women committed adultery by age forty, most doing so in their mid-thirties (416).

23. The film's reference to Richard's "animal" magnetism may provide another hint that the film mocks the response to Kinsey, who was accused of treating human sexual behavior as if it were animal behavior. For example, Bergler and Kroger write that Kinsey's "most dangerous fallacy is the confirmation of the postulate that the 'human animal' (Kinsey's favorite term) is a machine-like figure who discharges sex *without* the element of tender love. This is exactly the attitude of the neurotic man, who views woman merely as an instrument of coitus; it is exactly the attitude normal women justifiably complain about" (185).

24. See Cohan for a connection of these phenomena to "the burden of breadwinning" (64).

25. A number of critics have suggested that The Girl is a nonentity; Bolton, following Babington and Evans, suggests that she might even be a figment of Richard's imagination (Bolton 97; Babington and Evans 229). My analysis will show how Monroe performs a woman troubled by the double standard but torn between

the benefits of having sex appeal and the drawbacks of being thought of as a walking sexual fantasy. See also "The Seven Year Itch" in *Weekly Variety*; Armstrong; Barton; Harvey; Jon Lewis; Mobilio; Piercy; and Sinyard and Turner. In the film *Insignificance* (1985), Nicholas Roeg's fictional "Monroe" (Teresa Russell) states that The Girl is "a figment of this guy's imagination."

26. While the joke at the time would have been that Fisher, a pop singer not a classical musician, illustrated the age and taste gap between Richard and The Girl, the allusion perhaps becomes ironic after Fisher's marriage to Debbie Reynolds ended because of his scandalous affair with Elizabeth Taylor.

27. See chap. 5 of Nadel's *Containment Culture* on brinkmanship.

28. See also Norris; Reiss; and Morse.

29. See also Hitschmann and Bergler; C. Lewis; and Cryle and Moore. Kroger and Freed argue that "in many cases, frigidity 'represent[ed] the natural behavior of the highly moral and cultured woman [. . . for] it is the direct characteristic of the respectable woman not to feel sexual pleasure but to reject everything sexual as indecent or at best to submit but passively to the male'" (526).

30. Established in 1930 (but not fully effective until 1934), the Production Code Administration strove to uphold public morals while avoiding censorship from outside the industry. To ensure that their films would receive a seal of approval, filmmakers followed Production Code provisions on the treatment of crime, sex, language, costuming, religion, and "national feeling," among other topics. However, screenwriters and censors upheld the letter of the Code but often skirted its spirit. See, for example, Weinberger. Until 1953, films without the seal were not exhibited in major theaters. For discussions of the Production Code, see Jacobs; Doherty; and Leff and Simmons.

31. See also both Winton and Phillips.

32. The material cut from the film because of censorship adds little in the way of scandal. Two scenes—one where the plumber reaches into The Girl's bathwater to retrieve a wrench he has dropped, and one in which The Girl says, "I feel sorry for you men in your hot pants"—were cut. Breen negotiated for only two shots, not three, of The Girl's skirt blowing in the subway breeze, and advised producer Frank McCarthy to eliminate reference to glands, and to cut away before MacKenzie rolls over onto Helen in Richard's hayride fantasy (F. McCarthy).

33. Breen wrote to producer McCarthy: "We would like to suggest you substitute something less pointed than the line by the girl, 'I was nude'. Perhaps you might consider using something to the effect of 'I didn't have too much on'. This is important in view of Richard's later reaction (page 42) to the girl's picture. As presently described, it is an unacceptable reaction to nudity, but, if the element of nudity were removed, we think it would be acceptable" (Breen).

34. J. Johnson argues that "the play is democratic, its sexuality equally distributed among all the characters, while the film goes out of its way to neutralize everyone but Monroe, all the overt sexuality safely wrapped up in her image" (74). Johnson insists that the film therefore cannot send the same message of gender reversal "that makes the stage version more subversive, relevant and powerful" (74), but, as I argue, Monroe's sexpot persona also makes Cherie subversive.

35. For reviews praising Monroe's acting in this film, see Crowther's "The Screen" and "The Proof of Marilyn."

36. That *Bus Stop* received the Production Code Administration seal of approval reveals both the waning influence of the body and that the film's producers thought the audience would accept the sexually charged material. *Bus Stop* was one of the first films Shurlock censored, and many of his suggestions were ignored. For example, while Shurlock argued that "Bo's line '. . . I wanta be in bed by ten o'clock' together with Cherie's reaction to it is unacceptably sex-suggestive," both remained in the film. The filmmakers also ignored the suggestion to "substitute some expression other than '. . . to practice on . . .' in Virge's dialogue with Bo," and, while Shurlock insisted that "the line 'Ya tryin' a tell me he never—' appears to have an unacceptable suggestive flavor," this line also remains in the film. Thus, it is evident that Virge intends for Bo to have a sexual interlude, and that Cherie expects him to treat her as just a sexual interlude.

37. Kinsey explains, "The slower responses of the female in coitus appear to depend in part upon the fact that she frequently does not begin to respond as promptly as the male, because psychologic stimuli usually play a more important role in the arousal of the average male, and a less important role in the sexual arousal of the average female." She is also "more easily distracted" and then has to start over (Kinsey et al. 627). See also both Kelly and Butterfield.

38. For other analyses of Kinsey's reports that allude to the 1920s, see Ditzion; Havemann; and Hurst. See also Reumann.

39. More than the flapper style, Sugar's costumes call to mind pre-Code costuming (or lack thereof). In *King Kong* (1933, dirs. Merian Cooper and Ernest Schoedsack), for example, Fay Wray wore a sheer blouse, and *Tarzan and His Mate* (1934, dir. Cedric Gibbons) featured an extended nude-swimming scene.

40. For critical interpretations of the film's androgyny and homosexuality, see Cohan; Bell-Metereau; Garber; and Lieberfeld. Sikov points out that the film ends with "two hidden penises" in the same relationship, but also laments that "theirs is a love that dare not speak its name" (146).

41. Several biographers have speculated that Monroe might have been homosexual or bisexual. Her first dramatic coach, Natasha Lytess, claims to have had a relationship with Monroe, and Monroe supposedly admitted to liaisons with

Marlene Dietrich and Joan Crawford. See Banner's biography and Jerris's less reputable *Marilyn Monroe: My Little Secret.*

42. According to the *New York Daily News*, Jorgensen's story was more popular than that of the infamous alleged spies Julius and Ethel Rosenberg, executed in June 1953 (Meyerowitz 66). In addition to several *New York Daily News* stories, Jorgensen's story formed the basis of a five-part *American Weekly* series in February and March 1953, and appeared in at least twenty other magazines during the 1950s. See www.christenejorgensen.org for many of these articles. See also Meyerowitz.

43. Butler draws on the 1929 work of psychoanalyst Joan Riviere in "Womanliness as Masquerade." Film theorist Mary Ann Doane uses Riviere's theory of the "masquerade" to theorize female spectatorship as structured, like a masquerade, by distance from the female body on screen in "Film and the Masquerade" and "Masquerade Reconsidered."

44. Of course, Wilder also includes shots of Sugar's behind that follow the conventions of what Mulvey has termed "the male gaze," but he underscores how conventional these shots are when he uses them for Jerry and Daphne or delays using them for Monroe.

45. For a year, Wilder wrote about fashion and beauty tips as a woman named Billie for the Berlin newspaper *Tempo*. He brought Billie's drag confidante Barbette in from Germany to train Curtis and Lemmon (Gemünden 116).

46. For other commentary on how cross-dressing transforms the characters' identities, see Armstrong; Bell-Metereau; Dick; Cardullo; French; Garber; Gemünden; Grindon; and Sikov.

47. See also Lundberg and Farnham; M. Robinson; Kroger and Freed (cited in C. Lewis); Bergler and Kroger.

48. See also Meyer; Frank; M. Robinson; Cohan; and Reumann.

49. A similar dress design, using what designer Orry-Kelly called "nude soufflé," appears in both the seduction scene and the film's final scene. The dress was sensational: "Moviegoers, mesmerized by the sensuous swaying of her close-to-nude breasts during the song, had a surprise coming. When she finished the number and turned her back to the camera, the dress turned out to be backless— down to M.M.'s tailbone. The effect elicited gasps from audiences" (Nickens and Zeno 113).

50. This message is reinforced in the crosscut scenes of Daphne leading Osgood on the dance floor, which suggest that Junior isn't the only man who likes his woman assertive—Daphne secures a proposal from a millionaire by taking charge, just as Sugar hopes to do. Sinyard and Turner, and French, also comment on the male passivity in this scene.

CHAPTER 5 — THE ACTRESS AND HER METHOD

1. Even Twentieth Century-Fox executives, including Darryl Zanuck, recognized that *River* was a weak film. A memorandum on the script dictated by Zanuck noted: "It will come alive only if two hot personalities like Mitchum and Monroe meet head on—then you will have fireworks but otherwise it will lay an egg in spite of the suspense, excitement and scenery" (Memorandum).

2. *Photoplay* reported on her refusal to report to work on *Pink Tights* because the studio "hadn't consulted her on the script" (York 40).

3. Monroe had to appear in *Business* to be cast in *The Seven Year Itch* (1955, dir. Billy Wilder) and, because she wanted to work with Billy Wilder, she took the part.

4. Jack Cole choreographed the numbers for both films, so their similarities are not surprising.

5. See, for example, "The Dostoevsky Blues": "Marilyn already has a strong ally in fun-loving Director Billy (*Sabrina*) Wilder, who insists that he would like to see Marilyn play in *The Brothers Karamazov*. After that, he grinned, he would be delighted to direct her in such Hollywoodish sequels as *Seven Brides for the Brothers Karamazov, All the Brothers Were Karamazovs, The Brothers Karamazov Join the WACs*, and, of course, *The Brothers Karamazov Meet Abbott & Costello*" (75).

6. In the 1952 story "Temptations of a Bachelor Girl," "Monroe" states that she works from six A.M. to seven P.M. at the studio, then comes home and learns her lines (44). Similarly, the fictional "Cal York" writes in a 1952 *Photoplay* gossip column that Monroe was diligently studying acting (32), and in 1954 a *Movieland* writer praises Monroe's ambition and ability to get others to help her improve ("Too" 60).

7. The workings of viewer identification are not simple. While, according to apparatus theory, the film directs viewers to identify with the goals and desires of the protagonist, later theorists have advanced a more complicated picture of audience identification. Cowie's *Representing the Woman* proposes that the act of watching a film is an act of shifting identifications driven by fantasy (71, 114). Thus the viewer at alternating moments may identify with minor characters, with the antagonists, and with stars.

8. This criticism seems to dog Method actors in particular, such as Shelley Winters, Al Pacino, and Robert De Niro, "who consistently construct character from their own unique expressive mannerisms, [and thereby] 'act themselves' in a variety of roles" (Counsell 58).

9. Monroe tried to take control of her own career first in April 1954, the same month she earned a top performer award from *Photoplay*.

10. Monroe was not the first actress to walk out on the studio for more money and more control over her film roles. Greta Garbo had done so in 1926 (Schatz 42–43), and Bette Davis held out for nearly a year before getting Warner Bros. to concede to her demands in 1937 (Schatz 218–220). Davis also worked to earn her own corporation from Warner Bros. in 1943 (Schatz 318). However, part of these women's star persona was their tough-minded careerism—unlike Monroe, they were not considered naive and vulnerable.

11. See also Kouvaros; Conroy; and Wexman for discussions of how the Method dramatizes the split between inner life and outer persona, which often constitutes much of the drama in Method performances.

12. Strasberg discusses the misunderstandings of his use of emotional memory in his *A Dream of Passion*; see 113, 122. His daughter, Susan, also discusses this theory in her memoir (85) and credits him with trying to clarify affective memory for Monroe by saying, "Yes, we want your feelings and sensitivity but we want you to be able to arouse them from the things you consciously give to your imagination, not to what is unconsciously elicited" (S. Strasberg 137).

13. Strong studies of film acting exist, of course, including Naremore's *Acting in the Cinema*, Wexman's *Creating the Couple: Love, Marriage, and Hollywood Performance*, and Hollinger's *The Actress: Hollywood Acting and the Female Star*. A number of anthologies also address film acting, including Lovell and Kramer's collection *Screen Acting*, Wojcik's *Movie Acting: The Film Reader*, and Taylor's *Theorizing Film Acting*.

14. Reviewer Crowther describes her in much the same way: "She doesn't have to act in a picture, she just has to wiggle, bat her eyes, twist her mouth in those oval contortions and speak vapidly in that tooth-paste voice" ("Look" X1).

15. Olivier, it seems, was more committed to a British style of acting than many others of the period; Rollyson points out that many of Olivier's contemporaries, including Michael Redgrave and Paul Scofield, had used Stanislavskian methods in the 1950s (*Marilyn* 129).

16. Hirsch (328) has pointed out that this scene demonstrates how Monroe created character without dialogue, drawing on her Method training.

17. Rollyson reminds us of another context for this remark: Monroe "represented a certain kind of American sensitivity to the individual which, in its extreme form, provokes Elsie to worry about the fate of an imprisoned politician, Wolffstein—just as Monroe pestered Miller and Rosten to offer Indonesian prime minister Sukarno refuge when she learned that he was in danger of being deposed" (*Marilyn* 130).

18. See Savran for more on Miller's House Committee on Un-American Activities appearances and political work.

19. Near the end of the film, Amanda will also speak to the need to recognize the difference between actor and character, telling of an actor who got so into playing Abraham Lincoln that "he looks like Lincoln, he talks like Lincoln, but he won't be satisfied until he gets *shot!*"

20. Audiences have any number of biographical details they could draw on here—Monroe's relationship with her mother, her suicide attempts, her nude photos, not to mention, if audiences were *Confidential* readers, potential affairs with Frank Sinatra and Montand.

21. Reviewers were divided: despite not being very good, according to Stanley Kaufmann, the film "makes Miss Monroe pleasantly available to her fans" ("Stars" 20). The *Time* reviewer, on the other hand, notes that "there is a lot of Marilyn to admire these days, but it is still in fine fettle" and "the comic counterpoint of fleshy grandeur and early Shirley Temple manner is better than ever," reading Monroe's performance as the highlight of the film ("New" 88).

22. *The Misfits* also asks Clift and Gable to play themselves. Gable notoriously lived with women outside of marriage (he was featured in a 1939 *Photoplay* article on "Hollywood's Unmarried Husbands and Wives," though the article's intent was to help him secure a divorce so he could marry Carole Lombard [Baskette]). *The Misfits* echoes this scenario when Gay and Roslyn unapologetically live together outside of marriage. Clift's 1956 car accident, alternately read as a genuine accident and an attempt at self-destruction, and the way it marred Clift's face, led viewers "to read [his performances] for signs of physical and mental suffering" (Lawrence 180). His role in *The Misfits* alludes to his accident: in his first scene in the film, he says, in a phone conversation with his ma, "My face is fine, it's all healed up." This line prompts viewers to read the rest of his performance—as a self-destructive, withdrawn, drunken cowboy—as Clift playing himself.

23. Reviews were generally negative, calling *The Misfits* a "rambling, banal [film], loaded with logy profundities" ("New" 68), "a dramatic failure" (Angell 87), and "a complex maze of introspective conflicts, symbolic parallels and motivational contradictions, the nuances of which may seriously confound general audiences" ("Film Review" 3). Others criticized the film's psychoanalytic undertones. Croce wrote in the British journal *Sight and Sound* that the film was for "a graying mass of nailbiters to whom words like 'personal adjustment,' 'conformism,' and 'communication' sum up the entire burden the human conscience has to bear in mid-century America" (142), and Bellow used the film to illustrate the overly psychological tone of the period's movies.

24. Paula Strasberg, Monroe's dramatic coach, remarked to James Goode, who was writing *The Making of the Misfits* and was present throughout the

production, "It's much more difficult to play yourself than someone you've never met. . . . It was essential [for Strasberg to coach her] because so much of it was close to her" (qtd. in Goode 259). Miller admitted, "Roslyn's dilemma was [Monroe's], but in the story it was resolved" (*Timebends* 466). Miller says he wrote himself into Gable's character (*Timebends* 473).

25. Today's critics are also conflicted regarding Monroe's role. Leaming argues that Monroe played Roslyn with "the terror of a woman hunted by various men," emphasizing Monroe the victim (366). Banner, on the other hand, refers to Roslyn as "a pantheistic force of nature, never more radiant, never more wise," emphasizing Monroe the goddess (355). In addition, Goldstein recognizes in Roslyn a staunch antiwar figure predating the Vietnam era and a critic of genocide, and notes, "That Roslyn can embody such a range of moral imperatives—not, admittedly, without straining dramatic credibility—speaks well for the relevance of *The Misfits* in a feminist era" (118). Goldstein overstates Roslyn's response to Vietnam, which is loosely metaphorical, but significantly claims Roslyn is a feminist heroine within this context.

26. See Bailey's chapter on *The Misfits* for an extended reading of how the film was conceived of as Monroe "playing herself."

27. Just after meeting her, Gay tells her, "I think you're the saddest girl I ever met," calling attention to the questions circulating in the press regarding whether Monroe was the happy person she appeared to be onscreen or infinitely sad. In his autobiography, Miller writes about this period: "I knew by this time that I had initially expected what she satirized as 'the happy girl that all men loved' and had discovered someone diametrically opposite, a troubled woman whose desperation was deepening no matter where she turned for a way out" (*Timebends* 466). Roslyn calls attention to the disparity between Gay's assessment of her and that of others, remarking, "I'm usually told how happy I am." Gay replies, "That's because you make a man feel happy."

28. Churchwell traces how the press represented Monroe and her brand of sex appeal as "natural," beginning with the earliest fan magazine stories and the *Playboy* centerfold story. Thus, *The Misfits*, by aligning Roslyn with nature, subverts this convention of describing her as a sex symbol, making her alignment with nature threatening to the extent that it makes her unavailable to men; see also Goldstein 116–117.

29. This is another aspect of Roslyn's character that resembles Monroe. See, in particular, McCann; Rollyson's *Marilyn*; and Bigsby. See also A. McIntyre's story on the production, in which she notes that Monroe "becomes at once the symbol of impartial and eternal availability, who yet remains simultaneously forever pure—and a potentially terrible goddess whose instincts could also deal death and

whose smile, when she directs it clearly at you, is exquisitely, heart-breakingly sweet" (74).

30. In the 1957 draft, when Roslyn offers Guido money for the horses, and he tells her, "Everything has to die," she says, "That's not the same as being destroyed, is it? Is it the same?" (144). She aligns herself with "the thing that get's [*sic*] eaten" and insists, "It can't be that way. We're human, we're supposed to understand . . ." (Miller, *The Misfits* 1957, 145). Roslyn's eloquent pleas for sympathy are absent in the final version, making her calling the men "murderers" near the film's climax seem less rational.

31. See also Coetzee 66.

32. Monroe had a reputation for forgetting lines in many of her films—most famously, perhaps, when she struggled with the line "It's me, Sugar" when filming *Some Like It Hot* (1959, dir. Billy Wilder).

33. Robert Lewis, a critic of Strasberg's approach to the Method who, in the spring and summer of 1957, gave lectures on how it could be used to reconnect to the play's text, rather than the actor's psyche, insisted that "the 'I-don't-feel-it-that-way' problem" should be solved by finding a justification "to use his technique to do what is required of him and not allow his technique to prevent him from doing it" (R. Lewis 79).

Although her acting was criticized throughout her career, Monroe's face tells the story in so many scenes in *The Misfits* that her acting skill is evident. However, when critics complimented her acting, they undermined her appearance: "Miss Monroe has seldom looked worse; the camera is unfailingly unflattering. But there is a delicacy about her playing, and a tenderness that is affecting" ("'The Misfits' Provocative" 3). The title of Dick Williams's review sums up what he noticed about Monroe's performance: "Marilyn Still Needs a Good Girdle."

CHAPTER 6 — CONCLUSION

1. Axelrod's 1950 theatrical version of *The Seven Year Itch* was not based on Monroe's persona, but critics have frequently remarked that the character of The Girl in Wilder's 1955 film adaptation of the play is clearly based on Monroe—The Girl has modeled nude, and very obviously fulfills the role of sexual fantasy in the film. In contrast, the character of Rita Marlowe is clearly based on Monroe, and is the only consistent feature between the stage and screen versions of *Will Success Spoil Rock Hunter?*

2. *Time* quoted Monroe as saying, "Sex is a part of nature, and I'll go along with nature" ("To Aristophanes" 80).

3. See "To Aristophanes." That these suicide attempts were common knowledge becomes clear upon reading the 1962 profiles by Levy, written before Monroe's death, and Meltsir, written after her death.

4. This perception of Monroe becomes clearest in fan letters, including those by Darone; Tompkins; and Adler. (These letters are discussed in more detail in chapter 2.)

5. De Vito and Tropea write about how Monroe has been represented in novels, films, and plays since the 1950s in their *The Immortal Marilyn*. Essays in Block's edited collection *Fan Phenomena: Marilyn Monroe* attest to Monroe's continual cultural recirculation—on YouTube (in both music video tributes and fan impersonations) as well as in more official re-creations such as NBC's *Smash* (2012–2013) or the film *My Week with Marilyn* (2011, dir. Simon Curtis).

WORKS CITED

"5,940 Women." *Time*, Aug. 24, 1953: 51–54, 56, 58.

Abel, Michael. Report to Darryl Zanuck on story of *How to Marry a Millionaire*, Oct. 23, 1952. Box 4, Folder 3. Twentieth Century-Fox Collection, Cinematic Arts Library, University of Southern California, Los Angeles, CA.

Adams, Clifford. *Preparing for Marriage*. New York: E. P. Dutton, 1951.

Adler, Gloria. "Letters: Marilyn Monroe." *Life*, Aug. 28, 1964: 21.

Affron, Charles. *Star Acting: Gish, Garbo, Davis*. New York: Dutton, 1977.

Alberoni, Francesco. "The Powerless 'Elite': Theory and Sociological Research on the Phenomenon of the Stars." In *Sociology of Mass Communication*, ed. Denis McQuail, 75–98. Baltimore, MD: Penguin, 1972.

"All about Eve: Kinsey Reports on American Women." *Newsweek*, Aug. 24, 1953: 68, 70, 71.

Alpert, Hollis. "Sexual Behavior in the American Movies." *Saturday Review* 39 (1956): 9–10, 38.

"Also Showing." *Time*, Feb. 9, 1953.

Andrews, David, and Christine Andrews. "Film Studies and the Biocultural Turn." *Philosophy and Literature* 36.1 (Apr. 2012): 58–78.

Angell, Roger. "Misfire." *New Yorker*, Feb. 4, 1961: 87–88.

"Announcing This Year's Photoplay Gold Medal Award Winners." *Photoplay*, Apr. 1954: 20–21.

Arbuthnot, Lucie, and Gail Seneca. "Pre-Text and Text in *Gentlemen Prefer Blondes*." In *Issues in Feminist Film Criticism*, ed. Patricia Erens, 112–125. Bloomington: Indiana University Press, 1990.

Armstrong, Richard. *Billy Wilder, American Film Realist*. Jefferson, NC: McFarland, 2000.

Arnold, Eve. *Marilyn Monroe: An Appreciation.* New York: Alfred A. Knopf, 1987.

Ashley, James. *The Silver Age of Hollywood Movies, 1953–1963, Vol. 1: Marilyn Monroe.* N.p., 2015. Kindle.

Association of Motion Picture Producers. "Hollywood Production Code." Rev. Dec. 11, 1956. Jack Hirshberg Papers, Censorship, Margaret Herrick Library, Academy of Motion Picture Arts and Sciences, Los Angeles, CA.

A. W. "Niagara Falls Vies with Marilyn Monroe." *New York Times,* Jan. 22, 1953: 20.

Axelrod, George. *The Seven Year Itch.* New York: Random House, 1953.

Babington, Bruce. *British Stars and Stardom: From Alma Taylor to Sean Connery.* New York: Manchester University Press, 2001.

Babington, Bruce, and Peter Evans. *Affairs to Remember: The Hollywood Comedy of the Sexes.* Manchester: Manchester University Press, 1989.

Badman, Keith. *Marilyn Monroe: The Final Years.* New York: St. Martin's Press, 2010.

Bailey, Peter. "Misfittings: *The Misfits* as Marilyn Monroe's Spiritual Autobiography." In *Star Bodies and the Erotics of Suffering,* ed. Rebecca Bell-Metereau and Colleen Glenn, 193–219. Detroit, MI: Wayne State University Press, 2015.

Balázs, Béla. *Theory of the Film—Character and Growth of a New Art.* Trans. Edith Bone. New York: Dover, 1970.

Ball, Terence. "The Politics of Social Science in Postwar America." In *Recasting America: Culture and Politics in the Age of Cold War,* ed. Lary May, 76–92. Chicago: University of Chicago Press, 1989.

Banita, Georgiana. "Re-Visioning the Western: Landscape and Gender in *The Misfits.*" In *John Huston: Essays on a Restless Director,* ed. Tony Tracy and Roddy Flynn, 94–110. Jefferson, NC: McFarland, 2010.

Banner, Lois. "The Creature from the Black Lagoon: Marilyn Monroe and Whiteness." *Cinema Journal* 47.4 (Summer 2008): 4–29.

———. *Marilyn: The Passion and the Paradox.* New York: Bloomsbury, 2012.

———. *MM—Personal: From the Private Archive of Marilyn Monroe.* New York: Abrams, 2011.

Banning, Margaret Culkin. "What Women Won't Tell Dr. Kinsey." *Cosmopolitan* 131 (Sept. 1951): 44–45, 108, 110.

Barbas, Samantha. *Movie Crazy: Fans, Stars, and The Cult of Celebrity.* New York: Palgrave Macmillan, 2001.

Barley, Rex. "DiMaggio Sad Boy at Series." *Daily Mirror,* Oct. 4, 1954: 1, 9.

Baron, Cynthia. "Crafting Film Performances: Acting in the Hollywood Studio Era." In *Screen Acting,* ed. Alan Lovell and Peter Krämer, 31–45. London: Routledge, 1999.

Baron, Cynthia, and Sharon Marie Carnicke. *Reframing Screen Performance*. Ann Arbor: University of Michigan Press, 2008.

Barris, George. *Marilyn: Her Life in Her Own Words*. New York: Birch Lane Press, 1995.

Barthes, Roland. *Mythologies*. Trans. Annette Lavers. New York: Hill and Wang, 1972.

Barton, Ruth. "Rocket Scientist! The Posthumous Celebrity of Hedy Lamarr." In *In the Limelight and under the Microscope: Forms and Functions of Female Celebrity*, ed. Su Holmes and Diane Negra, 82–102. New York: Continuum, 2011.

Barton, Sabrina. "Face Value." In *All the Available Light: A Marilyn Monroe Reader*, ed. Yona Zeldis McDonough, 120–141. New York: Simon and Schuster, 2002.

Basinger, Jeanine. *The Star Machine*. New York: Alfred A. Knopf, 2007.

———. *A Woman's View: How Hollywood Spoke to Women, 1930–1960*. Hanover, NH: Wesleyan University Press, 1993.

Baskette, Kirtley. "Hollywood's Unmarried Husbands and Wives." *Photoplay*, Jan. 1939: 22–23, 74.

Batdorff, Virginia Roller. "American Women vs. the Kinsey Report." *American Mercury* 77 (Aug. 1953): 121–124.

Baty, S. Paige. *American Monroe: The Making of a Body Politic*. Berkeley: University of California Press, 1995.

"Behavior, after Kinsey." *Time*, Apr. 12, 1948: 79–80.

Bell-Metereau, Rebecca. *Hollywood Androgyny*. 2nd ed. New York: Columbia University Press, 1993.

Bellow, Saul. "The Mass-Produced Insight." *Horizon*, Jan. 1963: 111–113.

Belton, John. *Widescreen Cinema*. Boston, MA: Harvard University Press, 1992.

Bender, James, "How Much Women Change—and How Little." *Reader's Digest*, July 1947: 127–128.

Benzel, Kathryn. "The Body as Art: Still Photographs of Marilyn Monroe." *Journal of Popular Culture* 25.2 (1991): 1–29.

Bergler, Edmund. *Neurotic Counterfeit-Sex: Impotence, Frigidity, "Mechanical" and Pseudosexuality, Homosexuality*. New York: Grune and Stratton, 1951.

Bergler, Edmund, and William Kroger, *Kinsey's Myth of Female Sexuality: The Medical Facts*. New York: Grune and Stratton, 1954.

Bergquist, Laura. "Check Your Sex Life against the New Kinsey Report." *Pageant*, Oct. 1953: 16–25.

Berlant, Lauren. "Intimacy: A Special Issue." In *Intimacy*, ed. Lauren Berlant, 1–8. Chicago: University of Chicago Press, 2000.

Betsky, Aaron. "The Enigma of the *Thigh Cho*: Icons as Magnets of Meaning." In *Icons: Magnets of Meaning*, ed. Aaron Betsky, 20–51. San Francisco: Chronicle, 1997.

Bigsby, Christopher. *Arthur Miller: A Critical Study*. Cambridge: Cambridge University Press, 2005.

Biltereyst, Daniel. "Censorship, Negotiation and Transgressive Cinema: *Double Indemnity*, *Some Like It Hot* and Other Controversial Movies in the United States and Europe." In *Billy Wilder, Movie-Maker: Critical Essays on the Films*, ed. Karen McNally, 145–158. Jefferson, NC: McFarland, 2011.

Biskind, Peter. *Seeing Is Believing: How Hollywood Taught Us to Stop Worrying and Love the Fifties*. New York: Pantheon, 1983.

Blaine, Diana York. "'We Are Going to See the King': Christianity and Celebrity at Michael Jackson's Memorial." In *Michael Jackson: Grasping the Spectacle*, ed. Christopher Smit, 191–206. Farnham, UK: Ashgate, 2012.

Bliven, Bruce. "Hullabaloo on K-Day." *New Republic* 129 (Nov. 9, 1953): 17–18.

Block, Marcelline. *Fan Phenomena: Marilyn Monroe*. Bristol: Intellect, 2015.

Bode, Lisa. "The Afterlives of Rudolph Valentino and Wallace Reid in the 1920s and 1930s." In *Lasting Screen Stars: Images that Fade and Personas that Endure*, ed. Lucy Bolton and Julie Lobalzo Wright, 159–171. London: Palgrave Macmillan, 2016.

Bolton, Lucy. *Film and Female Consciousness: Irigaray, Cinema and Thinking Women*. New York: Palgrave Macmillan, 2011.

"Bombs, H and K: Newspapers' Attitude toward the Kinsey Report." *Newsweek*, Aug. 31, 1953: 57.

Bongard, David. "Don't Bother to Knock." *LA Daily News*. Core Collection Files, *Don't Bother to Knock*, Margaret Herrick Library, Academy of Motion Picture Arts and Sciences, Los Angeles, CA.

Boozer, Jack. "The Lethal Femme Fatale in the Noir Tradition." *Journal of Film and Video* 51.3–4 (1999/2000): 20–35.

Borde, Raymond, and Étienne Chaumeton. "Towards a Definition of *Film Noir*." In *Film Noir Reader*, ed. Alain Silver and James Ursini, 17–26. New York: Proscenium, 2001.

Bowman, Henry. *Marriage for Moderns*. 2nd ed. New York: McGraw-Hill, 1948.

Brackett, Charles. *Niagara* final shooting script, May 15, 1952. Charles Brackett Papers, *Niagara*, Box 4, Folder 29, Margaret Herrick Library, Academy of Motion Picture Arts and Sciences, Los Angeles, CA.

———. *Niagara* treatment, Sept. 6, 1951. Charles Brackett Papers, *Niagara*, Box 4, Folder 27, Margaret Herrick Library, Academy of Motion Picture Arts and Sciences, Los Angeles, CA.

Brackett, Charles, Walter Reisch, and Richard Breen. *Niagara* script, Sept. 14, 1951. Charles Brackett Papers, *Niagara*, Box 4, Folder 28, Margaret Herrick Library, Academy of Motion Picture Arts and Sciences, Los Angeles, CA.

Brand, Harry. "Biography of Marilyn Monroe," 1956. Jack Hirshberg Papers, Box 5, Marilyn Monroe, Margaret Herrick Library, Academy of Motion Picture Arts and Sciences, Los Angeles, CA.

Braudy, Leo. "'No Body's Perfect': Method Acting and 50s Culture." *Michigan Quarterly Review* 35.1 (1996): 191–215.

Breen, Joseph. Letter to Frank McCarthy, Aug. 18, 1954, Motion Picture Association of America, Production Code Administration Records, Margaret Herrick Library, Academy of Motion Picture Arts and Sciences, Los Angeles, CA.

Brégent-Heald, Dominique. "Dark Limbo: *Film Noir* and the North American Borders." *Journal of American Culture* 29.2 (2006): 125–138.

Brown, Peter. *Kim Novak: Reluctant Goddess*. New York: St. Martin's Press, 1986.

Brown, Peter, and Patte Barham. *Marilyn: The Last Take*. New York: Mandarin, 1993.

Bruce, William. "Meet the New Marilyn Monroe." *Movieland* 12.11 (Nov. 1954): 44–45, 62–64.

Bulcroft, Kris, Linda Smeins, and Richard Bulcroft. *Romancing the Honeymoon: Consummating Marriage in Modern Society*. Thousand Oaks, CA: Sage, 1999.

Burgess, Ernest, and Harvey Locke. *The Family: From Institution to Companionship*. New York: American Book Company, 1945.

Burgess, Ernest, and Paul Wallin. *Engagement and Marriage*. Chicago: J. B. Lippinscott, 1953.

Burr, Ty. *Gods Like Us: On Movie Stardom and Modern Fame*. New York: Pantheon, 2012.

Buskin, Richard. *Blonde Heat: The Sizzling Screen Career of Marilyn Monroe*. New York: Billboard, 2001.

"'Bus Stop' Great Picture in Boxoffice and Artistry." *Hollywood Reporter*, Aug. 14, 1956: 3, 9. Core Collection Files, *Bus Stop*, Margaret Herrick Library, Academy of Motion Picture Arts and Sciences, Los Angeles, CA.

Buszek, Maria Elena. *Pin-Up Grrrls: Feminism, Sexuality, Popular Culture*. Durham, NC: Duke University Press, 2006.

Butler, Judith. *Gender Trouble: Feminism and the Subversion of Identity*. New York: Routledge, 1999.

Butterfield, Oliver. *Planning for Marriage*. Princeton, NJ: D. Van Nostrand, 1956.

———. *Sexual Harmony in Marriage*. New York: Emerson, 1953.

Byars, Jackie. "The Prime of Miss Kim Novak: Struggling Over the Feminine in the Star Image." In *The Other Fifties: Interrogating Midcentury American Icons*, ed. Joel Foreman, 197–223. Urbana: University of Illinois Press, 1997.

Cahn, Robert. "The 1951 Model Blonde." *Collier's*, Sept. 8, 1951: 15, 50–51.

"Can You Measure Love?" *Time*, May 17, 1954: 75.

Cantril, Hadley. "Sex without Love." *The Nation* 177 (Oct. 10, 1953): 294–296.

Capote, Truman. *Breakfast at Tiffany's*. New York: Vintage, 1995.

Cardullo, Bert. "Farce, Dreams, and Desire: *Some Like It Hot* Re-Viewed." *Cambridge Quarterly* 39.2 (2010): 142–151.

Carnicke, Sharon Marie. "Lee Strasberg's Paradox of the Actor." In *Screen Acting*, ed. Alan Lovell and Peter Krämer, 75–87. London: Routledge, 1999.

Carpozi, George, Jr. *Marilyn Monroe: "Her Own Story."* New York: Universal-Award House, 1973.

Carroll, Harrison. "'Some Like it Hot' Is Hilarious Farce for Marilyn, Tony, Jack." *Herald*, Apr. 9, 1959. Billy Wilder Papers, Margaret Herrick Library, Academy of Motion Picture Arts and Sciences, Los Angeles, CA.

Cavan, Ruth. *American Marriage: A Way of Life*. New York: Thomas Y. Crowell, 1959.

Celello, Kristin. *Making Marriage Work: A History of Marriage and Divorce in the Twentieth-Century United States*. Chapel Hill: University of North Carolina Press, 2009.

Chandler, Charlotte. *Nobody's Perfect: Billy Wilder, A Personal Biography*. New York: Simon and Schuster, 2002.

Chapple, John. "Editorial." *Ashland Press*, Mar. 16, 1949.

Charyn, Jerome. *Joe DiMaggio: The Long Vigil*. New Haven, CT: Yale University Press, 2011.

Christensen, Harold. *Marriage Analysis: Foundations for Successful Family Life*. 2nd ed. New York: Ronald Press, 1958.

Churchwell, Sarah. *The Many Lives of Marilyn Monroe*. New York: Picador, 2005.

Citrin, Mrs. Marion. "Letters: M.M." *Time*, May 28, 1956: 4.

Clark, Colin. *My Week with Marilyn*. New York: Weinstein, 2011.

———. *The Prince, the Showgirl, and Me*. New York: Weinstein, 2011.

Clark, Danae. *Negotiating Hollywood: The Cultural Politics of Actors' Labor*. Minneapolis: University of Minnesota Press, 1995.

Coetzee, J. M. "*The Misfits*." In *Writers at the Movies: Twenty-Six Contemporary Authors Celebrate Twenty-Six Memorable Movies*, ed. Jim Shepard, 63–67. New York: HarperCollins, 2000.

Cohan, Steven. "Cary Grant in the Fifties: Indiscretions of the Bachelor's Masquerade." *Screen* 33.4 (1992): 394–412.

———. *Masked Men: Masculinity and the Movies in the Fifties*. Bloomington: Indiana University Press, 1997.

Cohen, Lisa. "The Horizontal Walk: Marilyn Monroe, CinemaScope, and Sexuality." *Yale Journal of Criticism* 11.1 (1998): 259–288.

Cook, Pam. *Nicole Kidman*. Hampshire, UK: Palgrave Macmillan, 2012.

Coontz, Stephanie. *Marriage, a History: From Obedience to Intimacy or How Love Conquered Marriage*. New York: Viking, 2005.

Conroy, Marianne. "Acting Out: Method Acting, the National Culture, and the Middlebrow Disposition in Cold War America." *Criticism* 35.2 (1993): 239–263.

Conway, Michael, and Mark Ricci. *The Films of Marilyn Monroe*. New York: Cadillac, 1964.

Corber, Robert. *In the Name of National Security: Hitchcock, Homophobia, and the Political Construction of Gender in Postwar America*. Durham, NC: Duke University Press, 1993.

Corder, Ada. "Letters: Marilyn." *Time*, Aug. 17, 1962: 3.

Corwin, Jane. "Orphan in Ermine." *Photoplay*, Mar. 1954: 61, 106–109.

Coughlan, Robert. "Changing Roles in Modern Marriage." *Life*, Dec. 24, 1956: 108–114.

Counsell, Colin. *Signs of Performance: An Introduction to Twentieth-Century Theatre*. London: Routledge, 1996.

Cowie, Elizabeth. "*Film Noir* and Women." In *Shades of Noir: A Reader*, ed. Joan Copjec, 121–165. London: Verson, 1993.

———. *Representing the Woman: Cinema and Psychoanalysis*. Minneapolis: University of Minnesota Press, 1997.

Creadick, Anna. *Perfectly Average: The Pursuit of Normality in Postwar America*. Amherst: University of Massachusetts Press, 2010.

Crist, Steve, ed. *André de Dienes: Marilyn Monroe*. Cologne, Germany: Taschen, 2015.

Croce, Arlene. "Review of *The Misfits*." *Sight and Sound* (Summer 1961): 142.

Crowther, Bosley. "Look at Marilyn!" *New York Times*, June 12, 1955: X1.

———. "Of Size and Scope: The Wide Screen Viewed in the Light of 'How to Marry a Millionaire.'" *New York Times*, Nov. 15, 1953: X1.

———. "The Proof of Marilyn." *New York Times*, Sept. 9, 1956: X1.

———. "The Screen: Marilyn Monroe Arrives." *New York Times*, Sept. 1, 1956: F19.

———. "To Be Frank with You." *New York Times*, Apr. 26, 1959: X1.

Cryle, Peter, and Alison Moore. *Frigidity: An Intellectual History*. New York: Palgrave Macmillan, 2011.

Curtis, H. M. Letter to Charles Brackett, Feb. 24, 1953. Charles Brackett Papers, *Niagara*, Box 4, Folder 34, Margaret Herrick Library, Academy of Motion Picture Arts and Sciences, Los Angeles, CA.

Curtis, Tony. *The Making of* Some Like It Hot: *My Memories of Marilyn Monroe and the Classic American Movie*. New York: Wiley, 2009.

Darone, Mrs. Maurice P. Letter to Hedda Hopper, Aug. 25, 1962. Hedda Hopper Papers, Marilyn Monroe, Margaret Herrick Library, Academy of Motion Picture Arts and Sciences, Los Angeles, CA.

Das, Sonya. *The American Woman in Modern Marriage*. New York: Philosophical Library, 1948.

Davidson, Bill. "Kinsey: On the Difference between Men and Women." *Collier's* 132 (Sept. 4, 1953): 19–21.

Davidson, Bill, and Emily Mudd. "How Dr. Kinsey's Report on Women May Help Your Marriage." *Collier's* 132 (Sept. 18, 1953): 112–117.

De Cordova, Richard. *Picture Personalities: The Emergence of the Star System in America*. Urbana: University of Illinois Press, 1990.

De Dienes, Andre, and Steve Crist. *Marilyn*. Cologne, Germany: Taschen, 2002.

De Lauretis, Teresa. *Alice Doesn't: Feminism, Semiotics, Cinema*. Bloomington: Indiana University Press, 1984.

D'Emilio, John, and Estelle Freedman. *Intimate Matters: A History of Sexuality in America*. New York: Harper and Row, 1988.

Derry, Charles. *The Suspense Thriller: Films in the Shadow of Alfred Hitchcock*. Jefferson, NC: McFarland, 1988.

De Saussure, Ferdinand. *Course in General Linguistics*. Trans. Roy Harris. London: Duckworth, 1983.

Desjardins, Mary. *Recycled Stars: Female Film Stardom in the Age of Television and Video*. Durham, NC: Duke University Press, 2015.

De Vito, John, and Frank Tropea. *The Immortal Marilyn: The Depiction of an Icon*. Lanham, MD: Scarecrow Press, 2007.

"Diamonds Are a Girl's Best Friend," additional lyrics. *Gentlemen Prefer Blondes. History of Cinema: Series 1: Hollywood and the Production Code: Selected Files from the Motion Picture Association of America Production Code Administration Collection*, Margaret Herrick Library, Academy of Motion Pictures Arts and Sciences, Los Angeles, CA. Microfilm.

Dick, Bernard. *Billy Wilder*. Updated ed. New York: De Capo Press, 1996.

Dickos, Andrew. *Street with No Name: A History of the Classic American Film Noir*. Lexington: University Press of Kentucky, 2002.

"Did Yves Cause Marilyn's Collapse?" *Movieland and TV Time*, Dec. 1960: 13.

Dietrich, John. Letter to Hedda Hopper, June 5, 1952. Hedda Hopper Papers, Marilyn Monroe, Margaret Herrick Library, Academy of Motion Picture Arts and
Sciences, Los Angeles, CA.

Dimendberg, Edward. *Film Noir and the Spaces of Modernity*. Cambridge, MA:
Harvard University Press, 2004.

Dinter, Charlotte. "What Marilyn Couldn't Tell the Doctor." *Photoplay*, Oct. 1959:
43, 93–95.

Dione, Jill. "Body Image: Fashioning the Postwar American." PhD diss., University of Pittsburgh, 2009.

Ditzion, Sidney. *Marriage, Morals and Sex in America: A History of Ideas*. New
York: Bookman Associates, 1953.

Doane, Mary Anne. "The Close-Up: Scale and Detail in the Cinema." *Differences:
A Journal of Feminist Cultural Studies* 14.3 (2003): 89–111.

———. *The Emergence of Cinematic Time: Modernity, Contingency, the Archive*.
Cambridge, MA: Harvard University Press, 2003.

———. *Femmes Fatales: Feminism, Film Theory, Psychoanalysis*. New York:
Routledge, 1995.

———. "Masquerade Reconsidered: Further Thoughts on the Female Spectator."
Discourse 11.1 (1989): 42–54.

Doherty, Thomas. *Hollywood's Censor: Joseph I. Breen and the Production Code
Administration*. New York: Columbia University Press, 2009.

———. *Pre-Code Hollywood: Sex, Immorality, and Insurrection in American Cinema, 1930–1934*. New York: Columbia University Press, 1999.

"Don't Bother to Knock." Motion Picture Association of America, Production
Code Administration Records, *Don't Bother to Knock*, Margaret Herrick Library,
Academy of Motion Picture Arts and Sciences, Los Angeles, CA.

"The Dostoevsky Blues." *Time*, Jan. 24, 1955: 75.

Dougherty, James. "Marilyn Monroe Was My Wife." *Photoplay*, Mar. 1953: 47–49,
75, 78–85.

Dratler, Jay, and Gina Kaus. "If I Could Re-Marry." Twentieth Century-Fox Collection (We're Not Married, 4-.1). Cinematic Arts Library, University of Southern California, Los Angeles, CA.

Drury, Allen. "Arthur Miller Admits Helping Communist-Front Groups in '40's."
New York Times, June 22, 1956: 1, 9.

Dubinsky, Karen. *The Second Greatest Disappointment: Honeymooning and
Tourism at Niagara Falls*. New Brunswick, NJ: Rutgers University Press,
1999.

Dudley, Fredda. "How a Star Is Born." *Photoplay*, Sept. 1950: 38–41, 100–102.

———. "How a Star Is Born." *Photoplay*, Nov. 1950: 52–55, 91–94.

Durgnat, Raymond. "Paint It Black: The Family Tree of the *Film Noir*." In *Film Noir Reader*, ed. Alain Silver and James Ursini, 37–51. New York: Proscenium, 2001.

Duvall, Evelyn, and Reuben Hill. *When You Marry*. New York: Association Press, 1953.

Duvall, Sylvanus. *101 Questions to Ask Yourself before You Marry*. New York: Association Press, 1954.

Dyer, Richard. "*A Star Is Born* and the Construction of Authenticity." In *Stardom: Industry of Desire*, ed. Christine Gledhill, 132–140. London: Routledge, 1991.

———. "Four Films of Lana Turner." In *Star Texts: Image and Performance in Film and Television*, ed. Jeremy Butler, 214–239. Detroit, MI: Wayne State University Press, 1991.

———. *Heavenly Bodies: Film Stars and Society*. 2nd ed. London: Routledge, 2004.

———. "Postscript: Queers and Women in Film Noir." In *Women in Film Noir*, ed. E. Ann Kaplan, 123–129. London: British Film Institute, 2000.

———. "Resistance through Charisma: Rita Hayworth and *Gilda*." In *Women in Film Noir*, ed. E. Ann Kaplan, 115–122. London: British Film Institute, 2000.

———. *Stars*. London: British Film Institute, 1982.

Ebert, John David. *Dead Celebrities, Living Icons: Tragedy and Fame in the Age of the Multimedia Superstar*. Santa Barbara, CA: Praeger, 2010.

Egelston, Janet, Rebecca Church, Edith Lyday. "Letters: The Women." *Time*, Mar. 16, 1953: 12.

Ehrat, Johannes. *Cinema and Semiotic: Peirce and Film Aesthetics, Narration, and Representation*. Toronto: University of Toronto Press, 2005.

Ellis, Albert. "Introduction." In *Sex Life of the American Woman and the Kinsey Report*, ed. Albert Ellis, 3–22. New York: Greenberg, 1954.

———. "Ten Indiscreet Proposals." *Pageant*, Nov. 1958: 6–15.

Ellis, John. *Visible Fictions: Cinema: Television: Video*. Rev. ed. London: Routledge, 1982.

Emmett, Robert. "Sex and Sin in Hollywood." *Photoplay*, Jan. 1956: 30–31, 74.

"End of Famous Marriage." *Life*, Nov. 21, 1960, 87–90.

Enelow, Shonni. *Method Acting and Its Discontents: On American Psycho-Drama*. Evanston, IL: Northwestern University Press, 2015.

Erickson, C. O. Letter to John Huston, Jan. 27, 1961. John Huston Papers, C. O. Erickson, Margaret Herrick Library, Academy of Motion Picture Arts and Sciences, Los Angeles, CA.

"Fantastic Summer Realities." *Life*, Aug. 30, 1954: 18.

Farris, Jocelyn. *Jayne Mansfield: A Bio-Bibliography*. Westport, CT: Greenwood Press, 1994.

Ferguson, Kevin. "Panting in the Dark: The Ambivalence of Air in Cinema." *Camera Obscura* 77 (2011): 32–63.

Filene, Peter. *Him/Her/Self: Gender Identities in Modern America*. Baltimore, MD: Johns Hopkins University Press, 1998.

"Film Review: 'The Misfits.'" *Variety*, Feb. 1, 1961: 3.

"Film Review: 'Some Like it Hot.'" *Variety*, Feb. 25, 1959.

Finkelstein, Adrian. *Marilyn Monroe Returns: The Healing of a Soul*. Charlottesville, VA: Hampton Roads, 2006.

"First Report from First Preview, from Howard Strickling, February 16, 1950." John Huston Papers, Margaret Herrick Library, Academy of Motion Picture Arts and Sciences, Los Angeles, CA.

Frank, Lawrence. "How Much Do We Know about Men?" *Look*, May 17, 1955: 52, 53–54, 57–58, 60.

Franse, Astrid, and Michelle Morgan. *Before Marilyn: The Blue Book Modeling Years*. New York: Thomas Dunne, 2015.

Fraterrigo, Elizabeth. *Playboy and the Making of the Good Life in Modern America*. New York: Oxford University Press, 2009.

Frazer, G. "Readers Inc." *Photoplay*, Nov. 1962: 4.

Freedgood, Anne. "Dr. Kinsey's Second Sex." *Harper's Magazine* 207 (Sept. 1953): 21–27.

Freeman, Lucy. "Sex and Emotional Health." In *Sex Life of the American Woman and the Kinsey Report*, ed. Albert Ellis, 59–75. New York: Greenberg, 1954.

French, Brandon. *On the Verge of Revolt: Women in American Films of the Fifties*. New York: Frederick Ungar, 1978.

Friedan, Betty. *The Feminine Mystique*. New York: W. W. Norton, 1963.

Frost, Jennifer. *Hedda Hopper's Hollywood: Celebrity Gossip and American Conservatism*. New York: New York University Press, 2011.

Gallup, George. "Two American Institute of Public Opinion Surveys on the Kinsey Reports." In *Sexual Behavior in American Society: An Appraisal of the First Two Kinsey Reports*, ed. Jerome Himelhoch and Sylvia Fleis Fava, 379–382. New York: W. W. Norton, 1955.

Gamson, Joshua. *Claims to Fame: Celebrity in Contemporary America*. Berkeley: University of California Press, 1994.

Gans, Eric. *Carole Landis: A Most Beautiful Girl*. Jackson: University Press of Mississippi, 2008.

Garber, Marjorie. *Vested Interests: Cross-Dressing and Cultural Anxiety*. New York: Routledge, 1997.

Gates, Philippa. *Detecting Women: Gender and the Hollywood Detective Film*. Albany, NY: State University of New York Press, 2011.

Gemünden, Gerd. "All Dressed Up and Running Wild: *Some Like it Hot* (1959)." *A Foreign Affair: Billy Wilder's American Films.* New York: Berghahn, 2008. 100–121.

"Gentlemen Prefer Blondes." *Variety*, June 23, 1953.

Geraghty, Christine. "Re-Examining Stardom: Questions of Texts, Bodies and Performance." In *Reinventing Film Studies*, ed. Christine Gledhill and Linda Williams, 183–201. London: Arnold, 2000.

Gerould, Christopher. *Sexual Practices of American Women.* New York: Zenith, 1953.

Giedt, F. Harold. "Changes in Sexual Behavior and Attitudes Following Class Study of the Kinsey Report." In *Sexual Behavior in American Society: An Appraisal of the First Two Kinsey Reports*, ed. Jerome Himelhoch and Sylvia Fleis Fava, 405–416. New York: W.W. Norton, 1955.

Gilbert, James. "Family Culture." *Another Chance: Postwar America, 1945–1985.* Chicago: Dorsey Press, 1986. 54–75.

Girelli, Elisabetta. *Montgomery Clift, Queer Star.* Detroit, MI: Wayne State University Press, 2014.

Gledhill, Christine. "Introduction." In *Stardom: Industry of Desire*, ed. Christine Gledhill, xiii–xx. London: Routledge, 1991.

———. "*Klute* 1: A Contemporary Film Noir and Feminist Criticism." In *Women in Film Noir*, ed. E. Ann Kaplan, 20–34. London: British Film Institute, 2000.

———. "Signs of Melodrama." In *Stardom: Industry of Desire*, ed. Christine Gledhill, 207–231. London: Routledge, 1991.

Glitre, Kathrina. "Conspicuous Consumption: The Spectacle of Widescreen Comedy in the Populuxe Era." In *Widescreen Worldwide*, ed. John Belton, Sheldon Hall, and Steve Neale, 133–143. Bloomington: Indiana University Press, 2010.

"Go Easy." *Time*, Feb. 23, 1953: 102.

Goldstein, Laurence. "*The Misfits* and American Culture." In *Arthur Miller's America: Theater and Culture in a Time of Change*, ed. Enoch Brater, 109–134. Ann Arbor: University of Michigan Press, 2005.

Goode, James. *The Making of* The Misfits. New York: Limelight Editions, 1986.

Grafton, Samuel. "Man Talk: The Intelligent Woman's Monthly Guide to a Reasonably Happy Marriage." *Good Housekeeping*, Mar. 1953: 44, 209.

———. "Man Talk: The Intelligent Woman's Monthly Guide to a Reasonably Happy Marriage." *Good Housekeeping*, Apr. 1953: 46, 316.

———. "Man Talk: The Intelligent Woman's Monthly Guide to a Reasonably Happy Marriage." *Good Housekeeping*, May 1953: 44, 199–200.

Graham, Sheilah. "Hollywood's Lost Ladies." *Photoplay*, Nov. 1953: 52–53, 113–115.

———. "Is Hollywood Carrying Sex Too Far?" *Photoplay*, Feb. 1953, 36–37, 84.

———. "Marilyn Talks about Joe and Babies." *Modern Screen*, Sept. 1954. http://www.marilynmonroe.ca/camera/mags/ms54a.htm.

———. "Why Gentlemen Prefer Blondes." *Photoplay*, June 1953: 52–53, 97–98.

Gray, Marijane. "Commercializing Marilyn Monroe." *Immortal Marilyn*, Feb. 17, 2016. https://www.immortalmarilyn.com/commercializing-marilyn-monroe.

Greenson, Ralph. "On Screen Defenses, Screen Hunger, and Screen Identity." *Journal of the American Psychoanalytic Association* 6 (1958): 242–262.

Griffin, Susan. *Pornography and Silence: Culture's Revenge against Nature*. New York: Harper and Row, 1981.

Griffith, Richard. *LA Times*. August 5, 1952. Core Collection Files: *Don't Bother to Knock*, Margaret Herrick Library, Academy of Motion Picture Arts and Sciences, Los Angeles, CA.

Grindon, Leger. *The Hollywood Romantic Comedy: Conventions, History, Controversies*. West Sussex, UK: Wiley-Blackwell, 2011.

Grossberg, Lawrence. "Is There a Fan in the House? The Affective Sensibility of Fandom." In *The Adoring Audience: Fan Culture and Popular Media*, ed. Lisa Lewis, 50–65. London: Routledge, 1992.

Grossman, Julie. *Rethinking the Femme Fatale in Film Noir: Ready for Her Close-Up*. New York: Palgrave Macmillan, 2009.

Groves, Gladys Hoagland. "Marital Sex Intercourse." In *Sex Life of the American Woman and the Kinsey Report*, ed. Albert Ellis, 139–157. New York: Greenberg, 1954.

Guiles, Fred Lawrence. *Legend: The Life and Death of Marilyn Monroe*. New York: Stein and Day, 1984.

Hall, Stuart. "Encoding, Decoding." In *The Cultural Studies Reader*, ed. Simon During, 90–103. London: Routledge, 1993.

Hamilton, Marybeth. *When I'm Bad, I'm Better: Mae West, Sex, and American Entertainment*. New York: Harper Collins, 1995.

Handel, Leo. *Hollywood Looks at Its Audience: A Report of Film Audience Research*. Urbana: University of Illinois Press, 1950.

Handyside, Fiona. "Let's Make Love: Whiteness, Cleanliness and Sexuality in the French Reception of Marilyn Monroe." *European Journal of Cultural Studies* 13.3 (2010): 291–306.

Hansen, Miriam. *Babel and Babylon: Spectatorship in American Silent Film*. Cambridge, MA: Harvard University Press, 1991.

Happy Mother. "Open Letter to Marilyn." "Readers Inc." *Photoplay*, Mar. 1959: 10.

Harbert, Ruth. "Out and About in Hollywood." *Good Housekeeping*, Apr. 1953: 19.

Harvey, Brett. *The Fifties: A Woman's Oral History.* San Jose, NM: ASJA Press, 2002.

Harvey, James. *Movie Love in the Fifties.* New York: Alfred A. Knopf, 2001.

Harvey, Sylvia. "Woman's Place: The Absent Family of Film Noir." In *Women in Film Noir,* ed. E. Ann Kaplan, 35–46. London: British Film Institute, 1998.

Haskell, Molly. *From Reverence to Rape: The Treatment of Women in the Movies.* 2nd ed. Chicago: University of Chicago Press, 1987.

Haspiel, James. *Marilyn: The Ultimate Look at the Legend.* New York: Henry Holt, 1991.

Hattersley, Ralph. "Marilyn Monroe: The Image and Her Photographers." In *Marilyn Monroe: A Composite View,* ed. Edward Wagenknecht, 57–79. Philadelphia: Chilton, 1969.

Havemann, Ernest. "The Kinsey Report on Women." *Life,* Aug. 1953: 41–42, 45–46, 48, 53–54, 56.

Heath, Stephen. *Questions of Cinema.* Bloomington: Indiana University Press, 1981.

Henaghan, Jim. "Marilyn Monroe . . . Lovable Fake." *Motion Picture,* Nov. 1953: 33, 67–68.

Hermes, Joke. "Media Figures in Identity Construction." In *Rethinking the Media Audience: The New Agenda,* ed. Pertti Alasuutari, 69–85. London: Sage, 1999.

Higashi, Sumiko. *Stars, Fans, and Consumption in the 1950s: Reading Photoplay.* New York: Palgrave Macmillan, 2014.

Himes, Norman. *Your Marriage.* 2nd ed., rev. Donald Taylor. New York: Rinehart, 1955.

Hirsch, Foster. *A Method to Their Madness: The History of the Actors Studio.* New York: Norton, 1984.

Hitschmann, Eduard, and Edmund Bergler. *Frigidity in Women: Its Characteristics and Treatment.* New York: Nervous and Mental Disease Monographs, 1948.

Hoffman, Alexander. Letter to Hedda Hopper, Aug. 5, 1962. Hedda Hopper Papers, Marilyn Monroe, Margaret Herrick Library, Academy of Motion Picture Arts and Sciences, Los Angeles, CA.

Hoig, Bob. "Letters: M.M." *Time,* May 28, 1956: 4.

Holliday, Lucy. *A Night in with Marilyn Monroe.* New York: Harper, 2015.

Hollinger, Karen. *The Actress: Hollywood Acting and the Female Star.* New York: Routledge, 2006.

Hollingsworth, Cregg. "Readers Inc." *Photoplay,* June 1952: 8.

"Hollywood Topic A-Plus." *Life,* Apr. 7, 1952: 101–104.

Holmes, Marjorie. "What Became of the Girl *You* Married?" *Better Homes and Gardens,* Sept. 1952: 130, 200–201, 203.

———. "What Became of the Man I Married?" *Better Homes and Gardens*, May 1952: 6, 9, 255–257.

"Honeymooners, Beware." *Time*, Aug. 15, 1955.

Hopper, Hedda. "Marilyn Monroe Tells the Truth to Hedda Hopper." *Photoplay*, Jan. 1953: 36–37, 85–86.

———. "Marilyn's Life Saga of Broken Dreams: Acting Career End Foreseen by Star, Columnist Believes." *LA Times*, Aug. 7, 1962: IV8.

Horton, Donald, and R. Richard Wohl. "Mass Communication and Para-Social Interaction: Observations on Intimacy at a Distance." In *Inter/Media*, ed. Gary Gumpert and Robert Cathcart, 32–55. New York: Oxford University Press, (1956) 1979.

"How to Be Marriageable." *Ladies' Home Journal*, Mar. 1954: 46–47, 96.

Hurst, Fannie. "Nourishing." *Life* 35 (Aug. 24, 1953): 59, 62, 65.

Huston, John. *John Huston: An Open Book*. New York: Alfred A. Knopf, 1980.

"'I Dress for Men,' Says Marilyn Monroe." *Movieland*, July 1952: 32–35, 76.

Inge, M. Thomas, ed. *Truman Capote: Conversations*. Jackson: University Press of Mississippi, 1987.

Jack, Albert. *Robert Kennedy: JFK: The Death of Marilyn Monroe: Who Didn't Kill Them*. Capetown: Albert Jack 2015. Kindle.

Jacobs, Lea. *The Wages of Sin: Censorship and the Fallen Woman Film, 1928–1942*. Berkeley: University of California Press, 1997.

Jameson, Fredric. *The Political Unconscious: Narrative as a Socially Symbolic Act*. Ithaca, NY: Cornell University Press, 1981.

Jerris, Tony. *Marilyn Monroe: My Little Secret*. New York: Zim Entertainment, 2010.

Johnson. Publicity. 20th Century-Fox. c. 1953. Jack Hirshberg Papers, Marilyn Monroe, Margaret Herrick Library, Academy of Motion Picture Arts and Sciences, Los Angeles, CA.

Johnson, Catherine. "Marriage and Money: How to Marry a Millionaire." *Film Reader* 5 (1982): 67–75.

Johnson, Hildegard. "3-D Pinup Girls." *Photoplay*, Sept. 1953: 42–45, 83.

———. "Hollywood vs. Marilyn Monroe." *Photoplay*, July 1953: 42–45, 98–99.

Johnson, Jeff. *William Inge and the Subversion of Gender: Rewriting Stereotypes in the Plays, Novels, and Screenplays*. Jefferson, NC: McFarland, 2005.

Johnson, Nora. "Sex and the College Girl." *Atlantic*, Nov. 1959: 57–58.

Jones, Elton. *The Unremarkable Death of Marilyn Monroe*. London: Samuel French.

Jordan, Jessica Hope. *The Sex Goddess in American Film, 1930–1965: Jean Harlow, Mae West, Lana Turner, and Jayne Mansfield*. Amherst, NY: Cambria Press, 2010.

Joyce, Alex. "Marilyn at the Crossroads." *Photoplay*, July 1957: 44–45, 90, 92.

Juncker, Clara. *Circling Marilyn: Text, Body, Performance*. Odense: University Press of Southern Denmark, 2010.

Kahn, Roger. *Joe and Marilyn: A Memory of Love*. New York: William Morrow, 1986.

Kaplan, E. Ann, ed. *Women in Film Noir*. London: British Film Institute, 2000.

Kauffman, Stanley. "Across the Great Divide." *New Republic*, Feb. 20, 1961: 26, 28.

———. "The Stars in Their Courses." *New Republic*, Feb. 3, 1960: 19–20.

———. *A World on Film: Criticism and Comment*. Westport, CT: Greenwood Press, 1966.

Kear, Adrian, and Deborah Steinberg, eds. *Mourning Diana: Nation, Culture, and the Performance of Grief*. London: Routledge, 1999.

Kelly, G. Lombard. *Sexual Feeling in Married Men and Women*. New York: Greystone Press, 1951.

Kidd, Elizabeth. "Sexual Behavior in the American Advertiser: Why the New Kinsey Study is Significant." *Printer's Ink*, Sept. 11, 1953: 41–43.

King, Barry. "Articulating Stardom." In *Stardom: Industry of Desire*, ed. Christine Gledhill, 167–206. London: Routledge, 1991.

———. "Embodying an Elastic Self: The Parametrics of Contemporary Stardom." In *Contemporary Hollywood Stardom*, ed. Thomas Austin and Martin Baker, 45–61. London: Arnold, 2003.

Kinsey, Alfred, Wardell Pomeroy, and Clyde Martin. *Sexual Behavior in the Human Male*. Philadelphia: W. B. Saunders, 1948.

Kinsey, Alfred, Wardell Pomeroy, Clyde Martin, and Paul Gebhard. *Sexual Behavior in the Human Female*. Philadelphia: W. B. Saunders, 1953.

"Kinsey Report in the Press." *America* 90 (Oct. 10, 1953): 30–31.

Knight, Arthur. "Time Listings." *Time*, Mar. 30, 1959: 94.

Knight, Timothy. *Marilyn Monroe: A Life in the Movies*. iFocus, 2015.. Kindle..

Kobal, John. *People Will Talk*. New York: Alfred A. Knopf, 1985.

Konkle, Amanda. "How to (Marry a Woman Who Wants to) Marry a Millionaire." *Quarterly Review of Film and Video* 31.4 (2014): 364–383.

Kouvaros, George. *Famous Faces Yet Not Themselves: The Misfits and Icons of Postwar America*. Minneapolis: University of Minnesota Press, 2010.

Krasner, David. "I Hate Strasberg: Method Bashing in the Academy." In *Method Acting Reconsidered: Theory, Practice, Future*, ed. David Krasner, 3–39. New York: St. Martin's Press, 2000.

Kroger, William S., and Charles Freed. "Psychosomatic Aspects of Frigidity." *JAMA: The Journal of the American Medical Association* 143.6 (1950): 526–532.

Krutnik, Frank. *In a Lonely Street: Film Noir, Genre, Masculinity.* London: Routledge, 1991.

Kutner, Nanette. "Don't Blame Yourself, Marilyn." *Photoplay* 47.1 (Jan. 1955): 43, 62.

Lal, Gobind Behari. "Science and Sex Conversion." *American Mercury*, Feb. 1953: 39–44.

Landis, Judson. "Time Required to Achieve Marriage Adjustment." In *Readings in Marriage and the Family*, ed. Judson Landis and Mary Landis, 160–180. New York: Prentice-Hall, 1952, 1953.

Landis, Judson, and Mary Landis. *Building a Successful Marriage.* 2nd. ed. Englewood Cliffs, NJ: Prentice-Hall, 1953.

Landis, Paul H. "The Changing Family." *Current History* 19.109 (1950): 151–153.

Lane, Laura. "Eeny, Meeny, Miny, Mo, Who Will Be the First to Go?" *Photoplay*, Mar. 1957: 38–41.

"Last Scene, Exit Unhappily." *Life*, Oct. 18, 1954: 53–4.

Lawrence, Amy. *The Passion of Montgomery Clift.* Berkeley: University of California Press, 2010.

Leaming, Barbara. *Marilyn Monroe.* New York: Crown, 1998.

Leder, Jane Mersky. *Thanks for the Memories: Love, Sex, and World War II.* Westport, CT: Praeger, 2006.

Lees, Hannah. "What Every Husband Needs." *Reader's Digest*, Oct. 1957: 137–140.

Leets, Laura, Gavin De Becker, and Howard Giles. "Fans: Exploring Expressed Motivations for Contacting Celebrities." *Journal of Language and Social Psychology* 14 (1995): 102–123.

Leff, Leonard, and Jerold Simmons. *The Dame in the Kimono: Hollywood, Censorship, and the Production Code.* 2nd ed. Lexington: University Press of Kentucky, 2001.

LeMasters, E. E. *Modern Courtship and Marriage.* New York: Macmillan, 1957.

"Letters: Bosomy Babes." *Time*, Dec. 8, 1952: 8, 11.

"Letters to the Editors." *Life*, June 15, 1953: 16.

Levine, Lena. *The Modern Book of Marriage: A Practical Guide to Marital Happiness.* New York: Bartholomew House, 1957.

Levitt, Linda. "Death on Display: Reifying Stardom through Hollywood's Dark Tourism." *Velvet Light Trap* 65 (2010): 62–70.

Levy, Alan. "Marilyn Monroe: 'A Good, Long Look at Myself.'" *Redbook*, Aug. 1962: 40, 74–77.

Lewis, Carolyn Herbst. *Prescription for Heterosexuality: Sexual Citizenship in the Cold War Era.* Chapel Hill: University of North Carolina Press, 2010.

Lewis, Jon. "1955—Movies and Growing Up . . . Absurd." In *American Cinema of the 1950s: Themes and Variations*, ed. Murray Pomerance, 134–154. New Brunswick, NJ: Rutgers University Press, 2005.

Lewis, Robert. *Method—or Madness?* New York: Samuel French, 1958.

Lieberfeld, Daniel. "Keeping the Characters Straight: Comedy and Identity in 'Some Like it Hot.'" *Journal of Popular Film and Television* 26.3 (1998): 128–135.

Little, Rev. Msgr. Thomas F. Letter to Geoffrey Shurlock, Mar. 5, 1959. Motion Picture Association of America, Production Code Administration Records, *Some Like It Hot*, Margaret Herrick Library, Academy of Motion Picture Arts and Sciences, Los Angeles, CA.

Loney, Glenn. *Unsung Genius: The Passion of Dancer-Choreographer Jack Cole.* New York: Franklin Watts, 1984.

Lovell, Alan, and Peter Krämer. "Introduction." In *Screen Acting*, ed. Alan Lovell and Peter Krämer, 1–9. London: Routledge, 1999.

———, eds. *Screen Acting.* New York: Routledge, 1999.

Lowe, Barry. *Atomic Blonde: The Films of Mamie Van Doren.* Jefferson, NC: McFarland, 2008.

Luce, Clare Boothe. "What Really Killed Marilyn." *Life*, Aug. 7, 1964: 68–78.

Lundberg, Ferdinand, and Marynia Farnham. *Modern Woman: The Lost Sex.* New York: Harper and Brothers, 1947.

Lyle, Jae. "Behind the Yves Montand, Marilyn Monroe, Arthur Miller Triangle." *Photoplay*, Oct. 1960: 32, 70–71.

MacCannell, Dean. "Marilyn Monroe Was Not a Man." *Diacritics* 17.2 (1987): 114–127.

Mailer, Norman. *Marilyn: A Biography.* New York: Grosset and Dunlap, 1973.

Malague, Rosemary. *An Actress Prepares: Women and the Method.* London: Routledge, 2012.

Maland, Charles. *Chaplin and American Culture: The Evolution of a Star Image.* Princeton, NJ: Princeton University Press, 1989.

Mallett, Richard. "At the Pictures: *How to Marry a Millionaire, Le Fruit Défendu*." *Punch*, Jan. 27, 1954: 162.

Maltby, Richard. "'A Brief Romantic Interlude': Dick and Jane Go to 3 ½ Seconds of the Classical Hollywood Cinema." In *Post-Theory: Reconstructing Film Studies*, ed. David Bordwell and Nöel Carroll, 419–433. Madison: University of Wisconsin Press, 1996.

———. "'Film Noir': The Politics of the Maladjusted Text." *Journal of American Studies* 18.1 (1984): 49–71.

Mandy, Arthur. "Frigidity." In *Sex Life of the American Woman and the Kinsey Report*, ed. Albert Ellis, 95–109. New York: Greenberg, 1954.

Manning, Dorothy. "The Woman and the Legend." *Photoplay*, Oct. 1956: 58–61, 96–98.

Marchant, Linda. "Still Famous: Fixing the Star Image of Diana Dors in the Photography of Cornel Lucas." In *Lasting Screen Stars: Images That Fade and Personas That Endure*, ed. Lucy Bolton and Julie Lobalzo Wright, 261–276. London: Palgrave Macmillan, 2016.

"Marilyn and the Mustangs." *Time*, Aug. 8, 1960: 57.

"Marilyn at 30 Finds Kinsey Comforting." *LA Times*, June 3, 1956. Constance McCormick Collection: Marilyn Monroe, Vol. 2. Cinema and Television Library, University of Southern California, Los Angeles, CA.

"Marilyn Monroe in a Remarkable Recreation of Fabled Enchantresses." *Life*, Dec. 22, 1958: 138–145.

Marshall, David. *The DD Group: An Online Investigation into the Death of Marilyn Monroe*. New York: iUniverse, 2005.

Marshall, P. David. *Celebrity and Power: Fame in Contemporary Culture*. 2nd ed. Minneapolis: University of Minnesota Press, 2014.

Martin, Pete. *Will Acting Spoil Marilyn Monroe?* New York: Doubleday, 1956.

May, Elaine Tyler. *Homeward Bound: American Families in the Cold War Era*. New York: Basic, 2008.

Mayer, Geoff. *Roy Ward Baker*. Manchester: Manchester University Press, 2004.

Mayne, Judith. *The Woman at the Keyhole: Feminism and Women's Cinema*. Bloomington: Indiana University Press, 1990.

McCann, Graham. *Marilyn Monroe*. New Brunswick, NJ: Rutgers University Press, 1988.

McCarthy, Frank. Letter to Billy Wilder and Charles Feldman, Mar. 1, 1955. Motion Picture Association of America, Production Code Administration Records, *The Seven Year Itch*, Margaret Herrick Library, Academy of Motion Picture Arts and Sciences, Los Angeles, CA.

McCarthy, Todd. *Howard Hawks: The Grey Fox of Hollywood*. New York: Grove Press, 1997.

McDonald, Paul. *Hollywood Stardom*. Maden, MA: Wiley-Blackwell, 2013.

———. *The Star System: Hollywood's Production of Popular Identities*. London: Wallflower, 2000.

McGarr, Maj. Gen. Lionel. Letter, Feb. 16, 1954. *Property from the Life and Career of Marilyn Monroe*, Julien's Auctions Catalog, Beverly Hills, CA, Dec. 6, 2014: 41.

McGilligan, Patrick. *Cagney: The Actor as Auteur*. South Brunswick, NJ: A. S. Barnes, 1975.

McGreevy, Patrick Vincent. *Imagining Niagara: The Meaning and Making of Niagara Falls*. Amherst: University of Massachusetts Press, 1994.

McIntyre, Alice T. "Making the Misfits or Waiting for Monroe or Notes from Olympus." *Esquire*, Mar. 1961: 74–81.

McIntyre, Howard. "Letters: M.M." *Time*, June 4, 1956: 6.

McLean, Adrienne. *Being Rita Hayworth: Labor, Identity, and Hollywood Stardom*. New Brunswick, NJ: Rutgers University Press, 2004.

———. "Betty Grable and Rita Hayworth: Pinned Up." In *What Dreams Were Made Of: Movie Stars of the 1940s*, ed. Sean Griffin, 166–192. New Brunswick, NJ: Rutgers University Press, 2011.

———. "The Thousand Ways There Are to Move: Camp and Oriental Dance in the Hollywood Musicals of Jack Cole." In *Visions of the East: Orientalism in Film*, ed. Matthew Bernstein and Gaylyn Studlar, 130–157. New Brunswick, NJ: Rutgers University Press, 1997.

McMillan, Rob. "Giant Marilyn Monroe Statue Attracts Attention." *KABC*, May 17, 2012. http://abclocal.go.com/kabc/story?section=news/local/inland _empire&id=8666611.

McNulty, Bishop. Letter to Eric Johnston, Mar. 5, 1959. Motion Picture Association of America, Production Code Administration Records, *Some Like It Hot*, Margaret Herrick Library, Academy of Motion Picture Arts and Sciences, Los Angeles, CA.

McPartland, John. *Sex in Our Changing World*. New York: Rinehart, 1947.

Mead, Margaret. "She Has Strength Based on a Pioneer Past." *Life*, Dec. 24, 1956: 26–27.

Melody, M. E., and Linda Peterson. *Teaching America about Sex: Marriage Guides and Sex Manuals from the Late Victorians to Dr. Ruth*. New York: New York University Press, 1999.

Meltsir, Aljean. "MM-Tribute." *Photoplay*, Nov. 1962: 36, 78–81.

"Memorandum on Final Script of 4-7-53 (D. Z. Dictated to Audrey Blanchard)," Apr. 22, 1953. *River of No Return*, Box 5, Folder 8, Twentieth Century-Fox Collection, University of Southern California, Los Angeles, CA.

Meyer, Agnes. "Women Aren't Men." *Atlantic Monthly*, Aug. 1959: 32–36.

Meyerowitz, Joanne. *How Sex Changed: A History of Transsexuality in the United States*. Cambridge: Harvard University Press, 2002.

Meyers, Jeffrey. *The Genius and the Goddess: Arthur Miller and Marilyn Monroe*. London: Hutchinson, 2009.

———. *John Huston: Courage and Art*. New York: Crown Archetype, 2011.

Miller, Arthur. *The Misfits* script, 1957. John Huston Papers, *The Misfits*, Margaret Herrick Library, Academy of Motion Picture Arts and Sciences, Los Angeles, CA.

———. *Timebends: A Life*. New York: Harper and Row, 1987.

Miller, Douglas. "Hollywood in Transition." *The Fifties: The Way We Really Were*. New York: Doubleday, 1975. 314–43.

Miller, Margaret. Letter. *Life*, Aug. 24, 1962: 19.

Miracle, Berniece Baker, and Mona Rae Miracle. *My Sister Marilyn: A Memoir of Marilyn Monroe*. Lincoln, NE: iUniverse, 2003.

"'Misfits' Carrying 'Adults Only' Tag Ducks Legion 'C.'" *Variety*. John Huston Papers, Publicity—clippings. Margaret Herrick Library, Academy of Motion Picture Arts and Sciences, Los Angeles, CA.

"'The Misfits' Provocative, Stimulating Production." *Hollywood Reporter*, Feb. 1, 1961: 3.

Mobilio, Albert. "Scratching Tom Ewell's Itch." In *All the Available Light: A Marilyn Monroe Reader*, ed. Yona Zeldis McDonough, 53–59. New York: Simon and Schuster, 2002.

Monroe, Marilyn. "Make It for Keeps." *Photoplay*, July 1951: 37, 92.

———. "The Men Who Interest Me." *Pageant*, Apr. 1954: 55.

———. "My Beauty Secrets." *Photoplay*, Oct. 1953: 34–35, 76.

———. "Temptations of a Bachelor Girl." *Photoplay*, Apr. 1952: 44–45, 95.

———. "The Truth about Me, as Told to Liza Wilson." Part 1. *American Weekly*, Nov. 16, 1952.

———. "The Truth about Me, as Told to Liza Wilson." Part 2. *American Weekly*, Nov. 23, 1952.

"The Monroe Reforms, Changed Marilyn Promised in Film Bow." *Gentlemen Prefer Blondes, Exhibitor's Campaign Book*, 15. Core Collection Files, *Gentlemen Prefer Blondes*, Margaret Herrick Library, Academy of Motion Picture Arts and Sciences, Los Angeles, CA.

Montagu, Ashley. "Where Kinsey Went Wrong." *McCall's* 81 (Dec. 1953): 37, 123, 124.

Montaigne, Lewis. *The Origins and Nature of Marriage*. New York: Citadel Press, 1953.

Moore, Isabel. "Why Women Hate Marilyn Monroe." *Movieland*, Oct. 1952: 25–28, 66, 70.

Morin, Edgar. *The Stars*. Trans. Richard Howard. Minneapolis: University of Minnesota Press, 2005.

Morse, Benjamin. *Sexual Behavior of the American College Girl*. New York: Lancer, 1963.

Mosby, Aline. "Nude Calendar Beauty at Last Is Identified." *Los Angeles Herald Examiner*, Mar. 13, 1952.

Moseley, Rachel. *Growing up with Audrey Hepburn: Text, Audience, Resonance*. Manchester: Manchester University Press, 2002.

Moskin, J. Robert. "The American Male: Why Do Women Dominate Him?" *Look*, Feb. 4, 1958: 77–80.

Mudd, Aron and Emily Krich. *Man and Wife: A Source Book of Family Attitudes, Sexual Behavior and Marriage Counseling*. New York: Norton, 1957.

Mulvey, Laura. "Afterthoughts on 'Visual Pleasure and Narrative Cinema' Inspired by *Duel in the Sun*." *Framework* 15 (1981): 12–15.

———. *Death 24x a Second: Stillness and the Moving Image*. London: Reaktion, 2006.

———. "*Gentlemen Prefer Blondes*: Anita Loos/Howard Hawks/Marilyn Monroe." In *Howard Hawks American Artist*, ed. Jim Hillier and Peter Wollen, 214–228. London: British Film Institute, 1996.

———. "Thoughts on Marilyn Monroe: Emblem and Allegory." *Screen* 58.2 (2017): 202–209.

———. "Visual Pleasure and Narrative Cinema." In *Feminism and Film*, ed. E. Ann Kaplan, 34–47. New York: Oxford University Press, 2000.

Munby, Jonathan. *Public Enemies, Public Heroes: Screening the Gangster from* Little Caesar *to* Touch of Evil. Chicago: University of Chicago Press, 1999.

Nadel, Alan. *Containment Culture: American Narratives, Postmodernism, and the Atomic Age*. Durham, NC: Duke University Press, 1995.

Naremore, James. *Acting in the Cinema*. Berkeley: University of California Press, 1988.

———. *More Than Night: Film Noir in Its Contexts*. Berkeley: University of California Press, 1998.

Nelson, Elyda. "The True Life Story of Marilyn Monroe." *Modern Screen*, Dec. 1952: 50–53, 84–85.

"New Films: Arthur Miller, Freud, and La Monroe." *Cue*, Feb. 4 1961. Core Collection Files, *The Misfits*, Margaret Herrick Library, Academy of Motion Picture Arts and Sciences, Los Angeles, CA.

Newland, Roger. "The Lies They Tell about Marilyn." *Silver Screen*, June 1955.

"New Picture: The Misfits." *Time*, Feb. 3, 1961: 68.

"The New Pictures: How to Marry a Millionaire." *Time*. Nov. 22, 1953: 115–116.

"The New Pictures: Let's Make Love." *Time*, Sept. 19, 1960: 88.

Nickens, Christopher, and George Zeno. *Marilyn in Fashion: The Enduring Influence of Marilyn Monroe*. Philadelphia: Running Press, 2012.

Norris, Kathleen. "Incredible." *Life*, Aug. 24, 1953: 59–60.

Ohmer, Susan. "Jean Harlow: Tragic Blonde." In *Glamour in a Golden Age: Movie Stars of the 1930s*, ed. Adrienne McLean, 174–195. New Brunswick: Rutgers University Press, 2011.

Oliver, Kelly and Benigno Trigo. *Noir Anxiety*. Minneapolis: University of Minnesota Press, 2002.

Olivier, Laurence. *Confessions of an Actor*. London: Simon and Schuster, 1982.

Orlay, Lt. James F. "Letters." *Life*, Mar. 22, 1954: 19.

Parsons, Louella. "Review: *The Asphalt Jungle*." *Cosmopolitan* 13 (June 1950): 122–123.

Patti, Lisa. "Everybody's All-American: The Posthumous Rebranding of Marlon Brando." In *Lasting Screen Stars: Images that Fade and Personas that Endure*, ed. Lucy Bolton and Julie Lobalzo Wright, 189–199. London: Palgrave Macmillan, 2016.

Paul, Julie. "Too Much Fire." *Motion Picture* 85.2 (Mar. 1953): 50, 63–64.

Pehowski, Marian. "Letters: M.M." *Time*, June 4, 1956: 6.

Peirce, Charles Sanders. *Collected Papers of Charles Sanders Peirce*. 5 vols. Ed. Charles Hartshorne and Paul Weiss. Cambridge, MA: Harvard University Press, 1932.

———. "Logic as Semiotic: The Theory of Signs." In *Philosophical Writings of Peirce*, ed. Justus Buchler, 98–119. New York: Dover Publications, 1955.

Pepitone, Lena, and William Stadiem. *Marilyn Monroe Confidential: An Intimate Personal Account*. New York: Simon and Schuster, 1979.

Peters, David. *Marilyn Monroe: All You Have to Know*. N.p., 2015. Kindle.

Peterson, Jennifer. "The Front Lawn of Heaven: Landscape in Hollywood Melodrama circa 1945." *Camera Obscura* 25.2 (2010): 119–158.

Phillips, Gene. *Some Like It Wilder: The Life and Controversial Films of Billy Wilder*. Lexington: University Press of Kentucky, 2010.

Piercy, Marge. "Looking Good." In *All the Available Light: A Marilyn Monroe Reader*, ed. Yona Zeldis McDonough, 103–108. New York: Simon and Schuster, 2002.

"Pin Up #2." *Photoplay*, Mar. 1951: 23–24.

Place, Janey, and Lowell Peterson, "Some Visual Motifs of Film Noir." In *Film Noir Reader*, ed. Alain Silver and James Ursini, 65–76. New York: Proscenium, 2001.

Pomerance, Murray. *Johnny Depp Starts Here*. New Brunswick, NJ: Rutgers University Press, 2005.

———. "A Passing Node: *The Asphalt Jungle*." In *John Huston as Adaptor*, ed. Douglas McFarland and Wesley King, 23–42. Albany: State University of New York Press, 2017.

Popkin, Henry. "Arthur Miller out West." *Commentary* 31 (May 1961): 433–435.

Powdermaker, Hortense. *Hollywood: The Dream Factory. An Anthropologist Looks at the Movie-Makers*. Boston: Little, Brown, 1950.

Pullen, Kirsten. *Like a Natural Woman: Spectacular Female Performance in Classical Hollywood*. New Brunswick, NJ: Rutgers University Press, 2014.

Pye, Douglas. "Running Out of Places: Fritz Lang's *Clash by Night*." *CineAction* 52 (2000): 12–17.

Redmond, Sean. "Intimate Fame Everywhere." In *Framing Celebrity*, ed. Su Holmes and Sean Redmond, 27–43. London: Routledge, 2006.

Reiss, Ira. *Premarital Sexual Standards in America*. New York: Free Press of Glencoe, 1960.

Renzi, Thomas. *Screwball Comedy and Film Noir: Unexpected Connections*. Jefferson, NC: McFarland, 2012.

Reumann, Miriam. *American Sexual Character: Sex, Gender, and National Identity in the Kinsey Reports*. Berkeley: University of California Press, 2005.

"Review: 'Clash by Night.'" *Variety*, Dec. 31, 1951.

Reynolds, Robert Grey. *Marilyn Monroe: New York City*. Smashwords, 2015.. Kindle.

"The Rich Middle Income Class." *Fortune*, May 1954: 97.

Riesman, David. *The Lonely Crowd*. New Haven, CT: Yale University Press, 2001.

Riviere, Joan. "Womanliness as Masquerade." *International Journal of Psychoanalysis*. 10 (1929): 303–313.

Robinson, David. "M M." In *Marilyn Monroe: A Composite View*, ed. Edward Wagenknecht, 142–147. Philadelphia: Chilton, 1969.

Robinson, Marie. *The Power of Sexual Surrender*. Garden City, NY: Doubleday, 1959.

Rodowick, David. "Madness, Authority, and Ideology: The Domestic Melodrama of the 1950s." In *Home Is Where the Heart Is*, ed. Christine Gledhill, 268–280. London: British Film Institute, 1990.

Roeper, Richard. "Marilyn Monroe's Giant Blowing Skirt Sculpture Brings Out the Worst." *Chicago Sun-Times*, July 17, 2011.

Rogers, Ariel. "'Smothered in Baked Alaska': The Anxious Appeal of Widescreen Cinema." *Cinema Journal* 51.3 (2012): 74–96.

Rogers, Cowan and Jacobs. "Biography of Marilyn Monroe." Jack Hirshberg Papers, Box 5, Marilyn Monroe. Margaret Herrick Library, Academy of Motion Picture Arts and Sciences, Los Angeles, CA.

Rogoff, Gordon. "Lee Strasberg: Burning Ice." *Tulane Drama Review* 9.2 (1964): 131–154.

Rojek, Chris. *Celebrity*. London: Reaktion, 2001.

Rollyson, Carl E., Jr. *Female Icons: Marilyn Monroe to Susan Sontag*. New York: iUniverse, 2005.

———. *Marilyn Monroe: A Life of the Actress*. Ann Arbor, MI: UMI Research, 1986.

Rose, Jacqueline. *Women in Dark Times*. London: Bloomsbury, 2014.

Rosen, Marjorie. *Popcorn Venus*. New York: Avon, 1974.

Rosenthal, Herbert. "Sex Habits of American Women." *Pageant*, Feb. 1950: 126–135.

Rowe, Kathleen. *The Unruly Woman: Gender and the Genres of Laughter*. Austin: University of Texas Press, 1995.

Rowland, Todd. "Marilyn Poses Nude—Again." *Photoplay* (Sept. 1962): 45–50, 86–87.

Rushing, Robert. "Gentlemen Prefer Hercules: Desire | Identification | Beefcake." *Camera Obscura* 23.3 (2008): 159–191.

Ryan, Amie. *Marilyn: Loved by You*. Seattle: JavaTown Press, 2016. Kindle.

Salzberg, Ana. *Beyond the Looking Glass: Narcissism and Female Stardom in Studio-Era Hollywood*. New York: Berghahn, 2014.

Sauer, Theodore, D.S.C. Letter to Charles Brackett, Feb. 27, 1953. Charles Brackett Papers, *Niagara*, Box 4, Folder 34. Margaret Herrick Library, Academy of Motion Picture Arts and Sciences, Los Angeles, CA.

Savran, David. *Communists, Cowboys, and Queers*. Minneapolis: University of Minnesota Press, 1992.

Saxton, Martha. *Jayne Mansfield and the American Fifties*. Boston: Houghton Mifflin, 1975.

Scannell, Mrs. John. "Letters: M.M." *Time*, June 4, 1956: 8.

Schatz, Thomas. *Hollywood Genres*. New York: McGraw-Hill, 1981.

Scheinfeld, Amram. "What's Wrong with Sex Studies." *Cosmopolitan* 135 (Aug. 1953): 16–19.

Schickel, Richard. *Intimate Strangers: The Culture of Celebrity in America*. Chicago: Ivan R. Dee, 2000.

Schleier, Merrill. "Fatal Attractions: 'Place,' the Korean War, and Gender in *Niagara*." *Cinema Journal* 51.4 (2012): 26–43.

Schmich, Mary. "Bad Taste, and on Such a Large Scale." *Chicago Tribune*, July 15, 2011. http://articles.chicagotribune.com/2011-07-15/news/chi-0715schmich-column_1_statue-bad-taste-photos.

Schultz, Margie. *Ann Sheridan: A Bio-Bibliography*. Westport, CT: Greenwood Press, 1997.

The Seven Year Itch, Publicity Clippings. Billy Wilder Papers, Box 6, Folder 76, Margaret Herrick Library, Academy of Motion Picture Arts and Sciences, Los Angeles, CA.

"The Seven Year Itch." *Weekly Variety*, June 8, 1955: 6. Motion Picture Association of America, Production Code Administration Records, *The Seven Year Itch*,

Margaret Herrick Library, Academy of Motion Picture Arts and Sciences, Los Angeles, CA.

"Sex or Snake Oil." *Time*, Jan 11, 1954: 14.

Shakespeare, Britney Grimm. *Marilyn Monroe Vampire Diaries Romance*. CreateSpace, 2015.

Shaw, Sam, and Norman Rosten. *Marilyn among Friends*. New York: Henry Holt, 1972.

Sheen, Rev. Fulton J. "How to Stay Married though Unhappy." *Good Housekeeping*, Feb. 1953: 59, 116–120.

Shingler, Martin. *Star Studies: A Critical Guide*. Hampshire, UK: Palgrave Macmillan, 2012.

Short, T. L. "The Development of Peirce's Theory of Signs." In *The Cambridge Companion to Peirce*, ed. Cheryl Misak, 214–240. Cambridge: Cambridge University Press, 2004.

———. *Peirce's Theory of Signs*. New York: Cambridge University Press, 2007.

Shumway, David. *Modern Love: Romance, Intimacy, and the Marriage Crisis*. New York: New York University Press, 2003.

Shurlock, Geoffrey. Letters to Frank McCarthy, Jan. 13, 1956, and Mar. 15, 1956. Motion Picture Association of America, Production Code Administration Records, *Bus Stop*, Margaret Herrick Library, Academy of Motion Picture Arts and Sciences, Los Angeles, CA.

———. Letter to Rev. Little. Mar. 18, 1959. "Some Like It Hot." In *Hollywood and the Production Code: Selected Files from the Motion Picture Association of America Production Code Administration Collection*. Woodbridge, CT: Primary Source Microfilm, 2006, microfilm.

Sikov, Ed. *Laughing Hysterically: American Screen Comedy of the 1950s*. New York: Columbia University Press, 1994.

Silver, Alain, and James Ursini, eds. *Film Noir Reader*. New York: Proscenium, 2001.

Silver, Alain, and Elizabeth Ward. *Film Noir: An Encyclopedic Reference to the American Style*. 3rd ed. Woodstock, NY: Overlook Press, 1992.

Silverman, Kaja. *The Subject of Semiotics*. New York: Oxford University Press, 1983.

Silvina, Dale. *Laurence Olivier and the Art of Film Making*. Cranbury, NJ: Associated University Presses, 1985.

Simmons, Jerold. "The Production Code under New Management: Geoffrey Shurlock, 'The Bad Seed,' and 'Tea and Sympathy.'" *Journal of Popular Film and Television* 22.1 (Spring 1994): 2–10.

Simpson, George. "Nonsense about Women." In *Sexual Behavior in American Society: An Appraisal of the First Two Kinsey Reports*, ed. Jerome Himelhoch and Sylvia Fleis Fava, 59–67. New York: W. W. Norton, 1955.

Singh, Domingo E. Letter to Charles Brackett, Mar. 25, 1953. Charles Brackett
    Papers, *Niagara*, Box 4, Folder 34. Margaret Herrick Library, Academy of Motion
    Picture Arts and Sciences, Los Angeles, CA.

Sinyard, Neil, and Adrian Turner. *Journey down Sunset Boulevard: The Films of
    Billy Wilder*. Ryde, Isle of Wight: BCW, 1979.

Skolsky, Sidney. "Wallach Scores in 'Misfits.'" *Citizen News*, Jan. 25, 1961: 14.

Smith, Murray. "*Film Noir* and the Female Gothic and *Deception*." *Wide Angle*
    10.1 (1988): 62–75.

Smith, Paul. *Clint Eastwood: A Cultural Production*. Minneapolis: University of
    Minnesota Press, 1993.

Smith, Susan. *Elizabeth Taylor*. Hampshire, UK: Palgrave Macmillan, 2012.

Sobchak, Vivian. *Carnal Thoughts: Embodiment and Moving Image Culture*.
    Berkeley: University of California Press, 2004.

Sokolove, Richard. Script reports/analyses to Charles Brackett, Mar. 18, 1952.
    Charles Brackett Papers, *Niagara*, Box 4, Folder 43. Margaret Herrick Library,
    Academy of Motion Picture Arts and Sciences, Los Angeles, CA.

Solomon, Matthew. "Reflexivity and Metaperformance: Marilyn Monroe,
    Jayne Mansfield, and Kim Novak." In *Larger Than Life: Movie Stars of the 1950s*,
    ed. R. Barton Palmer, 107–129. New Brunswick, NJ: Rutgers University Press,
    2010.

"Something for the Boys." *Time*, Aug. 11, 1952: 88.

Sonnet, Esther. "Girl in the Canoe: History, Teleology and the Work of Star Con-
    struction in the Early Roles of Marilyn Monroe." *Screen* 51.1 (Spring 2010): 54–70.

Sorokin, Pitirim. *The American Sex Revolution*. Boston: P. Sargent, 1956.

Spicer, Andrew. *Film Noir*. Harlow, UK: Pearson Education, 2002.

Spoto, Donald. *Marilyn Monroe: The Biography*. New York: HarperCollins, 1993.

Stacey, Jackie. *Star Gazing: Hollywood Cinema and Female Spectatorship*. London:
    Routledge, 1994.

Steinem, Gloria. *Marilyn: Norma Jeane*. New York: Henry Holt, 1988.

Stern, Bert. *Marilyn Monroe: The Last Sitting*. New York: Random House, 2007.

Sternheimer, Karen. *Celebrity Culture and the American Dream: Stardom and
    Social Mobility*. New York: Routledge, 2011.

Stever, Gayle. "Fan Behavior and Lifespan Development Theory: Explaining Para-
    Social and Social Attachment to Celebrities." *Journal of Adult Development* 18
    (2011): 1–7.

Stokes, Walter. *Modern Pattern for Marriage: The Newer Understanding of Mar-
    ried Love*. New York: Rinehart, 1948.

Stone, Hannah, and Abraham Stone. *A Marriage Manual: A Practical Guidebook
    to Sex and Marriage*. New York: Simon and Schuster, 1953.

Strasberg, Lee. *A Dream of Passion: The Development of the Method*. New York: Plume, 1988.

———. "Working with Live Material." *Tulane Drama Review* 9.1 (1964): 117–135.

Strasberg, Susan. *Marilyn and Me: Sisters, Rivals, Friends*. New York: Time Warner, 1992.

Studlar, Gaylyn. "Masochism and the Perverse Pleasures of the Cinema." In *Feminism and Film*, ed. E. Ann Kaplan, 203–225. New York: Oxford University Press, 2000.

———. *This Mad Masquerade: Stardom and Masculinity in the Jazz Age*. New York: Columbia University Press, 1996.

Taylor, Frank. Letter to Arthur Miller, Sept. 28, 1959. John Huston Papers, *The Misfits*—Frank Taylor, Margaret Herrick Library, Academy of Motion Picture Arts and Sciences, Los Angeles, CA.

———. Script notes. John Huston Papers, *The Misfits*—Frank Taylor. Margaret Herrick Library, Academy of Motion Picture Arts and Sciences, Los Angeles, CA.

Texier, Catherine. "French Kiss." In *All the Available Light: A Marilyn Monroe Reader*, ed. Yona Zeldis McDonough, 167–175. New York: Simon and Schuster, 2002.

Tolson, Andrew. *Mediations: Text and Discourse in Media Studies*. London: Arnold, 1996.

"There's Another Side of the Coin." *Modern Screen* 49.8 (July 1955): 82. Constance McCormick Collection: Marilyn Monroe, Vol. 2. Cinema and Television Library, University of Southern California, Los Angeles, CA.

"To Aristophanes and Back." *Time*, May 14, 1956: 74–80.

Tolson, Andrew. *Mediations: Text and Discourse in Media Studies*. London: Arnold, 1996.

Tomlinson, Doug, ed. *Actors on Acting for the Screen: Roles and Collaborations*. New York: Garland, 1994.

Tompkins, Joan. Letter to Hedda Hopper, Aug. 5, 1962. Hedda Hopper Papers, Marilyn Monroe. Margaret Herrick Library, Academy of Motion Picture Arts and Sciences, Los Angeles, CA.

"Too Hot Not to Cool Down?" *Movieland* 12.2 (Dec. 1954): 44–45, 60–61.

Tracy, Jack. "Marilyn Monroe/Frank Sinatra. Is It a Fling?/Or Is It a Thing?" *Photoplay*, Sept. 1961: 42–43, 81–82.

Tremper, Ellen. *I'm No Angel: The Blonde in Fiction and Film*. Charlottesville: University of Virginia Press, 2006.

Trilling, Diana. "The Death of Marilyn Monroe." In *Marilyn Monroe: A Composite View*, ed. Edward Wagenknecht, 125–141. Philadelphia: Chilton, 1969.

Turiello, James. *Marilyn: The Quest for an Oscar*. Los Angeles: Sandy Beach, 2015.

Turim, Maureen. *Flashbacks in Film*. New York: Routledge, 1989.

———. "Gentlemen Consume Blondes." In *Issues in Feminist Film Criticism*, ed. Patricia Erens, 101–111. Bloomington: Indiana University Press, 1990.

Turner, Graeme. *Understanding Celebrity*. London: Sage, 2004.

Tuska, Jon. *Dark Cinema: American Film Noir in Cultural Perspective*. Westport, CT: Greenwood Press, 1984.

"Unveiling of the New Monroe." *Life*, Aug. 27, 1956: 79–80, 82.

van Krieken, Robert. *Celebrity Society*. London, Routledge: 2012.

Vineberg, Steve. *Method Actors: Three Generations of an American Acting Style*. New York: Schirmer, 1991.

Vitacco-Robles, Gary. *Icon: The Life, Times, and Films of Marilyn Monroe, Vol. 1: 1926 to 1956*. Albany, GA: BearManor Media, 2015.

von Teese, Dita. *Your Beauty Mark: The Ultimate Guide to Eccentric Glamour*. New York: Dey Street, 2015.

Wager, Jans B. *Dames in the Driver's Seat: Rereading Film Noir*. Austin: University of Texas Press, 2005.

Walker, Alexander. "Body and Soul: Harlow and Monroe." In *Marilyn Monroe: A Composite View*, ed. Edward Wagenknecht, 148–161. Philadelphia: Chilton, 1969.

———. *Stardom: The Hollywood Phenomenon*. New York: Stein and Day, 1970.

Walters, Tony, ed. *The Mourning for Diana*. Oxford: Berg, 1999.

Warner, W. Lloyd. *Social Class in America: A Manual of Procedure for the Measurement of Social Status*. Chicago: Science Research Associates, 1949.

Wasson, Sam. *Fifth Avenue, 5 A.M.: Audrey Hepburn,* Breakfast at Tiffany's, *and the Dawn of the Modern Woman*. New York: HarperCollins, 2010.

Waterbury, Ruth. "Acting Marilyn Monroe Emerges in 'Misfits.'" *Los Angeles Examiner*, Sept. 4, 1960, 9, 10. Core Collection Files, *The Misfits*, Margaret Herrick Library, Academy of Motion Picture Arts and Sciences, Los Angeles, CA.

Weatherby, W. J. "The Misfits: Epic or Requiem?" *Saturday Review*, Feb. 4, 1961: 26, 27, 47.

Weaver, William R. "Showmen Select Ten Best Stars of Tomorrow." *Motion Picture Herald* 27 (Sept. 1952): 12, 14, 16.

Weinberger, Stephen. "Joe Breen's Oscar." *Film History* 17.4 (2005): 380–391.

We're Not Married!, first draft continuity, Oct. 16, 1951. Twentieth Century-Fox Collection (*We're Not Married!* Box 5, Folder 5), Cinematic Arts Library, University of Southern California, Los Angeles, CA.

Westbrook, Robert. "'I Want a Girl, Just Like the Girl That Married Harry James': American Women and the Problem of Political Obligation in World War II." *American Quarterly* 42.4 (1990): 587–614.

Wexman, Virginia Wright. *Creating the Couple: Love, Marriage, and Hollywood Performance*. Princeton, NJ: Princeton University Press, 1993.

Whitcomb, Jon. "Marilyn Monroe—The Sex Symbol versus the Good Wife." *Cosmopolitan*, Dec. 1960: 52–57.

Widdener, Margaret. "Cad's Paradise." *Good Housekeeping*, Oct. 1950: 55, 238–242.

Wilder, Billy, and I.A.L. Diamond. *Some Like It Hot* script, July 18, 1958. Mike Mazurki Papers, Margaret Herrick Library, Academy of Motion Picture Arts and Sciences, Los Angeles, CA.

Williams, Dick. "'The Misfits' One of Year's Strangest Films." John Huston Papers, *The Misfits*—reviews 1961. Margaret Herrick Library, Academy of Motion Picture Arts and Sciences, Los Angeles, CA.

Williams, Ivor. "The Pious Pornographers." *Playboy*, Oct. 1957: 24–26, 62, 64, 70, 72–74.

Williams, Raymond. *The Long Revolution*. Cardigan, Wales: Parthian, (1961) 2011.

Wills, David. *Marilyn: In the Flash*. New York: Dey Street, 2015.

Wills, Garry. *John Wayne's America: The Politics of Celebrity*. New York: Simon and Schuster, 1997.

Wilson, Earl. "New Type of Hollywood Girl." *Zanesville Times Recorder*, July 28, 1949: 4.

Winsten, Archer. Review: *The Seven Year Itch. New York Post*. 1955.

Winton, Gertrude. "Books and Authors Report on the Seven Year Itch," June 25, 1955. Billy Wilder Papers, Margaret Herrick Library, Academy of Motion Picture Arts and Sciences, Los Angeles, CA.

Wittels, Fritz. *The Sex Habits of American Women*. New York: Eton, 1951.

Wojcik, Pamela Robertson, ed. *Movie Acting: The Film Reader*. New York: Routledge, 2004.

Wolfe, Donald. *The Last Days of Marilyn Monroe*. New York: William Morrow, 2012.

Wollen, Peter. *Signs and Meaning in the Cinema*. Rev. ed. Bloomington: Indiana University Press, 1972.

"Wonderfully Wacky." *Newsweek*, Apr. 6, 1959: 113.

Wood, Robin. *Howard Hawks*. London: British Film Institute, 1981.

Woodward, Richard. "Iconomania: Sex, Death, Photography, and the Myth of Marilyn Monroe." In *All the Available Light: A Marilyn Monroe Reader*, ed. Yona Zeldis McDonough, 10–34. New York: Simon and Schuster, 2002.

Wright, Ellen. "'A Travesty on Sex': Gender and Performance in *Gentlemen Prefer Blondes*." In *Howard Hawks: New Perspectives*, ed. Ian Brookes, 125–141. London: British Film Institute, 2016.

Wright, Robert. Letter to "Producer of 'Niagara,'" Mar. 2, 1953. Charles Brackett Papers, *Niagara*, Box 4, Folder 34, Margaret Herrick Library, Academy of Motion Picture Arts and Sciences, Los Angeles, CA.

Wylie, Philip. *Generation of Vipers*. Normal, IL: Dalkey Archive Press, 1942.

Young, William, and Nancy Young, *The 1950s: Popular Culture through History*. Westport, CT: Greenwood Press, 2004.

Zanuck, Darryl. Memo to Charles Brackett, Oct. 30, 1952. Charles Brackett Papers, *Niagara*, Box 4, Folder 44, Margaret Herrick Library, Academy of Motion Picture Arts and Sciences, Los Angeles, CA.

———. Memo to Lew Schreiber, Jan. 22, 1952. Charles Brackett Papers, *Niagara*, Box 4, Folder 44, Margaret Herrick Library, Academy of Motion Picture Arts and Sciences, Los Angeles, CA.

Zolotow, Maurice. *Marilyn Monroe: An Uncensored Biography*. New York: Bantam, 1960.

———. "The Stars Rise Here." *Saturday Evening Post*, May 18, 1957: 44–45, 83–84, 86–88.

INDEX

acting: film, labor, 2, 9, 11–12, 146–148, 154, 161, 197; performance studies, 8–9, 23, 144–145, 206n14, 211n19, 225n13; the Method, 149, 153–154, 163–164; training, 24, 141, 144–146, 153–154, 168–170, 178, 209n2

acting, Monroe's: criticism of, 5, 53, 144, 145–146, 148, 155, 157, 164, 184, 185, 224n5, 225n14, 226n21; praise for, 53–54, 120–121, 157–158, 165, 174–175, 186–187, 211n16, 222n35, 224n6, 226n21, 228n33; playing herself because of the Method, 154, 156, 170, 224n8; playing herself in *The Misfits*, 174–175, 226–227n24, 227n26; playing herself in *The Prince and the Showgirl*, 161; playing herself offscreen, 19, 185–186; said to be playing herself by critics, 146, 148

Actors Studio, 150, 152, 161, 170, 208n31; Monroe at, 108, 155, 156–157, 186–187; Monroe's films after, 120, 141, 144, 158, 185

affective memory, 152, 154, 169, 171, 225n12

agency, star's, 8, 9, 11, 27, 145

All about Eve, 34, 35, 39–40, 42, 50, 141, 211n23

As Young as You Feel, 42

Asphalt Jungle, The, 34, 35–39, 42, 50, 209n35

audience, 24, 205–206n8, 207n22, 223n49; access to star, 30, 148; identification, 8; influence on studio, 19, 76; knowledge of offscreen persona, 159, 171, 176, 178, 193, 226n20; Monroe's appeal to, 5–6, 10, 11, 20, 23, 31, 35, 38, 54, 89, 95, 106, 136, 173, 175, 190, 196, 217–218n52, 222n36. *See also* fans

Axelrod, George, 10, 108, 109, 118, 120, 189, 192, 228n1

Bacall, Lauren, 18, 19, 86, 91, 92, 217n51

box office, 11, 13, 68, 106, 158, 207n19

Brackett, Charles, 68, 76

Breakfast at Tiffany's, 190–194

Breen, Joseph, 216n42, 221nn32–33. *See also* Production Code Administration

brinkmanship, 100, 114–115, 117, 123, 136, 198, 221n27

buildup, star, 4, 5, 23–25, 30, 48, 49, 52, 55

Bus Stop, 10, 20, 100, 107, 118–129, 140, 157, 192, 195, 209n35, 218n57; as adaptation, 222n34, 222n36

Capote, Truman, 191, 192, 193

censorship, 116, 118, 133, 191, 192, 221n30, 221n32. *See also* Production Code Administration

Chekhov, Michael, 146

Cinderella narrative, 16, 25, 30, 32, 192, 193, 216–217n44

CinemaScope, 77, 86, 89, 91–92, 93, 94–95, 154, 217n48, 217–218n52, 218n53

Clash by Night, 34, 43–48, 211n22

ABOUT THE AUTHOR

Amanda Konkle is an assistant professor of film studies and English at Georgia Southern University's Armstrong Campus in Savannah, Georgia.